Between Faith and Power

Between Faith and Power

Religious Freedom as Dynamic Engagement

WALTER R. RATLIFF

WIPF & STOCK · Eugene, Oregon

BETWEEN FAITH AND POWER
Religious Freedom as Dynamic Engagement

Copyright © 2020 Walter R. Ratliff. All rights reserved. Except for brief quotations in critical publications or reviews, no part of this book may be reproduced in any manner without prior written permission from the publisher. Write: Permissions, Wipf and Stock Publishers, 199 W. 8th Ave., Suite 3, Eugene, OR 97401.

Wipf & Stock
An Imprint of Wipf and Stock Publishers
199 W. 8th Ave., Suite 3
Eugene, OR 97401

www.wipfandstock.com

PAPERBACK ISBN: 978-1-7252-6329-1
HARDCOVER ISBN: 978-1-7252-6328-4
EBOOK ISBN: 978-1-7252-6330-7

Manufactured in the U.S.A.   10/07/20

For my family

Contents

Acknowledgments	ix
Introduction	1

PART ONE

1	From Scripture to the Modern Era	11
2	From the American Experiment to Postmodernism	33

PART TWO

3	Religious Freedom Advocacy and Pluralism	59
4	Ethics of Engagement	68
5	American Evangelical Political Mobilization	84
6	Rights, Development, and Religious Liberty in Egypt	113
7	The Institute for Global Engagement and Vietnam	140
8	Principles of Dynamic Engagement	172
Bibliography		189
Index		209

Acknowledgments

AT THE TOP OF those to thank is my wife for her loving and consistent support, and her interest in the topic. This project would not have been possible without her advice and encouragement throughout the entire process.

This book is the culmination of several years of work at Georgetown University and in the field. The scope of this work included working with a wide group of dedicated scholars and professionals across the country and across continents. My deep appreciation goes to Michael J. Kessler, managing director of Georgetown University's Berkley Center for Religion, Peace and World Affairs, for his editorial guidance on this project. I also extend my appreciation to Thomas Farr and Timothy Shah of the Religious Freedom Institute for their input and advice.

I would also like to thank the Georgetown Liberal Studies team, including Anne Ridder, Frank Ambrosio, Theresa Sanders, Terry Reynolds, Ariel Glucklich, and Trey Sullivan for their insights and dedication. I am a better scholar and educator because of my experience with these and many others at Georgetown.

I am grateful for the transparency and generous hospitality of the Coptic Evangelical Organization for Social Services and its director, Andrea Zaki Stephanous, for my time in Egypt researching their organization. Thanks also go out to Jennifer Cate and the team at Hands Along the Nile for providing connections and coordination. I am also grateful to Chris Seiple, president emeritus of the Institute for Global Engagement, for his insights and wisdom.

These and others deserve credit for improving the manuscript. Any errors or omissions are my own. My thanks also go out to Fairfax Community Church and Pastor Rod Stafford.

Introduction

A NUMBER OF YEARS ago, I was in Nigeria shooting a documentary about violence in the city of Kaduna that had killed hundreds of Muslims and Christians and set off interreligious violence around the country. My traveling companion was a human rights attorney who had fled Nigeria after being captured and tortured by the dictator Sani Abacha. It was his first trip to his home country since the 1999 democratic elections. We visited scenes of brutal violence, and spoke with local religious leaders on both sides to grasp what led to the riots. We also spoke with local religious charities that continue their work despite sectarian strife and government pressure.

One day, we pulled up in a light blue Peugeot to a vacant lot deep in Nigeria's capital city, Abuja. Several young men milled around the lot strewn with broken glass and empty plastic bottles. At the far end of the lot was a corrugated metal shack with a cardboard door. This was the "office" for the black market currency exchange. We were exchanging a few thousand American dollars into Nigerian naira for donations to an orphanage and other local charities. Exchanging money on the black market not only brought a better exchange rate, it prevented us from drawing a certain type of attention. Going to a bank to exchange the funds might end up with the money disappearing while we were questioned by suspicious government officials.

All eyes were on our sedan as a slender, crisply dressed man in a green polo shirt and long pants approached. Through the passenger window, my friend handed the young man in the polo shirt a stack of American bills amounting to several thousand dollars. The man tucked the wad of bills into a leather bag around his waist, and disappeared into the shack. He emerged a few moments later with two large paper grocery bags filled with bricks of Nigerian currency. There was a wide exchange rate between the U.S. dollar and the Nigerian naira, and high-denomination bills were rare. We were now very conspicuously stuffing many times the annual income of an average Nigerian into our car alongside an open roadway and under the gaze of an attentive neighborhood audience.

As we drove away, our driver's eyes kept darting from the road ahead to his rear-view mirror. We were being followed. With a high-speed turn that would make Starsky and Hutch proud, our driver dashed into a street lined with dilapidated apartment buildings. The car followed. He made a few more sudden turns through streets and alleys. The car followed. After a few more dramatic maneuvers and a sprint for the highway, our driver lost whoever was so intent on meeting us. An hour later, we delivered the funds to the local charities.

The money was raised among American churches and individuals concerned about humanitarian needs in this populous West African nation. Transmitting the money through official business or government channels in a country infamous for corruption would likely mean it would never reach the people who needed it the most. Though it came with some risk, working independently ensured in this case that the funds went where they were supposed to go. On the international stage, religious networks frequently cut across national boundaries, and often work independently of governments when they feel it is necessary, and often with some risk.

During the visit, I spoke to Nigeria's minister of information and culture, Jerry Gana. At the time, Christians and Muslims had clashed over the adoption of Sharia criminal law in certain states. The law included harsh sentences, including the amputation of a hand as punishment for theft.

> What happened in Kaduna and other places was not religious, it was political. It was designed to destabilize this government. The Nigerian constitution has a provision on the sanctity of human life, right? And the dignity of the human person. And the protection of that dignity. Therefore the constitution does not provide for, and allow for, government for whatever reason to hack people's hands. It's not there. So, where the constitution comes into conflict with this, the Constitution of the Federal Republic of Nigeria must prevail. Otherwise, there is no nation.[1]

Even though there were political and tribal factors in the violence between Muslims and Christians in Nigeria, the role of religion remained a central concern. Nigerian leaders involved in reconciliation efforts argued that it will take time to resolve many human rights issues in a country that has a very young democracy as well as deep ethnic, tribal and religious divisions. Kaduna's Methodist Archbishop, Benjamin Achigili, told me that

---

1. Ratliff, "Crisis in Kaduna," 5:18–6:10.

it may not be possible to address human rights concerns that spring out of economic problems and sectarian tensions until democracy in Nigeria is more secure: "It's very strange. These are the fevers of democracy that have come into Nigeria. We should learn to be patient with it, and go on to achieve what we want to achieve: freedom of the mind, freedom of speech, freedom of the people."[2]

My own interest in the relationship between rights, religion and government came into focus while I was contributing to *Christianity Today* as a Capitol Hill reporter during the passage of what eventually became the 1998 International Religious Freedom Act.[3] Not every news story carries with it issues of perennial and essential importance. This one sparked my interest in a deeper understanding of the issue.

The connection to religious liberty runs deep in my family. My maternal ancestors were German-speaking Mennonites who had migrated from country to country since the 16th century in search of religious freedom. In the late 19th century they were living in what is now Ukraine. Then, it was the breadbasket of the Russian Empire. Their move to the United States was prompted in large part by the looming threat that the Russian government would force members of their pacifist community into military service. South Russian Mennonites settled in Kansas and Oklahoma, the American breadbasket, hoping for a favorable environment in which to raise wheat and practice their faith.

Even in the early 20th-century Midwest, freedom from government restrictions and social hostilities remained elusive for American Mennonites. One instance related to mob violence in Kansas during World War I. A group of vigilantes arrived at a relative's Kansas farm intending to lynch two of the young men living there. They were offended that the family spoke German and refused to join the fight in Europe, based on their Anabaptist beliefs regarding nonviolence. The young Mennonite men they were looking for were away at the time, so the vigilantes burned down the barn instead.[4] At about the same time, when my grandmother was ten, her church in Inola, Oklahoma was burned down over the "military question." The congregation met in homes and schools until it was rebuilt in 1919.[5]

Other Mennonites in the area were not as lucky. More than a thousand conscientious objectors to military service were sent to the Ft. Leavenworth

---

2. Ratliff, "Crisis in Kaduna," 6:34–6:48.
3. Ratliff, "Congress May Merge Efforts." Ratliff, "New Religious Liberty Bill Unveiled."
4. Juhnke, "Mob Violence and Kansas Mennonites in 1918," 334–50.
5. Goertzen, "Inola Mennonite Brethren Church."

Military Penitentiary and other prison camps for violating the draft. More than half were Mennonite, and many were tortured by prison guards.[6] Some were chained to poles in extreme cold without protective clothing, or chased by guards on motorcycles across fields for sport. They also suffered beatings and stabbings at the hands of military personnel. Two Hutterian conscientious objectors died in Alcatraz after experiencing similar torture.[7]

My work on Mennonites and evangelicals over the past two decades dealt primarily with the forces at work in their relationships with Muslims. At the core of each of these projects was the idea that religious communities are driven by the values inherent in their traditions and the defining narratives they construct for themselves.

Through my research and reporting over the years, I noticed there is a direct relationship between how religious groups define themselves with respect to the state and those of other faiths and how effectively they advance rights in their home countries and abroad. The field of public religious engagement is as varied as the countries and communities where it takes place. This includes religious communities that see religious mandates, such as "love your neighbor," as a driving force in their reform efforts to improve the lives of those outside their community even as they seek greater religious liberty for themselves.

I found a prime example of this in Egypt while researching this book. A chapter is devoted to the Coptic Evangelical Organization for Social Services (CEOSS). Through this organization, Coptic evangelicals sponsor and train a spectrum of vulnerable groups and minorities in Egypt in how to become agents to protect their own human rights. During my time in Cairo and Upper Egypt, I met with a series of groups that CEOSS is helping, including urban working children, rural women, small-scale farmers, physically disabled adults and others. Coptic evangelicals are helping these and others, regardless of their faith, identify their rights according to Egyptian law and international norms, and build their capacity for securing those rights. By actively demonstrating their concern for others outside their own identity group, they make a strong argument for greater religious liberty and improved interreligious relationships.

Many major religious communities are at home discussing the theological basis for their ideas about human dignity claims, and how that relates to their public reform efforts. For example, a few years before the Rohingya Muslim crisis in Myanmar, Roman Catholic and Protestant leaders gathered in Yangon to find ways Catholic and Protestant churches could work

---

6. "Refused War Service; Get Long Prison Terms." Smith, *Mennonites*, 292.
7. Stoltzfus, *Pacifists in Chains*.

together to advance development that recognizes human rights in their Buddhist-majority emerging democracy. In his keynote speech at the event, Archbishop Charles Bo emphasized the role of the church in a country with a difficult human rights record:

> The Church is not just a non-governmental organization (NGO). Church is not just another civil society organization. The Church is a religious organization that affirms the existential dignity of every person, owing to his or her relationship with God. The Church is worried about all persons and the whole person.[8]

Bo called for religious groups to act as a watchdog in emerging democracies to ensure economic development did not come at the cost of human rights abuses and at the expense of the poor and vulnerable. In October 2019, Bo said he was pained by the "criminal" silence of religious leaders, including Buddhists and Christians, over the abuses suffered by Rohingya Muslims and other minorities in Myanmar.[9]

These and other examples are evidence of the dynamic role religion plays in a pluralistic and globalized world. This book focuses on one segment of that wide arena: how certain Protestant/evangelical groups have responded to pressing needs surrounding religious freedom in a set of pluralistic contexts. In a nutshell, this book examines the promotion of religious freedom among a representative selection of evangelical groups in order to define Dynamic Engagement, a set of ethical principles that take into account contemporary pluralism, best practices derived from the social sciences, and core debates within Protestantism over religion in public life.

Part one sets the stage in two chapters by offering an assessment of how current ideas about religion and public life emerged from the formation Scripture, through the Middle Ages to the contemporary era. It shows how the ideas behind phrases like, "we hold these truths to be self-evident, that all men are created equal," are packed with a long history of development, originating long before the values of equality and human dignity were considered self-evident.

Part two digs into the process by which values and cultural responses are being worked out today. The three case studies show how a representative selection of religious groups engage the public square with the tools of social movement framing and mobilization. Taken together the case studies present clear examples of the three modes of Protestant/evangelical group mobilization relevant to the contemporary context. This includes domestic

8. Bo, "Toward a Future," 91.
9. Carvalho, "Cardinal Complains of 'Criminal Silence.'"

American evangelicalism, which remains a powerful political force in the United States, as well as the work in the Global South by local and transnational organizations. This first case study looks at American evangelical mobilization for the 1998 International Religious Freedom Act (IRFA), and the subsequent anti-Sharia mobilization efforts within the same group. This case illustrates the critical role a pluralistic perspective plays in advancing or hindering religious freedom in the United States and introduces evidence contrasting the exclusive vs. inclusive approaches to religious freedom advocacy. While the successes of the IRFA campaign fit squarely into the model of successful mobilization models outlined by social scientists, the anti-Sharia campaign is an example of what constitutes failure by a social movement, with failure defined as co-option by another group, inability to gain a broader social consensus and the inability to extract legal or social advantages.[10]

The next case study examines efforts by Egypt's Coptic Evangelical Organization for Social Services (CEOSS). Coptic Christians in Egypt have suffered increasing persecution and violent social hostilities. The leaders of CEOSS believe violent extremism can be mitigated by addressing needs related to poverty, disenfranchisement, unemployment and other pressing social issues. They believe actively seeking to relieve these pressures will prevent some Egyptians from seeking violent remedies to their grievances. CEOSS remains closely engaged across different strata of government, from local councils to national leaders. This strategy emphasizes their unity with other Egyptians across demographic lines and keeps open a conduit for communicating their own concerns among government leaders. Their active pursuit of human rights across Egyptian society draws upon cooperation among both Muslim and Christian Egyptians to bolster a sense of cross-religious citizenship. In doing so, they have attained the support of each successive Egyptian regime. CEOSS's pluralistic approach has also reduced suspicions that could endanger its ability to remain politically and socially engaged.

The third case study examines the Institute for Global Engagement's (IGE) effort to address religious freedom concerns in the Global South, specifically in Vietnam. It shows how the leaders of IGE framed their nonproselytizing approach to engagement as fitting squarely within evangelicalism. At the same time, IGE employed what it calls a top-down, bottom-up approach by working among the country's political leaders, as well as representatives of religious groups that operate outside the country's power structures.

10. Gamson, *Strategy of Social Protest*, 29.

IGE and the other groups examined here are each exploring ways to address the religious freedom concerns they have identified in their unique contexts. The way these groups address these issues can either further their ability to freely engage the public square or lead to further conflict and religious restrictions. These case studies examined how each group identified issues entwined with religious liberty, framed the issues according to their ideological outlook, developed political resources to address the issue and mobilized their resources to bring about reform relevant to their context.

I also explored the limits of this type of religious mobilization through the theological critiques of leading Christian theologians and public intellectuals such as Reinhold Niebuhr and Stanley Hauerwas. These critiques highlight the paradox of Christians seeking to maintain the integrity of their faith while working with political power.

In 1975, William Gamson wrote a seminal study called *The Strategy of Social Protest*, in which he assessed a series of groups in American history that have attempted to gain influence with or extract concessions from those in political power. In the study, Gamson defined "success" for a social movement in two ways, either the group (and its agenda) gains acceptance in the larger culture, or the group extracts legal and social advantages as a result of their challenge to the political status quo. Gamson observed that the pursuit of success in social or political change is determined in large part by the how the group defines their goals, chooses their tactics, and how they organize around their goals. Gamson argued that how groups handle these challenges determines whether the group is successful in achieving the success they seek, whether they are co-opted by the agenda of another group, or otherwise fail in their pursuit of change.[11]

The Four Cs of Dynamic Engagement outlined in this study draw from the definition of success or effectiveness as outlined by social science researchers, and reflect practical observations observed in the field. They also take into account inherent concerns intertwined with values, tradition, and theology. The resulting principles draw from what has and has not been effective for these groups, often reflecting results that seem counterintuitive in today's age of polarization. I am a journalist and religion scholar, not an activist. These principles are not meant to endorse or condemn a particular branch of Christianity or theological outlook, or the actions of a particular group. Rather, they are a product of observation and analysis. It's part of an ongoing conversation. The term "Dynamic Engagement" reflects the ideas and practices of a wide group of leaders found in the case studies, including the dynamic citizenship of Coptic evangelical leader Andrea Zaki

---

11. Gamson, *Strategy of Social Protest*, 29–51.

Stephanous, the perspective of Chris Seiple of the Institute for Global Engagement, and others.

THE FOUR C'S OF DYNAMIC ENGAGEMENT:[12]

1. Conscience: Effective Christian leaders emphasized within their own communities the central role of the universal free conscience that appears in Scripture, theology, and tradition, and the implications of this in a pluralistic context.
2. Consistency: Effective Christian public engagement in defense of religious liberty was consistent in its emphasis on freedom and justice across religious and nonreligious boundaries.
3. Common Good: Effective religious freedom initiatives emphasized the role of faith groups serving the common good through participation in civil society.
4. Crossing Over: Effective religious freedom advocacy groups integrated their work with others across religious and social identity lines.

Underlying the Four C's is another "C": context. The task of the first part of the book will provide a survey of the historical context for religious liberty as a foundational component of modern human rights. It will pay particular attention to how theologians and leading political thinkers formed responses to the changing social and political environments they encountered over time, and how those responses shaped the values and norms we hold as self-evident today. This overview provides a context for the case studies and analysis found in the second part of the book. Many of the ideas and people discussed in the historical overview found part one recur in part two, either on stage or lurking behind the scenes.

---

12. These "Four C's" don't have direct relationship to Catherine Albanese's "Four C's of Religion: Creed, Codes, Cultus, Community." Even so, Albanese's work is recommended as a gateway into understanding the topic of religion itself. Albanese, *America, Religions and Religion*, 7–8.

PART ONE

1

From Scripture to the Modern Era

THE PAST 20 YEARS have established our time as an era of intense religious oppression. In Iraq and Syria, Christians and Yazidis faced extinction in their ancient homelands under the brutality of the Islamic State group. Rohingya Muslims faced violence and displacement in Myanmar. In China, millions of Muslim Uighers were targeted for Chinese reeducation camps based on their faith.[1] Chinese Christians have seen their government tear down crosses, demolish churches, and arrest their pastors.[2] In Egypt, Coptic Christians face bombings, shootings, kidnapping, and riots. This is just a sample of government restrictions and social hostilities involving faith and freedom in today's context. In an ever-shrinking, globalized world, millions of people of faith experience political or social hostilities that threaten their religious liberty and freedom of conscience.[3]

Advocates for those suffering violence and government oppression for their faith appeal to international norms like the Universal Declaration of Human Rights. Mary Ann Glendon of Harvard Law School noted that in 1948 "the framers of the Universal Declaration achieved a distinctive synthesis of previous thinking about rights and duties. After canvassing sources from North and South, East and West, they believed they had found a core of principles so basic that no nation would wish openly to disavow

---

1. Kang, "Leaked Data Shows China's Uighers Detained."
2. Tang, "Severe Crackdown in China."
3. Pew Research Center, "Latest Trends in Religious Restrictions and Hostilities."

them."[4] The declaration is among a vanishingly small group of documents that deal with values and ethics that have virtually unanimous support from the international community. Given the postmodern world we live in, this broad assent is remarkable, even if it falls short in practice around the world. The declaration sets up its list of human rights by rooting them in human dignity: "Whereas recognition of the inherent dignity and of the equal and inalienable rights of all members of the human family is the foundation of freedom, justice and peace in the world . . ."[5]

Directly tied to the ideas of human dignity and individual freedom in the declaration is the right of a free conscience and faith. Article 18 spells out the right of religious freedom as it relates to this core idea: "Everyone has the right to freedom of thought, conscience and religion; this right includes freedom to change his religion or belief, and freedom, either alone or in community with others and in public or private, to manifest his religion or belief in teaching, practice, worship and observance."[6]

History shows the normative value of religious liberty and other human rights wasn't always a universal value. In the West, it emerged on a parallel course with ideas about representative government and the rule of law. Some of the earliest writings about a free conscience emerged in the last centuries of the Roman Empire, a time when religion and public life were intimately intertwined, with official Roman religion occupying the social milieu with a variety of competing polytheistic, gnostic, and mystery religions.[7] Scholars argue the tectonic cultural changes during the final centuries of the Roman Empire were partially rooted in the shift from the polytheism of Roman religion, with its emphasis on ritual and outward acts of devotion, to the monotheism of Christianity, which emphasized the inward workings of one's own conscience, true vs. false religion, and worship of a deity that transcended earthly existence. The contemporary scholar Steven D. Smith says grasping the nature and future of today's polarized public square requires taking this religious orientation into account over time. He summons the work of William James and Emile Durkheim, who argue religion is humanity's connection to absolute realties, and that religion itself is an essential aspect of being human. Smith argues, "If James and Durkheim were right, then an effort to understand our history and even our current situation—our so-called

---

4. Glendon, *World Made New*, xviii.
5. "Universal Declaration of Human Rights," Preamble.
6. "Universal Declaration of Human Rights," Article 18.
7. Assmann, *Price of Monotheism*, 23.

culture wars—that does not take full account of our religious dimension seems foreordained to fail, and to distort."[8]

At the same time, some contemporary intellectuals are questioning the universality of religious liberty itself. They see religious liberty entwined with power and politics, and supportive of majority faiths and powerful nations. They argue the circumstances in which ideas surrounding religious freedom and liberty of conscience emerged swamp the timelessness of the ideas themselves.[9] Yet, a look at a broader sweep of history shows that, although religious freedom and liberty of conscience grew from a variety of contexts and ideas, they were integral with the growth of ideas surrounding universal human dignity and core human rights. They form a seamless garment of ideas that have led to human flourishing and the reduction of suffering, which the removal of one thread may lead to an unraveling of the whole. That said, one of the criticisms is the application of religious liberty laws favors a majority group, or is used as a tool for nations to exercise power over another. This study shows how concern for the less powerful as well as consistency in its application strengthens efforts to advance religious freedom and liberty of conscience in the public square.

One approach is to examine the intertextual nature of how religious groups define and redefine their meaning as a community in a given context. The term "intertextuality" originated as a literary term. The use of Hebrew Scriptures by Jesus and Paul the apostle to articulate the gospel of the New Testament, are classic instances of intertextuality in a religious canon.[10] The term "intertextuality" has also been expanded by theorists to discuss how groups bring their authoritative literature to bear on societal challenges they face, and how this interaction forms new ideas and recontextualizes old notions in the process.

In the context of religious freedom and the challenge of pluralism, the three main components of intertextuality are (a) the community: a group of people that are tied together by their culture and interests, (b) the canon: a set of texts that the community sees as authoritative, instructive, and inspirational, and (c) ideological and political challenges faced by the community in their historic setting, including those that arise from groups that have a different culture, canon, and set of interests.

Scriptures such as the Hebrew Bible and the New Testament are canonical for Christians in the classic sense. At the same time, there are cultural and political texts that are considered authoritative that occupy

---

8. Smith, *Pagans and Christians in the City*, 114.
9. Mahmood and Danchin, "Politics of Religious Freedom," 1–8.
10. Childs, *Biblical Theology of Old and New Testaments*, 226.

a secular role. In the United States, this includes documents such as the U.S. Constitution and the Declaration of Independence. With respect to the Constitution, there are contemporary debates over how strictly laws for today should adhere to the letter of the document, just as there have been debates for centuries over how communities should adhere to Scriptures. Even so, documents like the Constitution emerged from an interaction between groups (in this case the founding fathers), their lowercase "c" canon of philosophical and religious ideas, and the challenges they faced in colonial America. The Constitution and Declaration of Independence take their place in a new body of authoritative texts borne of this dynamic interaction. This new canon then informs how American communities form new laws and responses to cultural challenges of the day.

Religious communities around the world are steeped in this historic process of intertextual development. The capital "C" scriptural Canons for Christians, Muslims, and other groups may not change from one millennia to the next. However, the lowercase "c" canonical texts can have a profound impact on how their Scriptures are brought to bear on the challenges they experience over time. In this way, every religious community experiences a change in their cultural DNA over time according to the degree they engage the world around them. In this way, the operating ideas of a given group are rooted in the history that came before them as well as their current context.

This book shows how this process is at work among Protestant religious groups around the world with respect to religious liberty. Each of the cases presented in chapters five through seven digs into how a set of groups negotiate a response to religious freedom challenges. They offer a boots-on-the-ground look at the intertextual process. In order to better understand the context in which they operate, a type of drive through history is in order to see what is at work underneath the current trends. A review of biblical sources is followed by quick look at a selection of ideas and thinkers that helped form today's values of religious liberty and individual rights.

CONSCIENCE AND SCRIPTURE

The book of Job, one of the earliest in the Hebrew Bible, is a fascinating text that deals with a host of major themes. This includes the role of a free conscience in the distinction between humankind and animals. In the seventh chapter, Job laments his suffering and contemplates death. In the midst of this, Job asks "What is man that you should magnify him?" (7:17 NASB). In this context the term "magnify" could seem like the magnification that an ant receives from someone shining a magnifying glass in bright sunlight.

God's observation brings him into focus, but this attention is associated with suffering.

The answer to his question can be found in the book's first chapter. The first verse of Job's parable describes him as "blameless" and how he "feared God and turned away from evil." Even so, the adversary in Job 1:9–11 accuses God of being disingenuous when he points out Job's integrity. That is, he questions God's assertion that Job is freely worshipping God with an independent mind and will, rather than accepting or rejecting God as a conditioned response to comfort or hardship: "Have you not made a hedge around him and his house and all that he has, on every side? You have blessed the work of his hands, and his possessions have increased in the land. But stretch out your hand now, and touch all that he has, and he will curse you to your face."[11] The accusation challenges God's own veracity about what he claims about his creation of human beings. If righteousness is freely apprehended, it cannot be dependent on God's special protection, or necessarily fail under external pressure.

Job's parable is often used to explore the idea of theodicy. Yet there is also insight here about the nature of humanity. Job is presented by God as something above an automaton or animal driven by rewards or punishments. God allows terrible things to happen to Job in order to prove Job's innate freedom. That is, possessing a conscience independent of instincts or physical pressures is part of what it means to be human.

In Job's story, God allows a series of catastrophes to happen in every part of his life. His family, his wealth, and even his health were taken away. His friends offer a series of explanations that revolve around sins Job may have committed. His wife even presses him to "curse God and die."[12] He curses the day he was born, and argues with God, but he refuses to curse God or admit some sin brought about his suffering. He adheres to his faith in a powerful God that seems ambiguous to Job's personal welfare, but knows his innocence.[13] At the end of the book Job receives a new family and restored wealth and health.

Job questions God about his suffering, which parallels God's own claim to the Accuser that Job was blameless.[14] In the end, Job won the bet (or secured God's win) made with the Accuser by maintaining his belief and perspective despite his circumstances. The "hedge" that kept Job from

---

11. Job 1:10–11 NASB.
12. Job 2:9.
13. Job 16:19.
14. Job 31.

sinning was freely erected and maintained by Job himself.[15] The implicit result is God has been acquitted of creating a being whose freedom is swayed by divine protection or by external pressures.

New Testament

In the Sermon on the Mount, Jesus exhorts his followers to look after their own conscience and examine their own thoughts and motivations before condemning others (Matt 5–7). In response to whether it was permissible for God's people to pay taxes, Jesus delivered a reply that seemed to affirm the legitimacy of the state in its own domain: "Render unto Caesar the things that are Caesar's, and to God the things that are God's."[16] Taken with other saying of Jesus, including John 18:36, it also set forth a slow-motion revolution.[17] Steven Smith remarks that the idea that the world is divided between the earthly and heavenly domains unfurled over the centuries:

> This 'render unto' dualism persisted over the centuries in Christian thought: thence Augustine's two cities and, later, Luther and Calvin's two kingdoms. The Christian division of temporal and spiritual jurisdictions animated the papal campaign for 'freedom of the church'—a remote progenitor of American separation of church and state—and also, in a post-Reformation and Protestant development, the movement for freedom of the 'internal church' of conscience.[18]

Paul the apostle wrote of having faith rooted in an individual's response to God with one's own heart and mind, versus membership in a particular tribe, nation, or social strata.[19] In 1 Corinthians 8–10, Paul also discusses the idea that believers are responsible for their own decision-making when it comes to eating meat used in a pagan ritual. The rights of the individual are held as the benchmark, except in cases where the use of that meat may injure the conscience of a fellow believer. That is, one believer *ought to* set aside their right to a certain behavior to maintain a loving stance toward others. In this way, cultivating care for others is tied to the freedom of the individual to make their own spiritual and practical decisions. For those following their own convictions, Paul emphasizes God is the ultimate judge,

---

15. Job 1:10.
16. Matt 22:21 KJV.
17. "My kingdom is not of this world . . ."
18. Smith, *Rise and Decline*, 142.
19. Rom 10:9–17.

and that individuals have the responsibility for their own conscience, free of compulsion.[20]

A passage in Romans encapsulates the role of the free conscience in the individual effort to work out right and wrong, even beyond the benefit and authority of the Scriptures Paul and the early Christians adhered to: "For when Gentiles who do not have the Law do instinctively the things of the Law, these, not having the Law, are a law to themselves, in that they show the work of the Law written in their hearts, their conscience bearing witness and their thoughts alternately accusing or else defending them" (Rom 2:14–15 NIV). Other verses in the New Testament attest to the need for individuals to cultivate moral reasoning with respect to God, and to guard against a damaged conscience.[21]

These examples are by no means exhaustive of what the Old and New Testaments have to say on the subject. They represent a selection of foundational texts that have helped shape contemporary views regarding freedom of conscience, mutual responsibility, and even the immanent and transcendent domains. The next stop in how these ideas revolutionized Western thought is Roman North Africa at the turn of the Third Century.

Patristic Era

On July 17, 180 BCE, a few months after the death of Marcus Aurelius, seven men and five women faced the death penalty for their Christian faith. They were all from a small town outside Carthage, the empire's most important city in North Africa. Their trial and sentencing is recorded in the earliest known Christian text in Latin, *The Acts of the Scillitan Martyrs*.[22] Their spokesman, Speratus, told the Roman proconsul, Saturninus, that they were innocent of any wrongdoing: "We have never done ill, we have not lent ourselves to wrong, we have never spoken ill, but when ill-treated we have given thanks; because we pay heed to our Emperor [Christ]." Saturninus replied that they should swear an oath to the Roman emperor, Commodus. Speratus replied, "The empire of this world I know not; but rather I serve that God, whom no man has seen, nor with these eyes can see. I have committed no theft; but if I have bought anything I pay the tax; because I know my Lord, the King of kings and Emperor of all nations."[23] At the end of the

---

20. 1 Cor 4:2–5; 10:29
21. Heb 10:22; 1 Tim 4:2
22. Lightfoot, *Apostolic Fathers*, 599.
23. A reference to 1 Tim 6:15–16.

trial, the group refused an offer of 30 days to reconsider. As a result, they were immediately beheaded for their Christian faith.

This moment in early church history came at a turning point in the Roman Empire and for Christianity in the Roman World. Commodus's reign was marked by his megalomaniacal behavior, including his appearances in the gladiator ring. By the time he was assassinated (strangled by his personal trainer in a bathtub, not killed in the ring as in the movie *Gladiator*), the *Pax Romana* was endangered by political infighting and corruption. While the stability of the Roman Empire teetered on the brink, the empire's Christian community was undergoing a transformation. Between 180 and 210, Christians made a "great leap forward," transforming themselves from "fringe groups of disreputable characters as depicted by Celsus to the respectable, empirewide organization."[24] This new era in Roman Christianity would produce some of its most important thinkers, including Tertullian.

Tertullian (c.150–240)

Tertullian was likely a young, legally trained Carthaginian at the time the Scillitan martyrs were put to death for their faith. He converted to Christianity fifteen years or more after the trial. After his conversion, he became a Christian apologist and author in the cosmopolitan city of Carthage. One popular claim to fame is that he coined the term "Trinity" to describe God. In contrast to his contemporary, Clement of Alexandria, who sought to bring Greek philosophy into close conversation with Christian theology, Tertullian famously declared "What has Athens to do with Jerusalem, or the Academy with the church?"[25] Among his surviving writings are an open letter addressed to a Roman proconsul named Scapula involved in the persecution of Christians. The chief aim of *To Scapula* (c. 212) is to answer false accusations against the Christian community, and argue for an end to persecution. He argued Christianity is both correct and superior in comparison with the accepted pagan styles of worship in the empire.

One of Tertullian's contributions to the conceptual history of religious freedom and church-state relations is found in his forceful rhetoric. He debunked accusations that Christian worship included morally outrageous acts such as incest and child sacrifice, and pointed out that the outrageous acts Christians were accused of were in fact features of pagan worship. He also broke from contemporary and subsequent doctors of the church by rejecting the compatibility of Greek philosophy and Christian theology. He

---

24. Barnes, *Tertullian*, 332.
25. Greenslade, *Early Latin Theology*, 36.

argued Christianity alone contained truth. Tertullian resisted the idea there were no limits to the empire's intrusion into religious practice and freedom of conscience.

His writing on the topic ranges from sarcastic to confrontational: "Let one man worship God, another Jupiter . . . let one—if you choose to take this view of it—count in prayer the clouds, and another the ceiling panels; let one consecrate his own life to his God, and another that of a goat."[26] He makes the case that worship according to one's own conscience is the only morally consistent position: "For see that you do not give a further ground for the charge of irreligion, by taking away religious liberty, and forbidding free choice of deity, so that I may no longer worship according to my inclination, but am compelled to worship against it. Not even a human being would care to have unwilling homage rendered him." In his *To Scapula*, he argues: "It is a fundamental human right, a privilege of nature that every man should worship according to his own convictions . . . It is assuredly no part of religion to compel religion—to which free-will and not force should lead us—the sacrificial victims even being required of a willing mind."[27]

Tertullian argued Christians are loyal members of the Roman Empire, who pray for the emperor even if they do not pray to him, and have been recognized by previous emperors as beneficial to Rome: "Marcus Aurelius also, in his expedition to Germany, by the prayers his Christian soldiers offered to God, got rain in that well-known thirst."[28]

Tertullian's style and the content of his arguments regarding religious freedom and church-state relations were unique to him in his day. Yet, components of Tertullian's arguments can be seen in later Christian thinkers and advocates, up to the modern age.

Augustine (354–480)

One hundred eighty miles west, and a century later, in the Roman city of Hippo Regius, lived one of the leading Christian thinkers of the early church, Augustine. The role of Augustine in the development of Western theology and philosophy cannot be understated. During his lifetime, the Roman Empire was under continuous threat from Germanic invaders. Theological and cultural challenges dogged the church as it continued to define and defend itself against competing religious sects.

---

26. Coxe et al., *Ante-Nicene Fathers*, 3:39.
27. Coxe et al., *Ante-Nicene Fathers*, 3:104.
28. Coxe et al., *Ante-Nicene Fathers*, 3:107.

In his view, the Roman Empire should have been an instrument for the preservation and spread of Christianity, which included the use of state authority to punish heresy.[29] His model for the role of imperial authority in religious affairs was the nation of Israel in the Old Testament. As often is seen is Augustine's theology, scriptural revelation can carry both a meaning congruent with the period in which it was written, as well as a prophetic meaning relevant to a current situation.

Relevant to the idea of the role of church and state is Augustine's concept of the city of God set against the earthly city. The book was written in the context of the sack of Rome by the Visigoths in 410. The city of God, embodied by the church, was in constant conflict with the earthly city. The conflict was a manifestation of the universal conflict between God and Satan. The book refuted polytheism, and pointed to the growing presence of the city of God as evidence that the evil ways of the earthly city were steadily being defeated. He predicted one day the earthly city would pass away, and the city of God would prevail. The idea is a dramatic extension of Jesus' idea that there was a domain of Caesar and that of God (Matt 22:21).

MIDDLE AGES

Nine hundred years later, the Roman Empire was an idealized memory in the West. Europe's population was booming, and the official religion was Christianity, with the ultimate spiritual authority resting with the pope in Rome. By the 13th century, the Crusades were waning, with the crusaders suffering defeats and Jerusalem and the Latin States returning to Muslim control. At the same time, through Jewish and Muslim texts, the works of Aristotle were rediscovered by European Christian scholars. Leading the way in synthesizing the works of Aristotle with Christian theology was Thomas Aquinas.

Thomas Aquinas (1225–1274)

Aquinas is often placed at the top of list among the doctors of church, alongside Augustine. His *Summa Theologica* covers a vast territory. Aquinas set his sights on creating a timeless picture of who God is, what creation and its inhabitants are, and (among other things) the proper definitions of the relationship between things of heaven and earth. The nature of religious liberty and church-state relations make their way into Aquinas's grand theological

---

29. Brown, "St. Augustine's Attitude to Religious Coercion," 110.

landscape. His view of religious liberty reflects his historical circumstances as a medieval theologian describing the relationship between the civil and religious spheres in the context of medieval Christendom.

Some of his ideas were ahead of their time, particularly regarding the virtue of rulers, and the right of those under the ruler to exercise a legitimizing role in who leads them. Aquinas asserted citizens should participate in the political community and obey earthly rulers.[30] Aquinas argued the theological virtues of the church and questions of obedience to God and the church occupied a higher place on the great chain of being than secular authority.[31] Citizens are expected to obey secular authorities insofar as they are just—a potentially revolutionary position given the political systems in place in his day.[32] In terms of religious freedom, non-Christian adherents, such as Jews, should not be compelled to change their beliefs or practices. Aquinas followed Augustinian thought to some extent with regard to the use of coercion within the church. According to Aquinas, Christians guilty of heresy can and should be punished by the state, including capital punishment for persistent heretics.[33]

THE MODERN PERIOD

A dramatic shift in trajectory took place at the end of the Middle Ages. The Reformation introduced a divergent path in church-state relations that would be increasingly realized in the following centuries. The Enlightenment and the advent of modernity advanced the notion of individual autonomy beyond both state and religious institutions.

Martin Luther (1483–1546)

At the forefront of the Reformation was Martin Luther. While Augustine, Aquinas, and other doctors of the church married Greek philosophy to Christian teaching in order to produce a model that wove the church's influence and earthly power, Martin Luther deconstructed the academy's role in governance, and outlined limitations of the Catholic Church's temporal authority. Luther argued that not only was the philosophy of Aristotle and others divorced from Christian teaching (as Tertullian argued), but its

---

30. Aquinas, *Summa Theologica*, 2-2.104.1.
31. Aquinas, *Summa Theologica*, 2-2.104.3.
32. Aquinas, *Summa Theologica*, 2-2.104.6.
33. Aquinas, *Summa Theologica*, 2-2.10.8.

conclusions were in opposition to the teachings of the New Testament.[34] *Contra* Augustine and Aquinas, Luther argued the use of force is not effective against heresy, and Christians should disobey rulers who seek to limit religious practices, such as reading unapproved books, because it oversteps the boundaries of secular authority.[35] He argued that even Muslims (i.e., "the Turk") should be able to worship freely, with Scripture and prayer as the primary tools to oppose unbelief.[36]

At the time Luther was redefining the role of the church and state, John Calvin was outlining the distinct roles of spiritual and temporal authority. Calvin saw the powers of the church and the state as separate, yet still in relationship with each other. Calvin argued the church plays a role in advancing the moral rule of the authorities. While Calvin saw a "twofold government" of man separated by earthly and spiritual concerns, he asserted the state should retain the "power of the sword"[37] to protect the church from idolatry, blasphemy, and other offenses in order to protect the social and moral order. Calvin argued believers should recognize that both good and bad authorities hold their office by the providence of God, and believers should offer them respect and obedience insofar as their commands do not violate the Christian faith.

Thomas More (1478–1535)

Among the Roman Catholic leaders of the period, the English philosopher and statesman Thomas More vociferously opposed the Protestant Reformation and the separation of the Church of England from the Church of Rome. More's last words before being beheaded in 1535 were that he was "the king's good servant, but God's first." This sentiment encompasses More's approach to God and government. He wrote of Christ having immense love for humanity, even suffering torment in order to redeem the human race.[38]

More viewed persecution of, for example, the Catholic clergy by the English monarchy as both illegal and against God's work in the world. His novel, *Utopia*, paints a picture of an unobtainable land ruled by humanistic reason, featuring common property and a high degree of religious toleration. The novel explores More's key philosophical question: "What is the

---

34. Luther, "Disputation against Scholastic Theology."
35. Luther, "On Secular Authority."
36. Luther, "Martin Luther."
37. Vandrunen, "Context of Natural Law," 516, 518.
38. Wegemer and Smith, *Thomas More Source Book*, 264.

best way of life, and is it achievable in a fallen world?"[39] With regard to religious freedom, *Utopia* embraces a wide-ranging right to freedom of conscience as a critical component to civic peace.[40]

Sebastian Castellio (1515–1563)

Sebastian Castellio was a Reformation pioneer of religious toleration and freedom of conscience. He was skeptical of any religious or political leaders identifying, much less punishing, someone as a heretic: "In truth those who today boast that they have the true orthodox religion as taught by the Catholic doctors, and who so boldly condemn others as heretics, as a matter of fact are no more in accord with these doctors than with the Gospel."[41] He delivered a critique of both Catholic and Protestant leaders supporting persecution with characteristic bluntness:

> See what we have come to. More and more we have degenerated, until now there is no dealing or disputing with a heretic save by the gallows, sword . . . But the best of ancient canons are opposed to this insolence in that they forbid the clergy for any reason whatever, let alone for faith or heresy, to kill or lay violent hands on anyone either directly or indirectly.[42]

The mid-17th century was a watershed period in the history of the modern West. In 1637, Rene Descartes published *Discourse on the Method of Rightly Conducting One's Reason and of Seeking Truth in the Sciences*. Descartes's quest to find a foundation for human knowledge, including both scientific and moral knowledge, exerted a tremendous influence on philosophy and natural sciences throughout the Enlightenment.

The same year Descartes published *Discourse*, citizens of the New World settlement of Providence, led by Roger Williams, signed a town agreement that distinguished citizenship from religious adherence. The agreement restricted the role of the government to "civil things," setting the stage for the separation of church and state enshrined in the Bill of Rights more than 150 years later. In 1648, the Peace of Westphalia established the modern nation-state as a sovereign entity on equal legal standing as other states. It also had a deep religious dimension. Princes decided the official religion of a given state, and a degree of religious freedom was acknowledged

---

39. Wegemer and Smith, *Thomas More Source Book*, 175.
40. Kessler, "Religious Freedom in Thomas More's Utopia," 207–29.
41. Castellio, *Concerning Heretics*, 187.
42. Castellio, *Concerning Heretics*, 194.

for adherents of religion outside of the official church. Just a few years after Westphalia, Hobbes published *Leviathan*. The book outlined the social contract characteristics of a modern state, including the notion that religion is subordinate to civil law and the wishes of the ruler. Each of these developments would fuel religious and political developments for centuries to come.[43]

Hugo Grotius (1583–1645)

Hugo Grotius was a Christian humanist credited with groundbreaking work on international law. In his time, the political order of Europe was undergoing massive political changes, culminating in the Peace of Westphalia, three years after his death. The rise of the nation-state as an independent power ended a series of long and bloody wars across Europe over Catholic-protestant divides. Issues related to religious freedom were central to the treaties signed in Westphalia. They stipulated that states could determine their own established religion within the menu of Catholicism, Lutheranism, and Calvinism. Those outside a given nation's established church had the right to practice their faith, with some limits, and meet in private.

Grotius drew from both philosophy (particularly Aristotle) and Christian theology (particularly natural law) to develop universal ideas about the role of the state and the individual. He pioneered ideas about international rule of law, and the idea of a universal set of human rights. Grotius envisioned the law between and within nations as more or less religiously neutral. Within Grotius's arguments, reason prevails over revelation when it comes to forming an organized society. For example, he paraphrased Aristotle's idea that the best state is that which is designed to create the best and happiest life for its citizens. He also cited the apostle Paul's assertion that supreme earthly power is the servant of good, allowing citizens to lead a peaceable, respectful, and godly life. Grotius argued the instrument for achieving Aristotle's and Paul's requirements is reason. The product of reason takes the form of natural law (versus a sectarian-based code). This universal view of reason's role in divining natural law, and the rights of the individual in pursuit of reason, was innovative in his time. It was poised to have tremendous influence in the new order after Westphalia. Coupling universal rights of the individual with a common legal understanding between countries was an important moment in the development of modern ideas.

43. Lilla, *Stillborn God*.

Thomas Hobbes (1588–1679)

In contrast to Grotius, Hobbes's materialism points to a different source and a much different conclusion regarding social organization. Grotius saw human insight as endowed by God as a means of discerning natural law. Hobbes saw human behavior as essentially a soulless mix of appetites and desires. Without a social contract in the form of government, life is "solitary, poor, nasty, brutish, and short."[44] Reasoning, under his definition, is nothing more than the mind reckoning, or adding and subtracting, and then comparing its results with the reckoning of others. Gone are the leaps of insight described by Aristotle and Grotius that help raise humanity into a special category from the rest of creation. In this system, all knowledge is essentially tentative and flawed. Hobbes's theories about what a human being is, and the epistemological consequences of this definition lay the foundation of how he defines social organization and government. In place of theologically based natural law, which has an implied common good and a divine origin, Hobbes speaks of the laws of nature which, in exchange for giving up certain rights and containing certain impulses, are designed to reduce the risk of strife between fellow human beings. In short, this social contract is built upon a desire to escape from the chaos that would otherwise ensue without political organization. If nothing else, political organization is ultimately a pragmatic exercise: "The Passions that encline men to Peace, are Feare of Death; Desire of such things as are necessary to commodious living; and a Hope by their Industry to obtain them."[45]

Though he comes from a materialist viewpoint, Hobbes spends a large portion of *Leviathan* discussing scriptural authority, the role of revelation and biblical ideas about religion and the state. Hobbes argued that the sovereign should determine the doctrine of a nation as a means to control the passions and conflicts that erupt over competing religious ideas and agendas. However, he said too much restraint on religious matters might be counterproductive: "A state can constrain obedience, but convince no error, nor alter the minds of them that believe they have the better reason. Suppression of doctrine does but unite and exasperate, that is, increase both the malice and power of them that have already believed them."[46] Hobbes also remains suspicious of the clergy, since they (as all men) will seek power, and therefore have the potential to jeopardize the sovereign's authority.

---

44. Hobbes, *Leviathan*, XIII.
45. Hobbes, *Leviathan*, XIII.
46. Hobbes, *Behemoth*, Dialogue 2.

Benedict de Spinoza (1632–1677)

With Spinoza, freedom of conscience emerged as a primary right upon which other human rights flow. In his *Theological-Political Treatise*, he envisions the study and interpretation of Scripture as a basis for political organization. Yet, Spinoza wields the full weight of Enlightenment naturalism against his interpretation of the Old and New Testament. He strips away the supernatural source of miracles and special revelation. In doing so, he argues the use of reason and imagination by free individuals is a fundamental part of human experience that should be protected and cultivated. He asserts democracy has emerged as the prime form of government in which the individual trades some rights to the state (such as the right to commit violence against an enemy) in order to secure freedom of conscience and expression. He argued only deeds detrimental to civil society should be punished, and individual pursuits of happiness through reason should be left alone: "Divine law, which makes men truly happy and teaches the true life, is universal to all men. We also deduced that law from human nature in such a way that it must itself be deemed innate to the human mind and, so to speak, inscribed upon it."[47] He later went on to write:

> It is not, I contend, the purpose of the state to turn people from rational beings into beasts or automata, but rather to allow their minds and bodies to develop in their own ways in security and enjoy the free use of reason, and not to participate in conflicts based on hatred, anger or deceit or in malicious disputes with each other. Therefore, the true purpose of the state is in fact freedom.[48]

Spinoza argues a state that protects the right of individuals to use their own reason and imagination and safely express themselves, promotes its own peace and stability:

> For in reality it is far from possible to make everyone speak according to a script. On the contrary, the more one strives to deprive people of freedom of speech, the more obstinately they resist . . . Hence, a government which denies each person freedom to speak and to communicate what they think, will be a very violent government whereas a state where everyone is conceded this freedom will be moderate.[49]

---

47. Spinoza, *Theological-Political Treatise*, 68.
48. Spinoza, *Theological-Political Treatise*, 252.
49. Spinoza, *Theological-Political Treatise*, 251, 255.

However, Spinoza argued the state properly reserves some religious restrictions. For example, religious institutions that desire to be the legitimizing authority for the state, or institutions that grow large enough to exert too much control in society, or encourage subversiveness, should be controlled by the sovereign in order to maintain stability.[50]

Pierre Bayle (1647–1706)

Pierre Bayle was a French Calvinist philosopher who continued the Enlightenment project of reinterpreting Scripture to align with reason. Before the Reformation, the monopoly on authority held by the Roman Catholic Church had implications in the development of religious tradition regarding politics and religious liberty. In Bayle's day, post-Reformation Europe had a variety of religious authorities, and the Enlightenment called into question the supernatural claims of Scripture and religious tradition.

Into this cultural and religious fray, Bayle took the traditional doctors of the church to task regarding religious compulsion. In contrast to Augustine, who advocated the use of state authority to quell varieties of religious expression, Bayle argued: "The literal Sense of the words, 'Compel 'em to come in,' is directly repugnant to the Spirit of the Gospel."[51]

He argued that, in the context of the life and teaching of Christ, arguing that God wants his servants to force worship on unbelievers of any type is contrary to accurate biblical teaching. Like Spinoza, who discarded literal interpretations of supernatural and prophetic claims, Bayle asserted the "compel them to come in" line in Luke 14:23 should be not be interpreted literally, but as an allegory whose interpretation should fit comfortably with the rest of Jesus' teachings: "He does not say that he drives the Flock before him with Rod or Whip, as forcing 'em into grounds against their will; no, he goes before 'em, and they follow him, because they know his Voice: which signifies his leaving 'em at full liberty to follow."[52]

Reflecting the plurality of religious authority in 17th-century Europe, Bayle points out that each sect of Christianity believes itself to have the true interpretation of the Bible's teaching, and that each should have the right to pursue that truth. He also identifies the double standard that Church authorities exercised between monarchs and subjects, often tolerating a king's heresy while persecuting a commoner for variant beliefs.[53]

50. Spinoza, *Theological-Political Treatise*, 249.
51. Bayle, *Philosophical Commentary*, 58.
52. Bayle, *Philosophical Commentary*, 70.
53. Bayle, *Philosophical Commentary*.

Bayle builds a case for wide religious toleration, including atheists. He argues for "true religion" as the basis for human morality. Yet, he says a tolerance of ideas is reasonably based on a person's actions in society, not their inward beliefs.[54] That is, an atheist, for example, should be able to live peacefully as an upstanding citizen, even though (from a philosophical standpoint) their morality is based on something other than altruism or love of God. On the other hand: "It is conceivable that amongst those criminals, ruffians and celebrated assassins who commit crimes of that sort there are some who have no religion, but the contrary is still more probable given that among the many malefactors who pass through the hangman's hands, there are none that are found to be atheists."[55] As a result, Bayle argues for freedom of conscience with regard to religious beliefs, and moderation in the state's enforcement with regard to moral behaviors that do not endanger the safety and security of its citizens.[56]

Roger Williams (1603–1683)

The Protestant theologian and founder of Providence Plantation, Roger Williams, holds a unique place in the development of American-style religious freedom. Though his Puritan contemporaries and fellow English theologians were also formulating types of religious liberty, Williams is credited with innovations in both the conceptual arguments protecting religious liberty as well as the relationship between civil and religious governance.

Williams argued religious freedom went beyond securing rights of free worship for a particular group, which the Puritans sought. He argued the conscience of the individual should itself not be violated, even labeling religious compulsion "soul rape."[57] For Williams, the right to private judgment is a sacred privilege that cannot be violated without moral implications: "the blood of so many hundred thousand souls of Protestants and Papists, spilt in the wars of present and former ages, for their respective consciences, is not required nor accepted by Jesus Christ the Prince of Peace."[58]

Like Hobbes, he argued the use of civil penalties against religious liberty only increases dissent: "God requireth not a uniformity of religion to be enacted and enforced in any civil state; which enforced uniformity (sooner or later) is the greatest occasion of civil war, ravishing of conscience,

---

54. Bayle, *Bayle*, 312.
55. Bayle, *Bayle*, 317.
56. Bayle, *Bayle*, 326.
57. Williams, *Bloudy Tenant*, 205.
58. Williams, *Bloudy Tenant*, 87.

persecution of Christ Jesus in his servants, and of the hypocrisy and destruction of millions of souls."[59]

Perhaps one of his most enduring points of influence is his contribution to the debate over boundaries between the civil and religious authority. By outlining clearer boundaries between the "Power of the Keys" (the church), and the "Power of the Sword," (civil government), Williams defined the contours of debates that continue to this day regarding the relationship between the government and religion. His ideas incorporated earlier arguments by other theologians and political philosophers. This includes Richard Hooker, who first used the term "wall of separation" with regard to church and state.[60] Williams expanded upon this idea, arguing a free conscience and free corporate worship should not be violated unless there is a compelling reason for the state to infringe upon religious liberty.

Williams saw the human conscience as an inviolable part of every person. He also saw the conscience as a pathway to God, nothing less than the voice of God within each person, and the way each person communicates with God. As such, freedom to follow one's conscience is the freedom to follow God's will versus the freedom to do anything one wishes. His argument follows that a violation of any person's conscience is a violation of human dignity. His vision was pluralistic from the start, seeing the rights of a free conscience being held by "Jews, Turks, Papists, Protestants, pagans" in addition to the varieties of Christian in his context.

Core ideas about the nature of human conscience fed Williams's ideas about the government's need to protect the right of a free conscience. These ideas revolved around noncoercion, equality, nonestablishment, and separationism. Williams sought to bring the force of law to bear on the protection of the rights of a free conscience, in contrast to legal persecution that violated conscience rights that were prevalent in his day.

His ideas were considered radical in their time. Copies of his religious freedom tract, "The Bloody Tenant," were burned as a threat to English law. A central feature of his argument is persecution by the government for the sake of conscience is a sacrilegious transgression on the part of the government because it interferes with God's work. Later thinkers, such as John Locke, and founding fathers, such as James Madison and Thomas Jefferson, expand his religious ideas regarding the free conscience into secular concepts of freedom of thought and the inviolability of individual rights. Those ideas found their way into the First Amendment enshrined in the American Constitution written more than a century after Williams's death.

---

59. Williams, *Bloudy Tenant*, 2.
60. Hooker, *Of the Laws of Ecclesiastical Polity*, 219–20.

John Locke (1632–1704)

John Locke was an English Enlightenment philosopher that had a tremendous influence on American political thought with respect to the essential rights of an individual, the origins of those rights, and the implications for a civil government. In contrast to some French Enlightenment thinkers, who embraced materialist rationalism, Locke argued reason itself was given by God, "the candle of the Lord" as he put it. In a similar vein as Williams, he argued divinely imparted reason should rightly be used to discern moral and civil knowledge.[61] Locke's theory combines ideas about liberal and rational society with the pursuit of moral and religious truth. Thomas Jefferson offered a distilled version of Locke's ideas in the preamble of the *Declaration of Independence*: "We hold these truths to be self-evident, that all men are created equal, that they are endowed by their Creator with certain unalienable Rights, that among these are Life, Liberty and the pursuit of Happiness."[62] A key difference being that Locke concluded the triplet with the right to secure property ownership versus Jefferson's pursuit of happiness.

Like other English thinkers of the day, Locke pressed for freedom of conscience and civil tolerance of a variety of religious beliefs:

> The care of souls is not committed to the civil magistrate, any more than to other men. . . . it appears not that God has ever given any such authority to one man over another, as to compel any one to his religion. Nor can any power be vested in the magistrate by the consent of the people; because no man can so far abandon the care of his own salvation as blindly to leave it to the choice of any other, whether prince or subject, to prescribe to him what faith or worship he shall embrace . . . All the life and power of true religion consists in the inward and full persuasion of the mind; and faith is not faith without believing.[63]

Locke argued it is not possible to construct a theory of common rights without God's sovereignty: "Want of a common judge with authority puts all men in a state of nature: force without right, upon a man's person, makes a state of war, both where there is, and is not, a common judge."[64] Current debates about religious liberty often hinge on the proper role of religion in civil society. Those who draw upon the French Enlightenment model of materialist rationalism often place human rights in opposition with nonrational religious

---

61. Forster, *John Locke's Politics of Moral Consensus*, 85.
62. Jefferson, "Declaration Of Independence."
63. Locke and Popple, *Two Treatises of Government*, 192.
64. Locke and Popple, *Two Treatises of Government*, 97.

beliefs, as opposed to the Lockean vision of religious expression that is part and parcel with reason and the rights of the individual.[65]

Immanuel Kant (1724–1803)

The exemplar of Enlightenment thinking was Immanuel Kant. He carried Descartes's foundation of reason to new heights with the idea of transcendental idealism: the idea that our minds can, through subjective reasoning, come to objective conceptions about what we observe in the world. Kant's ideas regarding reason had profound implications for philosophy, theology, and political organization, even into the postmodern era.

Kant's philosophy moved the location of moral authority from outside the individual (i.e., the church or Scripture), to the individual's mind. Subjective ethical reasoning carried the weight of objectivity, in what he called the "categorical imperative." Through right thinking and right action, it is up to individuals to harness their tendency for evil. Individuals program their intellect to work out the proper moral maxims. Rejecting "radical evil" is a process derived from subjective reasoning: "Man himself must make or have made himself into whatever, in a moral sense, whether good or evil, he is or is to become. Either condition must be an effect of his free choice; for otherwise he could not be held responsible for it."[66]

Kant realized even with the nature-given advantage of reason, individuals have a tendency to be selfish and unreasonable. Left alone, they often come to conclusions that are not advantageous to society, drawing on Augustine's observation that there are two loves in the human heart: that of God and the things of God, and that of the self, even to the point of contempt for God.[67] For Kant, this warps human nature and leaves room for evil. The result is distilled in Kant's summation of the individual's reasoning tendency outside of the constraints of society (using Isaiah Berlin's paraphrase): "Out of the crooked timber of humanity, no straight thing was ever made."[68] A feature of Kant's idealized vision of society (*gesellschaft*) was that members freely compete against one another within the limits of civility, in an environment of competition and even "pervasive antagonism" among its members. This competition forces each member to reach ever-greater heights of reason (like trees in a forest reaching for sunlight), straightening

---

65. Trigg, "Threats to Religious Freedom in Europe."
66. Kant and Greene, *Religion within the Limits of Reason Alone*, 154, 42, 52, 775.
67. Taylor, *Sources of the Self*, 366.
68. Berlin, *The Crooked Timber of Humanity*, 19.

the twisted reasoning tendencies of individuals.[69] Kant envisioned a utopian society that clung to the tree of reason, whose fruit nourished individual freedom, the rational pursuit of goodness, and the interior adoption of ethical principles. The idea of God was retained in Kant's system as a philosophically necessary presupposition for the existence of morality, but not particularly relevant beyond subjective moral reasoning.

The ideas from Kant and the leading figures covered in this survey were incorporated into the functional norms that play a role up to the present day. The next chapter traces the idea of religious liberty and a free conscience from the founding of the American republic to the postmodern era.

---

69. Kant, *Idee zu einer allgemeinen Geschichte*, 10, 23. "Aus so krummem Holze, als woraus der Mensch gemacht ist, kann nichts ganz Gerades gezimmert warden."

2

From the American Experiment to Postmodernism

DURING THE FORMATION OF the United States, the founders fought to shed the authority of the crown and form an ideological and political mechanism for transforming a group of colonies into a nation. John Locke and others provided the philosophical underpinnings of liberty that justified independence. One of the issues faced by the founders was the plurality of religious denominations and institutions among the states (Puritans and Baptists in Connecticut, Episcopalians in Virginia, Quakers in Pennsylvania, etc.).

The American model of religious freedom, enshrined in the Establishment Clause of the First Amendment, can be seen as a culmination of the conversation between Christian and secular Enlightenment thinking with regard to theology and the role of reason. Scholars and legal analysts continue to debate the origins and implications of the Establishment Clause. Some see the letter and spirit of the First Amendment, as well as the writings of leading historical figures such as Roger Williams and James Madison, as endorsing a model of religious freedom that excludes an explicit role of religious actors and ideas in the formation of public policy.

On the other hand, others see the American tradition of religious freedom rooted in the variety of Christian evangelical movements during the colonial era. For them, the Establishment Clause established a barrier against governmental interference in religious affairs. They argue the framers of the Constitution deliberately protected religious behavior and organization over the alternative understanding of individualistic "rights of conscience" prevalent in some circles during that time.[1]

William Penn (1644–1718)

William Penn, the founder of Pennsylvania and a leading figure in the history of American religious freedom, had a particularly egalitarian vision of the relationship between civil authority and religion. Penn argued for government by consent and mutually applicable laws, and the protection of personal property as an essential component of the pursuit of liberty. He advocated the use of civil authority to suppress vice and enforce public morality, but argued forcefully against persecution regarding matters of conscience which he said should be protected as an expression of man's nature. Penn was suspicious of Roman Catholics, whom he suspected of holding loyalties to a "foreign jurisdiction."[2] At the same time, Penn argued Quakers and others with variant religious views should be able to use their own ability to reason to determine religious truth, without being treated as a subordinate religious group by the state.

Elisha Williams (1694–1755)

Elisha Williams was another early figure who argued forcefully for the rights of a free conscience, rooted firmly in the idea that reason is a gift from God and therefore beyond the purview of civil regulation:

> The rights of Magna Charta depend not on the will of the prince, or the will of the legislature; but they are the inherent natural rights of Englishmen . . . And if there be any rights, any priviledges, that we may call natural and unalienable, this is one, viz. the right of private judgment, and liberty of worshipping God according to our consciences, without controul from human laws . . . This we hold, not from man, but from God: which therefore no man can touch and be innocent.[3]

---

1. McConnell, "Origins and Historical Understanding of Free Exercise of Religion," 1409–1517.
2. Penn and Murphy, *Political Writings of William Penn*, 129.
3. Williams, *Essential Rights and Liberties of Protestants*, 65.

James Madison (1751–1836)

James Madison was equally vigorous in his arguments against any state establishment of a religious denomination. In his "Memorial and Remonstrance against Religious Assessments," he upheld the idea that rights of conscience transcend civil authority, and extended the argument against establishment by pointing out the ills of governments that endorse a religion:

> During almost fifteen centuries has the legal establishment of Christianity been on trial. What have been its fruits? More or less in all places, pride and indolence in the Clergy, ignorance and servility in the laity, in both, superstition, bigotry and persecution. Enquire of the Teachers of Christianity for the ages in which it appeared in its greatest lustre; those of every sect, point to the ages prior to its incorporation with Civil policy.[4]

Madison also argued that a variety of religious sects, all regarded equally under the law, lessens the danger of religion becoming a tool of oppression:

> A religious sect may degenerate into a political faction in a part of the Confederacy; but the variety of sects dispersed over the entire face of it must secure the national councils against any danger from that source. A rage for paper money, for an abolition of debts, for an equal division of property, or for any other improper or wicked project, will be less apt to pervade the whole body of the Union than a particular member of it; in the same proportion as such a malady is more likely to taint a particular county or district, than an entire State.[5]

In this vision, members of the society compete with one another with mutual antagonism and competing interests. However, instead of reaching for idealistic heights of reason, the "crooked timbers of humanity" described by Kant instead create a log jam that prevents the domination of one group over others.

Thomas Jefferson (1743–1826)

When it comes to ideas regarding religious freedom, Jefferson is most often quoted from his letter to the Danbury, Connecticut Baptists, which mentions the "wall of separation between the Church and State."[6] Taken from its

---

4. Madison, "Memorial and Remonstrance against Religious Assessments," para. 7.
5. Madison, "Federalist Papers No. 10," para. 21.
6. Jefferson, "Jefferson's Letter to the Danbury Baptists," para. 2.

context, this phrase is used as a weapon on both sides of arguments about religion in public life. Given the prominence of religious freedom literally chiseled into Jefferson's own epitaph, it is worth noting briefly that he not only believed the government should not play a compulsive role in religious matters, such as forcing church membership or religious taxes on citizens, but also that the free conscience had a role in public life that transcends the state:

> Our civil rights have no dependence on our religious opinions any more than our opinions in physics or geometry. That therefore the proscribing any citizen as unworthy the public confidence, by laying upon him an incapacity of being called to offices of trust and emolument, unless he profess or renounce this or that religious opinion, is depriving him injuriously of those privileges and advantages, to which, in common with his fellow citizens, he has a natural right.[7]

Thomas Jefferson's writings complement Madison's arguments for an egalitarian relationship between government and a variety of religious groups. Among the points he makes in his *Notes on the State of Virginia* is the state should not concern itself with the peaceful interaction of a variety of religious actors: "[I]t does me no injury for my neighbour to say there are twenty gods, or no god. It neither picks my pocket nor breaks my leg . . . "[8] Like Madison, Jefferson sees value in a society with a variety of religious communities:

> Difference of opinion is advantageous in religion. The several sects perform the office of a *Censor morum* over each other. Is uniformity attainable? Millions of innocent men, women, and children, since the introduction of Christianity, have been burnt, tortured, fined, imprisoned; yet we have not advanced one inch towards uniformity. What has been the effect of coercion? To make one half the world fools, and the other half hypocrites.[9]

Jefferson, a deist, exerted tremendous influence in both thought and the formation of the founding policies of the United States. Likewise, Madison cannot be classified as evangelical (unlike his mentor, John Witherspoon). However their ideas were formed within a milieu of religious and revolutionary fervor, and drew upon both the passion and ideas of religious leaders who helped build the country over the previous 150 years.

7. Jefferson, "Act for Establishing Religious Freedom," para. 1.
8. Jefferson, "Notes on the State of Virginia," 169.
9. Jefferson and Washington, *Writings of Thomas Jefferson*, 401.

Colonial religious pluralism was mirrored by the host of others pluralisms in the early America. This includes the variety of economies, local cultures, sources of labor, and ideas about the proper form of government.[10] The founders constructed a system of checks and balances to limit federal power and mitigate differences between the states. This structure was formed around an innovative ideological core that drew from thinkers such as Locke, but was worked out in practical terms among the founders. The goal was first to establish and preserve the union. However, a constructive ideological component was needed to undergird pragmatic political structures and offer a vision that could hold together members of the union as one people amid their diversity. The identity of the United States, and the enduring example it provides for burgeoning democracies, is located squarely in this vision of freedom, equality, and opportunity that emerged from their efforts.

The current pluralistic environment has some parallels with the United States at its founding. Religious groups ranging from the Danbury Baptists to the Jewish community in Newport, Rhode Island worried about domination by majority religious groups or by the government itself. Furthermore, each state contained its own particular religious history, and a populace with a variety of religious and nonsectarian ideas. Jefferson and Madison observed the nation's pluralistic nature, including its own version of religious pluralism, and sought to make this pluralism a functional feature of national unity.

19TH-20TH CENTURY

A major effect of modernity is what Mark Lilla refers to as the "Great Separation."[11] As the understanding of the cosmos was disjoined from theology, political institutions and philosophy were separated from religious institutions. As a result, the path of an individual's enlightened self-determination was mediated by the new political structure based on the nation-state, and eventually liberal democratic secularism. In this view, governments are based on a grand social contract as characterized in Hobbes's *Leviathan*, requiring citizens to trade some levels of personal autonomy in exchange for a political order that delivered certain goods, such as civil law and security.

As a result, theology and the religious hierarchies no longer held direct lines of authority over the lives of either individuals or the state. Normative values claims were contested in a public space occupied by individuals and

10. Katkin, *Beyond Pluralism*, 105–24.
11. Lilla, *Stillborn God*, 55.

groups holding a variety of competing views. Protestant and Catholic theology in the late modern era developed different ways to come to terms with the new environment.

Catholic Responses (1893–Present)

In *Rerum Novarum* (1893), Pope Leo XIII delivered the church's response to conditions affecting the working class suffering from the effects of the Industrial Revolution, and the general lack of protective organizations (i.e., unions) to ensure they were not abused. In this encyclical, the state is recognized as any form of government that orders society according to natural law, protects private property, and encourages virtue among citizens. It is significant as a religious call from the church to social action, and a call for government to play a role in promoting the well-being of its citizens. Leo dismisses socialist remedies to the problem, saying the working class would be the first to suffer under this ideology. Rather, private property is a natural right that offers some degree of protection from oppression. It also urges fair treatment of the working class by the rich, according to divine principles.[12] Other encyclicals on Catholic social teaching followed in the 20th century that dealt with the need to rein in the ills of big industry, and the obligation of the wealthy to use their surpluses for the common good.

A document produced by the Second Vatican Council in 1965 that is of particular interest to this religious liberty is *Dignitatis Humanae*.[13] The document outlines the official Catholic stance on religious freedom and the right of a free conscience for Catholics and non-Catholics alike. Leading thinkers behind *Dignitatis Humanae* such as John Courtney Murray saw the rise of secularism on the global stage as the predominant trend, and proposed a new stance for the church. This included the legitimate recognition of many religious groups, advocating religious freedom for all. This development in Catholic theology recognized intellectual contributions regarding human dignity and moral autonomy, as well as the realities of modern secular political systems.

Dignitatis Humanae is a prime example of the church responding to contemporary challenges of modernity and secularism with a theological stance consistent with core traditional teachings. Part of the genius of the document is it recognizes the rights and position of competing religious groups in a secular regime without endorsing the theological or ecclesiastical content of those competing groups, or even giving up its internal

12. Leo XIII, "*Rerum Novarum.*"
13. *Dignitatis Humanae.*

regard as the true church. It demonstrates adaptability within the context of a solid ecclesiastical identity. As a result, far from spelling the end of the church's influence in contemporary society, this adjusted stance opened up an era of deep Catholic influence on the global stage, including the waves of democratization that occurred in predominantly Catholic countries. The emergence of the Catholic left in Latin America and changes in the church's approach to individualism and social justice following the Second Vatican Council helped usher new states into the family of democratic nations.

In 1991, Pope John Paul II issued *Centesimus Annus*, which built on previous encyclicals by asserting the rights associated with human dignity, particularly as they pertain to free association, private property, spiritual development, worship, fair compensation, and the universal obligation to pursue the common good. With regard to the church and state, John Paul identified the origins of modern totalitarianism as rooted in a denial of the transcendental dignity of every individual. He also asserted the church's role on this issue is to continually defend human dignity. With regard to democracies, he said governments have an obligation to protect rights that promote families, and some democracies have lost sight of the common good. John Paul also reminded members of the church that pursuit of the common good and care for the poor were included in the overall mission of the church to bring the gospel to the world, with social justice being an active commitment to love one's neighbor.

Karl Barth (1886–1968)

In *The Humanity of God,* the German Protestant theologian Karl Barth outlined a response to modernist theologians regarding the incarnation of Jesus Christ and its implications on history. Barth argued the humanity of God is forgotten in modernist theological responses, which act to the detriment of understanding God's interest in human beings. The thoroughly otherworldly Christ of modern theologians, Barth argues, puts up a barrier between people and God, making God unknowable. It also severs the intimate relationship between humanity and God. When it comes to ethics, Christian understanding remains incomplete when the humanity of God, through Jesus, is not understood or acknowledged. Our responses toward others, whether with saints or the reprobate, become more loving when we understand that through the humanity of God, Jesus is everyone's brother, and God is the father of all. This understanding reaches into the approach Christians take in the political realm.[14]

14. Barth, *Humanity of God*.

In other writings, including *The Epistle to the Romans* and *Community State and Church*, Barth argues both church and state (but especially the state) are infused with both the trappings of grace as well as the detrimental effects of sin. Barth's vision of the relationship of the church to the state can be seen as a series of concentric circles rather than a dichotomy between two domains, or the rule of one domain over another. Barth spoke of the present order as a temporary construct, or "mediated fellowship,"[15] that occupies a place in humanity's developing relationship with God. That is, the church itself is a function of the community of believers that are instrumental in bringing about the kingdom of God. Yet, humanity's imperfection also means people occupy a state of grace in their relationship to God, since sinfulness remains part of the human condition. As a result, the primary role the church plays in society is to preach the gospel and administer the sacraments, bring congregants together for prayer and worship, aid the disadvantaged, offer religious education, and other types of pastoral care.

In his description of the state, Barth conveys Calvin's interpretation of Romans 13, "Let everyone be subject to the governing authorities, for there is no authority except that which God has established. The authorities that exist have been established by God . . . " Barth reaffirms Calvin's opinion that the governing authorities act (once again in an ideal sense) as the lieutenants, or even vicars, of Christ insofar as their limited jurisdiction applies. The Christian is beholden to obey the ruling authorities and render their service to the community through the state since it is also an "external means of grace."[16] However, Barth, who was exiled from Germany during World War II after refusing to swear an oath to Adolf Hitler, emphasized a person is a Christian and member of the church first, and a citizen second. In cases where the state deviates from its divinely defined role, Barth argued Christians are obligated to reject it, or work to have it altered or renewed.

John Rawls (1921–2002)

In his book, *Political Liberalism*, Rawls attempted to answer the question: "How is it possible that there may exist over time a stable and just society of free and equal citizens profoundly divided by reasonable though incompatible religious, philosophical, and moral doctrines?"[17] The goal of Rawls's thesis is to articulate a view of the state as essentially a contractual arrangement between citizens, legitimated by the consensus and participation

---

15. Barth, *Ethics*, 441.
16. Barth, *Community, State, and Church*, 22.
17. Rawls, *Political Liberalism*, xxv.

of its members. Rawls recognizes the difficulty of a state that enforces compulsory power, yet does not favor one moral ideology (i.e., religious perspective) over another. Rawls's answer is to create a common ground of discourse where ideas are argued on their political merits aside from the comprehensive/foundational ideologies held by various religious groups.

Rawls's aim is to utilize rational argument to identify universally accepted moral laws on which policies are formed. He argued groups holding comprehensive doctrines unique to themselves do not have to give up those beliefs and values; rather they are to enter into a mode of discourse that appeals to a deliberative process that those outside the group can participate in. A critical feature of Rawls's vision for democratic discourse is the idea of overlapping consensus. This occurs when multiple groups in a society form similar conclusions regarding a particular value claim, even though the origin of that value claim may differ according to each group's doctrines. Rawls recognizes the tendency in a pluralistic society for groups with varying foundational perspectives to cluster around certain values and issues that overlap with groups holding similar values, and remain partitioned off from those with competing values. Yet, Rawls admits there are limits to this model: "Eventually, though, there comes a point beyond which the requisite agreement in judgment breaks down and society splits into more or less distinct parts that hold diverse opinions on fundamental political questions."[18]

POSTMODERN ERA

Today, many crucial questions face humanity. Among them: What does it mean to be human? What values flow from our definition of humanity? How do we manage the pluralistic nature of today's society? Answering these questions effectively is no easy task. Yet, effectively pursuing these questions is critical to avoiding a repeat of the abuses of the past, and addressing the existential threats to our collective future.

What makes our current religious and political environment one of the most vital and fascinating in human history is the present challenge of pluralism. On this side of the postmodern era, no particular methodology or worldview can enforce an absolute public claim to the knowledge and values we need in order to address the challenges of our time. Instead, a new model of inquiry, debate, and engagement is needed to handle the pressing questions of the age.

Historically, the development of science, religion, and political systems have relied on an authoritative stance of a group or ideology regarding

18. Rawls, *Theory of Justice*, 340.

the nature of reality and the role of the person. Switching to a dialogical model where humility, fallibility, and engagement with incommensurable worldviews can be difficult. However, outlining the parameters of this new type of engagement is one of the most important tasks facing our common future. Intellectual and political developments over the past four centuries have forever changed the role of religion, the state, and science in Western intellectual life. Tracing these developments reveals the crucial issues in Western thought that recur in contemporary debates.

The postmodern era dismantled the remaining idealistic claims of early Enlightenment thinkers. This set forth a reworking of how people know what they know, and how people form communities of meaning. The implications in the religious and political spheres are still being worked out. Before delving into the contemporary discourse on the subject, here is a brief look at a few major thinkers who helped define the postmodern era.

Søren Kierkegaard (1813–1855)

Kierkegaard acknowledged that although human senses are reliable, the historical truth of anything is elusive. Therefore a great amount of knowledge about the world is contingent upon either faith or a conscious deferral of conclusions. The fate of the skeptic is to keep his mind constantly in suspense. The tension between certainty and uncertainty forces the individual to remain in a precarious state or freely choose a path of faith that resolves the tension. With regard to the incarnation of Jesus Christ, the contradictions wrapped up in the idea that God emptied himself to become man require a level of faith and passionate belief that is fundamentally transformative for the person.

Kierkegaard attempts to construct a unifying concept around the idea of freedom, being, and historicity. What has happened in the past is not necessary, in that the past could have unfolded in any manner of ways. The future does not carry the feature of being necessary in that it can also unfold in different ways. Kierkegaard connects contingency and variability of events in time to freedom. The necessary exists out of time and is simply being. God exercises his own transcendent freedom by crossing the boundaries of necessary existence into the historical domain. In this way, God provides a limited freedom to man to reach toward the necessary/absolute through the paradox that God has created his presence in history. Just as history doesn't necessarily need to unfold in a certain way, so individuals are free to make the decision to cross into faith or not.[19]

19. Kierkegaard and Swenson, *Philosophical Fragments*.

Kierkegaard captures an essential feature of Enlightenment thinking when he describes the Socratic view: "Each individual is his own center, and the entire world centers in him, because his self-knowledge is a knowledge of God."[20] This takes on different forms among different thinkers. Kant, for example, argued individual reason is the path to understanding and the basis of moral action, and Christ is an abstract exemplar of the perfect autonomous moral agent.

Kierkegaard retains the Enlightenment idea of individual freedom and autonomy. However, he decisively departs from Enlightenment thinking when he describes God as a being who acts and exists entirely outside the individual. The individual remains an autonomous agent encountering the world through reason, feeling, etc. However, God acts to present a condition to individuals that brings them to a new understanding and way of life that is outside, and perhaps even contrary to reason: faith. This understanding is not merely a projection of the imagination; it is a willful action on the part of the individual to resolve the paradox in favor of the idea that the God-man (Christ) presents. God is able to bring the individual to a new state of understanding that supersedes the lower levels of reason and feeling.[21]

Is it convincing? Few people arrive and cultivate faith through considering rational proofs regarding the existence of God, etc. Often reliance on proofs to describe the reasonableness of faith comes after the acquisition of faith itself. Internally, these rational proofs are used to maintain the faith that is already there, shoring up the mental defenses against what Kierkegaard describes as the absurdity of the absolute paradox, or as a means to talk about what they believe to those outside of their faith.

Kierkegaard emerged as one of the harshest critics of the project to redefine theological categories along modern/Enlightenment lines. In *Philosophical Fragments*, he explores the classical claims of Christianity and outlines their paradoxical relationship to the conclusions that can be formed via rational thought. In the process of crafting a novel approach to the question of post-Enlightenment faith, he affirmed some of the key themes of the era. In doing so, he placed the locus of authority and decision-making within the individual.[22]

Kierkegaard outlines a way to faith for the individual that recognizes the miraculous claims in the Bible, particularly the idea Jesus was the incarnated Son of God. Rather than making bland assertions about God's historical actions and intentions, or abstracting the idea of Christ into merely an

20. Kierkegaard and Swenson, *Philosophical Fragments*, 9.
21. Kierkegaard and Swenson, *Philosophical Fragments*.
22. Kierkegaard and Swenson, *Philosophical Fragments*.

archetype like Kant, Kierkegaard described the individual resolving himself in favor of faith beyond sensory belief or a theory based on tangible evidence. That is, he affirmed G. E. Lessing's argument that necessary truths like the divinity of Jesus cannot be reached through historical evidence—even for first-century, first-hand witnesses. Further, he argued (like Hume) that objective knowledge remains elusive, and historical claims are by their nature unreliable. The individual remains in tension about these uncertainties, or makes a resolution to overcome them by making a decision that exceeds the available evidence: "The conclusion of belief is not so much a conclusion as a resolution, and it is for this reason that belief excludes doubt."[23]

The decision to accept the incarnation results in a comprehensive transformation of the person's outlook and behavior. In doing so, God is able to transcend the barrier and enter into the historical and therefore free existence of the individual. Once the individual makes the resolution for faith, God is able to meet the believer, providing the condition for understanding the truth. In comparison to some Enlightenment thinkers who seemed to slice off portions of religious belief and life that did not match their intellectual models, Kierkegaard corralled the intellectual paradoxes of faith claims into his system.

Kierkegaard's faith in the incarnation is not merely a jump in logic. He argued the incarnation itself builds a bridge between the unnecessary/historical and the necessary/eternal, which can be crossed by the individual willing to believe. In this way, Kierkegaard changes the question of epistemology and historicity to a question of whether the individual recognizes the limits of logical inquiry and resolves to accept truths found in the eternal domain.[24] While retaining the place of subjectivity, he expanded its landscape with regard to faith. Kierkegaard's influence can be heard in a wide range of religious voices, including Billy Graham whose hallmark of evangelism was asking revival audiences to make a freely considered decision to follow Christ.[25]

Adolf von Harnack (1851–1930)

While some thinkers simply discarded religious claims, or shoehorned a semblance of Christian ideas into their models (like Kant's Christ-as-archetype seems to do), others tried to reconcile modern ideas about reason with the claims of Scripture. Adolf von Harnack, among others, tried to query

---

23. Kierkegaard and Swenson, *Philosophical Fragments*, 80.
24. Michalson, "Lessing, Kierkegaard, and the 'Ugly Ditch,'" 324.
25. McLoughlin, *Modern Revivalism*, 514.

biblical passages for truths that stood up to rational inquiry, particularly the life and teachings of Jesus. This involved dissecting scriptural accounts in search of truths beyond the miraculous or metaphysical claims that offended reason. In doing so, he tried to tease out an essence of Christianity that stood up to rational thought based on historical investigation. In this respect, Harnack is an important counterpoint to Kierkegaard. The theological trajectories of these two thinkers seem to occupy two of the poles of thought with regard to contemporary discourse about religion in general, and Christianity in particular. The historical-critical approach to religion versus Kierkegaard's existential leap of faith continues to be rich fodder for contemporary debates.

For Harnack, the scholar's job is to separate the kernels of historicity from the husk of what was added later to the teachings of Jesus: "For in order to decide what of the past shall continue to be in effect and what must be done away with or transformed, the historian must judge like a king. Everything must be designed to furnish a preparation for the future, for only the discipline of learning has a right to exist which lays the foundation for what is to be."[26]

This eye on the future and the idea that faith and history were unfolding toward a maturity of the human race drew from Enlightenment idealism. For example, Harnack writes that accounts of demon possession were common in the first century, so it is understandable that they made their way into the New Testament. However, modern reason "is sufficient for declining to accept them."[27] There also seem to be significant elements of Kant's influence in Harnack's emphasis on internal morality as an important part of the coming kingdom of God. Where Kant abstracted the person of Christ, Harnack sought to find him in history. As a result of his historical investigation, he concluded, if nothing else, the essence of Christianity is ethical by nature.

Harnack seems suspicious of emotion (à la Schleiermacher) as a critical element of religion. In one portion of *What is Christianity?*[28] he cites religious emotion and enthusiasm as key features of new religious movements. However, he argues emotion naturally fades away in favor of dogma, ritual, and regulations. In effect, emotion is neither durable nor reliable.[29] Yet, he asserts love for both God and neighbor is the driving force behind ethical

---

26. Livingstone, *Modern Christian Thought*, 288.
27. Harnack and Saunders, *What is Christianity?*, 63.
28. Harnack and Saunders, *What is Christianity?*, 169.
29. Harnack and Saunders, *What is Christianity?*, 212.

behavior.[30] Harnack's project assumed from the beginning that something valuable to humanity would remain from an historical-critical inquiry into the life of Jesus. This involved deconstructing biblical passages according to what could be known about their historical setting, the possible motivations of the authors, and the credibility of some sayings of Jesus set against others deemed not as credible.

Where Kierkegaard and Harnack part company dramatically is in their views on the divine sonship of Jesus. Kierkegaard emphasizes the paradox of such a claim, yet refuses to discard it for those who have resolved their will toward faith. Harnack, however, modifies the traditional understanding of the incarnation to the point that Jesus is only the Son of God insofar that he has internalized an understanding of God as a father.[31] The supernatural claims in Scripture are placed in opposition to what reason holds against those claims, resulting in an understanding that filters what Scriptures say by what can be known according to modern understanding.

Harnack's project sought to find the objective wisdom underlying the supernatural metaphysics woven throughout the scriptural passages. However, there are certain problems this poses. If the historicity of anything found in the Bible can be disputed, one could also argue even the ethical components Harnack finds as the essence of Christianity are not necessarily unique or historical. Also, Harnack seems to be arbitrarily choosing moments in the development of Christianity to assert what he regards as the essence of the faith. The danger here is in choosing where the essence resides. Is it in the actual mind of Jesus? Is it in Jesus' teachings as spoken in the Sermon on the Mount? Some argue the essence of Christianity was decided during the First Council of Nicaea, regardless of what was spoken by Jesus centuries beforehand. Kierkegaard might say Harnack's objective is itself paradoxical in that it attempts to peel away the innovations of time to reach an original substance, which results in a dismantling of what it is trying to preserve.

Friedrich Nietzsche (1844–1900)

Nietzsche argued moral standards and ways of thinking flowed from the premodern into the modern era as historically contingent developments, rather than transcendentally necessary features of human life. By tracing a genealogy of ethical ideology through the ages in *Beyond Good and Evil*, Nietzsche argued moral claims are merely the products of history. Moreover,

---

30. Livingstone, *Modern Christian Thought*, 290.
31. Livingstone, *Modern Christian Thought*, 302.

the idea of "evil" itself emerges from a slave mentality. Nietzsche argues the ruling classes of ancient civilizations originally merely thought in terms of "good" and "bad" when it came to placing a value claim on a given object or situation. Good was an attribute of that which led to greater power, comfort, and prosperity. Bad hindered the same. Evil was a concept that arose from the slave castes as they attached a transcendent quality that did not burden the aristocratic class. As such, "good" came to reflect the values of a slave mentality: meekness was valued over exercise of power, obedience over ambition, etc. Qualities associated with the aristocratic caste (aggression, greed, etc.) took on the quality of "evil."[32]

Nietzsche argued Western civilization is based upon a fusion of and tension between the master and slave mentalities, which was reflective of the Greek (heroic) and the Hebraic (slave) cultural heritages. He argued the egalitarian impulses of the Enlightenment are a direct descendant of the slave perspective that has shaped European culture through the ages. He wrote that the foundational thinking found in, for example, Kant's categorical imperative, is merely another historically contingent value, an illusion dependent on a culturally conditioned perspective rather than a transcendent ideal. A person who recognizes the historical contingency of their own values and cosmology can critique their own understandings as merely products of history. At that point, they have the opportunity to choose their own path forward. Nietzsche posits there is no God, or if there is, he is irrelevant to man's own will to power in an impersonal universe. Like many of Nietzsche's ideas, the marrying of values with power would become an important attribute of postmodern thought over the next century.

Jean-François Lyotard (1924–1998)

The distrust of received traditions was a legacy of Nietzsche's ideas throughout the 20th century. In 1979, Lyotard grappled with these ideas when he imported the term "postmodern" from domains such as art and architecture into philosophy and sociology in his book, *The Postmodern Condition: A Report on Knowledge*. Lyotard argued humanity historically relied on metanarratives to make sense of the world. Metanarratives are grand stories endorsing metaphysical explanations, methods of inquiry, and inherent values claims. These have shaped cultures and provided meaning and values to societies throughout history.[33]

---

32. Nietzsche, *Beyond Good and Evil*, 70.
33. Lyotard, *Postmodern Condition*.

The postmodern period has brought about a new situation. Metanarratives themselves are held up for scrutiny. The net effect of the postmodern condition is the collapse of the metanarrative's defining nature. Lyotard observes that a particular style of "language game" is replacing metanarratives. These language games skirt claims to absolute truth in favor of acknowledging and validating a diversity of perspectives. The present moment is fraught with danger when it comes to governing nations containing a variety of groups holding incommensurable values and even ideas about what it means to be human.[34]

Lyotard argues technological advances in the last half of the 20th century have dramatically reshaped how knowledge is defined, processed, and legitimized. He argues, when it comes to decisions about what constitutes legitimate knowledge and what should be preserved as knowledge, governments and large corporations loom large as the holders of power. Therefore, language games are inherently political. A modification in the language changes the game itself.

Lyotard does not see science as escaping scrutiny over its own narrative. He observes, in the modern era, scientific knowledge was legitimated through a teleological lens. That is, it was oriented toward a goal of a full understanding of the world (Hegel), or the emancipation of humanity (Marx). In the technological/postmodern era, the scientific narrative has gained high legitimacy because it is very efficient in how it produces knowledge. It performs the best among other major narratives in producing data that can benefit a technological society's economy. Lyotard's criticism of this condition is not unlike Max Weber's "iron cage" or "shell as hard as steel."[35] Weber and Lyotard warn the rise of technology and science, at the expense of values that transcend production efficiency and economic gain, is a dehumanizing development.

Lyotard's remedy is the legitimation of science through "paralogy," or moving beyond the productive aspects of scientific knowledge to scrutinize the overarching rationality in which that knowledge was reached. In doing so, Lyotard offers a paradoxical explanation of how the idea of justice can once again enter into the equation: "Consensus has become an outmoded and suspect value. But justice as a value is neither outmoded nor suspect. We must thus arrive at an idea and practice of justice that is not linked to that of consensus."[36]

---

34. Lyotard, *Postmodern Condition*, 25.
35. Baehr, "'Iron Cage' and the 'Shell as Hard as Steel,'" 153–69.
36. Lyotard, *Postmodern Condition*, 66.

The postmodern era left the challenge of functional values in a pluralistic environment an open question. Political developments, which rely on some form of common ethics to govern society, generated a piecemeal set of functional values regarding the role of reason and individual autonomy in a secular system. Tension remained over the role of the many religious and nonreligious perspectives found in a secular society. During the past few decades thinkers from a variety of disciplines have explored new prospects for developing a path forward in this pluralistic environment.

Richard Bernstein (1932–)

A chief complaint against postmodernists is they leave the question of meaning, values, and intercommunal dialogue mired in relativism. Meanwhile, the many facets of globalization and the existential threats that came with it demand answers about how a world full of incommensurable ways of assigning meaning could move toward a mutually beneficial future. Richard Bernstein outlined a "new conversation" among philosophers that steers a course around relativism via practical reasoning and dialogue across disciplines.[37]

Drawing from Lyotard's observations, Bernstein argued the major societal shift of the age occurred during the last half of the 20th century, when the technological/bureaucratic society that valued economic efficiency above all else merged with scientific positivism. Bernstein disputed the idea that incommensurable ways of viewing the world could not meet at points of shared perspective, or learn from each other through sustained interdisciplinary dialogue. Through rational dialogue and practical reason, a way forward could be forged in a pluralistic environment. What lies over the horizon for humanity may not yet be known in a complete way. Even so, otherwise incommensurable traditions and methodologies that describe the world can enter into a common space where they can sharpen each other's perspectives and provide a variety of tenable ways of handling the issues facing humanity. The global assortment of linguistic and cultural groups are not necessarily closed to dialogue with others holding a different perspective.

Intellectuals such as Bernstein, Richard Rorty, and Richard Shusterman are often categorized as forming a school known as pragmatism (or neopragmatism to distinguish it from earlier developments under the same name). There are certain features of pragmatism expressed in common by Bernstein and his colleagues. First, they oppose the idea that any knowledge

---

37. Reynhout, *Interdisciplinary Interpretation*, 25.

rests upon a fixed foundation. We can make ourselves aware of our own foundational or interpretive assumptions by examining them as subjects. Second, any inquiry begins with certain interpretive prejudices, so no argument can be made without acknowledging it is fallible at some level. Third, the "self" has a social nature, and therefore exists in and is conditioned by a community. Inquiry should begin within the investigating context of a given community. Fourth, all inquiry exists within the larger context of a plurality of historically contingent perspectives, philosophical orientations, and traditions.[38]

Those engaged in the type of dialogue Bernstein deals with must recognize the interpretive limitations of their own perspective and at the same time consider the internal logic of the person holding another worldview. In today's world, this applies to both the scientist and theologian. Both scientism and some forms of theology point to incommensurability as justification for rejecting interdisciplinary engagement. Bernstein's project argues that a stable and ongoing conversation can be achieved beyond objectivism and relativism. The alternative to engagement is an endless power struggle between totalizing ideologies. For Bernstein, it is not enough to philosophically deconstruct worldviews. For the sake of humanity one must engage in reconstruction as well, as fragile and fallible as that reconstructive dialogue might be.

SCANNING THE HORIZON

What does that dialogue look like? Paul Ricoeur is among those who have blazed a philosophical path that avoids the false dilemma of objectivism versus realism. Ricoeur envisions dialogue among theologians and secular philosophers as a wager rather than a proclamation:

> I wager that I shall have a better understanding of the bond of the being of man and the being of all beings . . . That wager then becomes the task of verifying my wager and saturating it, so to speak, with intelligibility. In return, the task transforms my wager: in betting *on* the significance of the symbolic world, I bet at the same time *that* my wager will be restored to me in power of reflection, in the element of coherent discourse.[39]

According to this wager, the person enters into a nonprivileged public conversation that reflects their interpretive location, but recognizes the

38. Westbrook, "Pragmatists and Politics," 104–21.
39. Ricoeur, *Symbolism of Evil*, 355 (emphasis original).

limits of that perspective. Submitting one's argument requires putting it into a language that those from other perspectives can understand in their own context. The arguments themselves are changed and broadened in the process, as is the perspective of the thinker. Those engaging in dialogue from other perspectives must confirm or deny the argument according to their own perspectives through mutual intelligibility. Agreements on wagers may come and go, but mutually respectful dialogue, humble in its approach and recognizing the fallibility of one's own perspective, illuminates the path forward.

In contrast, absolutist approaches seem to perpetuate conflict, whether from particular orthodoxies of identity or from positivist postures found in scientism. Unfortunately, this seems to be the ethos of the day in the public square. Concerns for human rights, the benefits of scientific research, and the production of values by religious and nonreligious communities are all potential beneficiaries of constructive dialogue. An overemphasis on rights alone creates pockets of competing political factions that engage in perpetual conflict. Scientism runs the risk of moving science itself from a bracketed task of describing a portion of reality to a totalizing stance that purports to describe everything about reality. On the other hand, religious communities often abdicate their role in making an intelligible, interdisciplinary case for human values that make sense outside their own constituency.

In her *Draft for a Statement of Obligations*, Simone Weil offered a different starting point for shaping an individual's role in the public space. In short, Weil's point of departure was a "profession of faith" that there is an absolute outside of human experience that manifests itself in a "longing" for the good inside every person. This longing for the unreachable absolute forms a connection between every human being. This connection places people on equal footing with the other when it comes to their connection to the good. Inequalities arise in the areas of economics, accidents of birth, and other factors. However, the idea that humanity is bound together by the pursuit of the good has the ability to shape the political sphere.[40]

For Weil, the capital-"O" Obligation one has to another person is to remove roadblocks (or "privations of the soul") that hinder the pursuit of the good. This comes prior to the assertion of rights for oneself. In public life, this includes creating an environment of free intellectual expression, where no hermeneutical perspective holds an authoritative place of privilege. That is not to say anything goes: Weil views deliberate falsehoods and ideologies that negatively impact the Obligation and an individual's pursuit

---

40. Weil and Miles, *Simone Weil*, 207.

of the good as a threat to public health. The Obligation requires a love for others, and to facilitate their own pursuit of the good.[41]

The pragmatic approach to dialogue between individuals and communities of varying hermeneutic perspectives perhaps requires an element of Weil's vision of the Obligation under a certain definition of the word "love." Defining love as commitment and action to protect the good of another (distinct from an emotional or physiological response) forms a synonymous connection between love and Obligation. Yet, it is not a personal, saintly love that she is necessarily talking about, but one that is connected to a universal concept that cuts across the lines of relativism and objectivity. In other words, pragmatic discourse among different hermeneutical perspectives requires the element of love/Obligation in order to bootstrap the conversations that Bernstein and others see as a critical part of a better future.

Stanley Hauerwas (1940–)

The rules of argument for modern philosophers and theologians often revolve around universal abstract notions, such as: What is the self? How do people come to knowledge? Hauerwas identifies Christians as people defined by their own distinct narrative. The Christian faith deals with a particular people living under the assumptions and experiences of a particular story about God's unfolding of history. Modern philosophical secularism deals with universals of the human condition that cannot enter into a dialogue with the particulars of the Christian story without compromising its universal stance. Hauerwas argues that the incommensurability between modernity and Christianity is found in the nature of the two systems. Part of Hauerwas's thinking centers on the question of whether human beings are creatures who participate in the meaning of a universe created by God, or are merely another meaningless accident of evolution in a natural world that is contained unto itself. For Hauerwas, a theologian cannot accept the epistemological suppositions and rational ethical program of modernity without setting Christianity on a course to dissolution. He cites Kant, through works such as *Religion Through the Limits of Reason Alone*, as moving the locus of theology from the exterior relationship between God and humanity to interior rationality. By handing the interrogation of nature to a materialist form of science at the expense of natural theology, Hauerwas says modern theologians were left ultimately without the conceptual resources to make the Christian God intelligible according to modernity's terms.[42]

---

41. Weil and Miles, *Simone Weil*, 209.
42. Hauerwas, *With the Grain of the Universe*.

Reinhold Niebuhr (1892–1971)

Reinhold Niebuhr saw modern democracy as a crucial barrier against injustice when it was combined with a strong spiritual orientation. In *Moral Man and Immoral Society*, Niebuhr argued for the role of the church from a compelling sociological perspective. He argued reason is often subservient to the self-interests of a group, so reason itself cannot be the arbiter of justice and ethical action. Furthermore, societies have trouble dealing with the competing interests found among their constituent groups. The *immoral society* in his equation demonstrates a low capacity among large groups to possess a concern for others, which leads to an increasingly unrestrained will to power over others.

Yet, it is through the democratic system that individuals, Christians included, can exert their moral convictions in the public square. Niebuhr argues harmonious social relationships need to be cultivated using both a reasoned sense of justice as well as benevolent sentiments. Religion's critical role in a society is to rein in the spirit of selfishness that emerges within a society by employing sensitivities found in a distinctly religious perspective.

Nicholas Wolterstorff (1932–)

Nicholas Wolterstorff argues that the agenda of political theology engaged with the modern world is far from over. Wolterstorff revives and redefines the Calvinist idea of providence at work in the present secular age. That is, Christians who believe God works through history can retain a belief He is working in the world's present system and through parties and institutions that do not recognize Him in the same way the believer does. At the political level, this means engaging with others in a pluralistic environment on issues where values of human dignity and other public goods are held in common. This differs from, for example, John Rawls's view of overlapping consensus in that Rawls calls for a meeting point among political actors on the grounds of reason alone. Wolterstorff argues each may make their case with the full weight of their tradition as the basis for advocacy. He argues the Rawlsian experiment of reason-based consensus has failed to generate agreement, so the viable option is to recover a much more rounded dialogue among religious and nonreligious actors.

Wolterstorff does not deny the corrosive effects of a *Leviathan*-like state. However, he sees the state as nevertheless forming an instrument of God's providence:

> States are fallen powers. They are evil. They oppress and kill people. But what's the alternative? Chaos is the alternative. Human existence is impossible in conditions of chaos. Human existence needs order. And states—all states—secure order. Willy nilly they secure order. There cannot be a state that does not secure some degree of order. So given the necessity of order for human existence, states are historical necessities. Evil though they are, their continued existence is a manifestation of God's providential care for humankind. For God to abolish these structures would be to bring human existence in history to an end.[43]

Wolterstorff also sees the state as being under the judgment of God, even as it acts as, in some respects, a mediator of God's providential will. The Christian citizen participates in the secular political process in order to limit the evil that might be done by the state. Conversely, Christians who disengage from secular social and political participation have a degree of moral culpability for the evil that takes place in their state. Therefore, a political theology that recognizes the pluralistic environment of the present age is a necessary component of the role of the church. The theologian may hold views incommensurable with other actors in the public space, but that does not absolve the theologian from working out an ethic of engagement.

THE PATH FORWARD

De Tocqueville observed how unity amid pluralism manifested itself in early America. He noted the broad consensus regarding religion, common human dignity, and other "habits of the heart" among the majority of the population contributed to unity amid plurality in the early United States.[44] Some argue the increasing strains of individualism and the broadening of pluralism in American society that De Tocqueville's observed, alongside other effects of modernity, have splintered the American experiment in *E Pluribus Unum* ("Out of Many, One") over the past century.

In light of this, one could argue Jefferson's ideas on religious freedom and freedom of conscience are as historically contingent as plantation life at the turn of the 19th century. Yet, an examination sees the ideas of both religious and political freedom that Jefferson, Madison, Williams, and others advanced spring from a common root, and are flourishing today. That is, certain religious and civil rights are beyond the jurisdiction of the state, and need to be protected from unjust restriction by the powers that be. This basic

---

43. Wolterstorff, *Mighty and the Almighty*, 24.
44. De Tocqueville, *Democracy in America*, 383.

idea is not only enshrined in the American Constitution and Bill of Rights, it is also a basic assumption found in many modern representative governments, and a key concept of the Universal Declaration of Human Rights.

During the 19th century, there was what Steven Smith has dubbed a "soft constitutionalism" with respect to religious freedom.[45] Various doctrines, denominations, and movements competed in the American marketplace for adherents. This included the Baptist and Methodist movements of the Second Great Awakening, which expanded the traditional choices of denominational membership among Americans, even as the young nation itself was expanding westward. Even though there was a plurality of religious options, they all had a common thread of Christianity. De Tocqueville noted the "habits of the heart" that united 19th-century Americans, habits that were cultivated within the Christianities of early America.[46]

The "American Settlement" between political authority in government and moral authority in religion in its various forms lasted until about the mid-20th century. Modernity presented a new cultural challenge that discarded an assumed Christian grand narrative. This form of secularism called the moral authority of the church into question, and gave birth to human rights language that changed the subject from duty to God toward greater individualism and human equality.

Some thinkers in the modern era, such as Ernst Troeltsch, argued Christianity in itself says nothing when it comes directly to the idea of the state. However, religion has come to play a critical role in the normative values of the state, and the pursuit of what today are collectively categorized as social justice issues. Modernists viewed history as leaving behind metaphysical claims while transferring values rooted in a religious context to a secular-democratic context. Troeltsch and others argued, at the same time, Christianity abandoned the progressive march to democracy by acting as a legitimating institution for aristocratic rule. Therefore, Christianity's legacy at the beginning of the 20th century was simultaneously the rule of the few over the many, and the demand that those who rule do so in a way that advances the well-being of their subjects.[47] At best, this vision shows the church as offering benevolent elitism, at worst an institution that exists to paper over the moral culpability of oppressive regimes.

Yet, the transference of religious values to a modern secular milieu was called into question by influential figures such as Friedrich Nietzsche. For Nietzsche, intellectual honesty demanded unmooring society's values from

---

45. Smith, *Rise and Decline of American Religious Freedom*, 128.
46. Bellah, *Habits of the Heart*, 220.
47. Troeltsch, *Religion in History*.

any remaining semblance of transcendent truth, whether that of the church or of Enlightenment idealists such as Kant. For Nietzsche, the root of human endeavor was the will to power, to overcome both the slave mentality and the domination of the social systems built on this ideological foundation. For Nietzsche, all traditions and ethical systems are merely fictions which individuals are free to choose, alter, or discard entirely.[48]

Later 20th-century thinkers, such as the tremendously influential John Rawls, tried to skirt Nietzsche's observations and reclaim the ideal of objective, universal values. For Rawls, pluralism is justly handled by forming common public discourse around reason alone, rather than the inclusion of political arguments founded within the variety of comprehensive belief systems. For Rawls and other secularists, this system prevents one ideology from exerting undue control over others in a society, giving everyone a common voice. Yet, Rawls's system seems to fall short of the idea that all in a democratic republic are endowed with a free conscience that cannot be unduly restricted from public expression without violating an individual's dignity. Therefore a tension emerges between the ideals of classic secular liberalism, which diminishes the role of religion in the public square, with those ideas of representative government that place the free conscience outside of the political jurisdiction.

American debates about religious freedom in the United States and global religious freedom concerns are two sides of the same coin. Through international treaties, sanctions, and the work of transnational organizations, developing countries experience a degree of pressure with respect to human rights, including religious freedom. Today, religious liberty and conscience issues around the world continue to be a major cause of concern. The United States has led the advancement of global democracy, yet certain cultural and political factors have diminished the ability of the United States to remain a leader in this area. In the meantime, countries that view minority religious communities and religion itself as an impediment to the consolidated power of the state continue to oppress adherents around the world.

The ideas of these thinkers and leaders reach beyond the historical context in which they were formed, and helped shape the functional norms of democracy and human rights around the world today. The relevant point is that everyone is responsible for how they handle the received ideas that shape our world. We need to take stock of our responses with respect to the best ideas received from previous generations about how to construct a society that leads to greater human flourishing. The next section digs into how this is being worked out in today's context.

48. Bernstein, "Nietzsche or Aristotle?," 6–29.

PART TWO

3

Religious Freedom Advocacy and Pluralism

IN THE UNITED STATES and around the world, religious groups seek protection from encroaching government restrictions and rising social hostilities.[1] This issue remains at the forefront of many debates over the role of religious groups in society. The question arises as to whether current rhetoric and mobilization approaches are sufficient to address religious freedom concerns.[2]

The following chapters delve into the different modes of religious freedom advocacy at work among today's evangelical organizations. They examine how a cross-section of religious networks and organizations tackle the pursuit of religious freedom in the contemporary context. The principles of Dynamic Engagement emerge from the case studies examined here. In addition to sociological analysis of how Christian groups have mobilized in the public square, Dynamic Engagement draws upon current conversations on the role of Christians in a pluralistic secular society. This includes the perspective of those who would advocate a retreat from a public square they see as incommensurable with Christian ideals, as well as those who seek an enduring presence for Christians in civil and political life. The case studies cover three modes of religious freedom advocacy and public engagement:

1. Pew Forum on Religion and Public Life, "Lobbying for the Faithful."
2. Pew Research Center, "Latest Trends in Religious Restrictions and Hostilities."

- Local evangelical mobilization in the United States, exemplified by the passage of the 1998 International Religious Freedom Act and the anti-Sharia movement in the mid-2010s.
- Organizations operating in the Global South in countries with high social and political hostilities, exemplified by the work of the Coptic Evangelical Organization for Social Services.
- Religious freedom initiatives that traverse national boundaries, exemplified by the work of the Institute for Global Engagement in Vietnam.

Woven throughout the studies are examples of how Christian groups are changing the way they view their role in society, and debating internally how they should respond to the rapidly changing political and legal landscapes. Taking stock of those developments within this tradition will help define the trajectories ahead. Throughout the project, leaders in each case study find themselves in circumstances that are unique to a postmodern, pluralistic age in which many groups are struggling to find both protection for their constituencies and the freedom of faithful public expression.

METHODOLOGY

This study employs tools of social movement theorists. These tools best illustrate the anatomy of mobilization among groups seeking a remedy to an injustice or to advance a human right. In a nutshell, it is the process of a group identifying a grievance, raising support to address the grievance, and putting pressure on those in power for political change. This model constitutes the current paradigm of how reform is pursued in modern democracies by any number of groups representing a spectrum of ideologies.

This type of analysis provides a holistic assessment of how a movement forms, executes its agenda and goes into decline. Factors include the group's underlying ideology, how it defines its agenda, why members join, the resources used to advance the cause, and the consequences that flow from a group's public actions.[3] Social movement theory is actually a family of methods that attempt to explain the life cycle and effects of social movements, particularly those that have the objective of effecting a political or social change. It gets behind a group's behaviors to find the cultural and organizational resources that drive their public actions. This ranges from the various groups' ideological components, their ability to reach a certain audience, and their ability to move that audience.

3. Tarrow, *Power in Movement*, 33.

A social movement is defined here as a group engaged in collective action, drawing upon a dynamic interplay of factors to address a grievance or dissatisfaction with institutional or cultural context. The change sought by social movements ranges from changing laws for the self-protection of the group to prescriptive changes that a group wishes for the larger society in which it is situated.[4] The analysis techniques are inherently interdisciplinary, drawing upon a variety of tools that can help explain the collective action of a movement, its ability to locate and draw upon resources for mobilization, and how their behavior fits into the political process of a given context.

In recent decades, researchers have extended the field's range of the inquiry. For example, Sidney Tarrow observed that social movements are further defined by cultural resources like a shared understanding of the world, a relatively dense network of members, and organizational infrastructures that can rally the members toward collective action. He saw that a smaller group can be a forceful opponent to more powerful players in the public square if it can harness social networks and political infrastructure. At the same time, movements both large and small are subject to political opportunities that present themselves within the ebb and flow of contentious politics.[5]

Robert Benford and David Snow sought a method of identifying the internal processes in which like-minded social groups are organized into movements. They identified the role of "framing," or constructing a definition of the movement's grievance, as a critical component of a movement's mobilization. These grievances are applied to the cultural and political resources that a movement possesses, which launches a cycle of protest by the group. Benford and Snow observed that the way the grievance is framed is constrained by the culture and values of the group targeted for mobilization.[6]

The tools of social movement theory have proved useful for examining religious movements that have escaped the gaze of researchers in the past. Scholars such as Mayer Zald and John McCarthy identified religious organizations as crucibles of the type of social movement organization that this methodology is designed to describe. They see religious groups as one of the chief facilitating forces behind social movements, contributing to both the social fabric from which movements arise as well as the values and worldviews that helped drive how grievances are framed and political opportunities are seized.[7]

4. Edwards and Snow, "Resources and Social Movement Organization," 117.
5. Tarrow, *Power in Movement*, 15.
6. Benford and Snow, "Framing Processes and Social Movements," 611–39.
7. Zald and McCarthy, "Religious Groups as Crucibles of Social Movements," 67.

Since the September 11th attacks, religion as a catalyst for mobilization has captured the attention of social movement theorists. Religious groups are now facing classic social movement questions such as: "What are the motives for political activity by religious groups? By what means do these groups facilitate political action? What features and conditions of the political system provide them opportunities for effective political action?"[8]

John Hannigan observed that "spirituality and contemporary social movements are part of the same socio-cultural fabric." He noticed religious movements often express themselves as social movements as a means to defend themselves against a state or a dominant culture they find threatening. He also sees religious groups contending with other groups for a new status quo aligned with their values and worldview. He argues that underlying both religious and political/social involvement is an effort to resolve the tension between their personal religious lives and the contentious world of politics, "attempting to overcome the split between a public world of competitive striving and a private world that was supposed to provide the meaning and love that make competitive striving bearable."[9]

He observes that resources for religious movements have expanded in the age of globalization. Whereas religious movements once were primarily concerned with local and national issues, today's religious movements are able to communicate and coordinate with their co-religionists around the world.

As in other major world religions, the global family of Christian communities transcends national boundaries, cultures, and political affinities. As Christianity continues to grow, it is becoming less white, wealthy, and Western. Demographic shifts in the faith are underway, moving the religion's center of gravity from the West to the Global South.[10] In addition to the umbrella label "Christian," these communities carry distinct identities, formed through the dynamic interaction between their sacred texts, historical challenges, and the stories they construct about their place in the world.

Developing an understanding of how Christian groups in various contexts form their defining narratives and mobilize according to these narratives is an interdisciplinary task.[11] The subjects of mobilization (i.e., religious freedom, human rights, etc.) are examined with respect to how groups identify their grievances, frame their arguments in the public square, and pursue a remedy. The objective here is to illuminate how believers exercise their voice in the public square with regard to religious freedom as well

---

8. Wald et al., "Making Sense of Religion in Political Life," 121–43.
9. Hannigan, "Social Movement Theory and the Sociology of Religion," 321.
10. Jenkins, *Next Christendom*, 103.
11. White, *Content of the Form*, 121.

as how they view themselves as people of faith, citizens, and neighbors to those outside their faith.

Two approaches within the social movement framework that are particularly useful for this study are framing and resource mobilization. Framing theory examines how a group articulates an issue in a way that prompts their constituency into action.[12] Resource mobilization delves into the practical and ideological resources put into play by a social movement to advance its cause. Ziad Munson employed these approaches to examine the rise of the Muslim Brotherhood in Egypt and the mobilization of pro-life groups in the United States. The arc of similarities in his studies and this project warrant a brief look at the factors and effects he observed. In each case he took stock of the role theological and political ideas play in mobilization, in balance with other factors that draw participation from religious adherents.[13]

Munson's goals included identifying the role ideas play in mobilization with respect to organizational and political resources. In his study of Egypt's Muslim Brotherhood, he discerned factors that historically strengthened the group. In short, the Brotherhood's organizational structure made it easy for Egyptian Muslims to join and employed a structure that thwarted government efforts to repress the organization. He also observed that the group intertwined religious beliefs with its political agenda in such a way that it readily gained like-minded supporters, providing some resilience against government repression. Third, the Islamic message of the group was framed in such a way that it related directly to the daily lives of Muslim Egyptians.[14]

Operating as a protest movement from its founding in 1928 until 2011, the Muslim Brotherhood offered a religiously infused alternative to autocracy. Yet, the group's ideology proved troublesome when it took the reins of power. The group's failed effort to govern is often attributed to the Brotherhood's effort to monopolize power and undemocratically reshape Egypt according to its ideological vision.[15] Munson found its unique mix of social ideology and Islamic interpretation pervades the Brotherhood's historical structure and message. This contributed to its popularity and decades of resilience in the face of government efforts to stamp out the group, but it was not effective in building a government itself.[16]

Munson also examined the role of ideology as one among several resources for mobilization in his study of pro-life groups in the United States.

12. Benford and Snow, "Framing Processes and Social Movements," 611–39.
13. Munson, "Islamic Mobilization," 487–510.
14. Munson, "Islamic Mobilization," 507.
15. Kingley, "Egyptian Activists Hope for 'Second Revolution.'"
16. Munson, "Islamic Mobilization," 507.

He argued identifying *religion* as merely a set of ideological propositions does not account for all the mechanisms that accompany those beliefs, why those beliefs are employed and not others, and the limits of those beliefs with respect to the goals of a given group.

He also found that many activists joining pro-life mobilization efforts were not always drawn from the pool of true believers in the cause. Rather, participants came from a variety of theological and political perspectives, including pro-secular and pro-choice individuals, who changed or solidified their beliefs in the cause only after they had joined the group's mobilization efforts. Munson attributes this to the strength of institutional, social, and experiential factors that transcend ideological or theological commitments.[17]

Examining the inventory of resources used by religious movements further illuminates what is behind mobilization on a given issue. In addition to the ideological resources that contribute to the cohesiveness of the group, there are a series of boots-on-the-ground resources as well. This includes associations and coalitions formed specifically to address a grievance, as well as events such as public meetings, vigils, demonstrations and the like. Charles Tilly defined the purpose of the mobilization actions as WUNC displays, demonstrating the (W)orthiness of the cause, (U)nity of the group around the cause, the sufficient (N)umbers to give it credibility, and the (C)ommitment they have to overturn the status quo.[18]

The framing structures and the resources used for mobilization point to the nexus of two domains. The first domain incorporates the components of a religious community that inform the identity they wish to practice and protect. This includes products of their subculture, including in-group media, and their unique theological perspectives. It also includes the character of their worship, moral commitments of the community, and their ability to convince outsiders to join their cause. The second domain determines the capacity of a given religious community to participate in a pluralistic public square. This includes identifying shared political interests with other religious or nonreligious communities, emphasizing a larger national or ethnic identity, and by communicating their tangible contributions to the common good.

CASE STUDIES

The case studies that appear in this project were chosen according to the following criteria. First, taken together they present clear examples of the three

17. Munson, *Making of Pro-Life Activists*, 2279.
18. Tilly, *Contentious Performances*, 122.

modes of Protestant/evangelical group mobilization relevant to the contemporary context. This includes the form of domestic American evangelicalism that remains a powerful political force in the United States. The second case represents the rising importance of Protestant/evangelical groups in the Global South. The third case examines the role of globalized religious organizations that work across international boundaries to effect change.

The first case study compares evangelical mobilization behind the 1998 International Religious Freedom Act (IRFA) with contemporary mobilization among many evangelicals against the American Muslim community. This case illustrates the critical role a pluralistic perspective plays in advancing or hindering religious freedom in the United States. The story behind the mobilization effort to pass the 1998 International Religious Freedom Act demonstrates the practical importance of an approach to political pursuits that are inclusive of other religious and political groups. By organizing their political strategies with activists and policy experts across religious and party lines, evangelicals played a crucial role in landmark legislation that created institutions within the United States government designed to monitor religious freedom issues around the world. The story of how the final legislation came about demonstrates how concern for Christian persecution was used as an initial catalyst for mobilization, but viability for the legislation depended on a pluralistic approach that sought to protect religious freedom across the spectrum of faiths.

This example is contrasted with the anti-Sharia movement among evangelicals, which sought to characterize the American Muslim presence in the United States as a threat to the American court system and national security. Evangelicals were mobilized according to a problematic view of American Muslims, which resulted in legal efforts to restrict the Muslims from ostensibly attempting to introduce Islamic religious law into American courts. As anti-Sharia legislation failed to produce the results intended by evangelical activists, new lawsuits and model legislation were introduced designed to restrict the use of any religious law, including Catholic canon law and Jewish law, in binding arbitration by any religious community. In this way, a mobilization effort that sought to restrict the religious freedoms of one group resulted in a threat to many religious groups, including the evangelicals' Catholic allies.

The passage of IRFA legislation was a victory for evangelicals, with lessons to be learned about the nuts and bolts of effective mobilization. Likewise, the anti-Sharia mobilization efforts were a defeat for evangelicals seeking greater religious freedom at home and abroad due to the insularity of their efforts, the clear inconsistency between their call for greater Christian religious freedom and their campaign targeting Muslim Americans, the co-option of the evangelical movement by political players outside evangelicalism, and the overall failure of the effort to effect the change they desired. While the successes of the IRFA campaign fits squarely into the model of successful mobilization, the anti-Sharia campaign is as an example of what constitutes failure by a social movement outlined by Gamson: co-option by another group, inability to gain a broader social consensus, and the inability to extract legal or social advantages.[19]

The next case study examines efforts by Egypt's Coptic Evangelical Organization for Social Services (CEOSS). Since the Arab Spring, Coptic Christians in Egypt have suffered increasing persecution and violent social hostilities. CEOSS's civil society efforts are part of a twin strategy for governmental and societal engagement they hope will result in greater religious liberty and reduced social hostilities. The leaders of this organization believe violent extremism can be mitigated by addressing needs related to poverty, disenfranchisement, unemployment, and other pressing social issues. They believe actively seeking to relieve these pressures will prevent some Egyptians from seeking violent remedies to their grievances. CEOSS remains closely engaged across different strata of government, from neighborhood councils to national leaders. This strategy emphasizes their unity with other Egyptians across demographic lines and keeps open conduits for communicating their own concerns.

CEOSS's unique approach is set within the context of the Coptic evangelical community as a public service consistent with the teachings and values of their faith. The cause of mobilization is defined by what they see as the Christian imperative to help the poor and oppressed in their community, regardless of their faith or social status. This strategic effort to identify ways they may practice their faith in a country that ranks low in religious freedoms and demonstrate their commitment to the pluralistic public good provides a strong example of Dynamic Engagement at work.

CEOSS trains members of vulnerable communities to identify and secure their rights according to national and international law. Their active pursuit of human rights across Egyptian society relies on cooperation among both Muslim and Christian Egyptians to bolster a sense of cross-religious citizenship. In doing so, they have attained the support of each successive Egyptian regime. CEOSS's pluralistic civic approach has also reduced suspicions toward the organization that had the potential to endanger its ability to remain politically and socially engaged as a religious organization.

The third case study examines the Institute for Global Engagement's (IGE) effort to address religious freedom concerns across international

---

19. Gamson, *Strategy of Social Protest*, 29.

lines. This includes IGE's ongoing efforts to relieve human rights and religious freedom concerns in Vietnam. This case study illuminates the process by which an international religious freedom advocacy group situates itself within both its home religious community as well as on the international stage. It shows how the leaders of IGE endeavored to frame their nonproselytizing approach to engagement governments and religious groups as fitting squarely within the evangelical tradition.

IGE's strategy employs what it calls a top-down, bottom-up approach by working among the country's political leaders, as well as religious representatives who operate outside the country's power structures. IGE's leaders articulated the mission of the organization according to principles they find in Christian Scripture and in the evangelical tradition. At the same time, they worked to assess the religious freedom concerns felt by Christian minorities in Vietnam, as well as the concerns of both the Vietnamese and U.S. governments with respect to religious freedom for these minorities.

IGE and the other groups examined here are each exploring ways to address the religious freedom needs they have identified in their unique contexts. The way these groups address these issues can either further their ability to freely engage the public square or lead to further conflict and religious restrictions.

There is a substantial tradition of debate among Christians about the role of the faithful in public life. Competing normative claims tackle whether and to what degree Christians should engage the political process. Examining how believers approach civil and political life requires taking stock of the normative arguments that continue to shape how religious groups see themselves in a pluralistic secular society. Integral to this examination is the idea that a Christian approach to public engagement is consistent with the theological and moral outlook of the tradition itself. The following chapter outlines these debates as they relate to the contemporary context and provides the theological backdrop for the principles of Dynamic Engagement.

# 4

Ethics of Engagement

WHILE SOME CHRISTIAN THINKERS see the political process as necessary to preserve their community, others see it as impossible to engage without violating the integrity of the faith. Each hold a set of observations and warnings about the Christian witness in society. A touchstone in this project is Reinhold Niebuhr's observation in *Moral Man and Immoral Society*. In this book, Niebuhr contends that political behavior among large religious groups runs counter to the moral ideals of its members, and almost inevitably veers into a power-play rooted in self-interest. This project tests his assertion that Christian political behavior in the contemporary political context almost inevitably tends toward a predatory stance against competing groups in society.[1]

Niebuhr argued this inclination has a bearing on how Christians should approach public life and the pursuit of justice and human rights:

> The most perfect justice cannot be established if the moral imagination of the individual does not seek to comprehend the needs and interests of his fellows . . . Any justice which is only justice soon degenerates into something less than justice. It must be saved by something which is more than justice [that is, love].[2]

According to Niebuhr, a Christian group or movement that does not cultivate a broader perspective of the common good is condemned to

---

1. Niebuhr, *Moral Man and Immoral Society*, 84.
2. Niebuhr, *Moral Man and Immoral Society*, 258.

perennial conflict and a spiral of immorality and injustice. The evidence presented in this project seems to align with Niebuhr's observations that seeking religious freedom for one's religious community without a concern for all members of a pluralistic society defeats the overall project of addressing a need within the common good, and ultimately defeats the quest of the group to look after its own interests.[3]

Niebuhr's argument remains relevant when examining the rhetoric of contemporary identity politics, from which religious freedom is often argued. Some examples emerge among the cases that counter Niebuhr's pessimistic view of group behavior. These examples show, when grounded in an ethic that meets the realities of a pluralistic context, religious freedom advocacy by Christian groups can help mitigate cycles of political and social polarization.

The definition of an ethic here is the collectively determined set of guidelines for conduct.[4] Engagement in public life includes both political activity (mobilization to support or oppose legislation, running for political office, etc.) and civil society participation (relief organizations, education partnerships, service organizations, churches, etc.). In this study, what makes the ethic Christian is the specific way practitioners in the various Christian traditions see the world and frame their public arguments in light of their Scriptures and moral traditions.

Christians are a diverse community. Protestants in particular are a fractious bunch, with evangelicals, progressives, Pentecostals, and others all offering competing visions of the Christian way of life. As Christian ethicist Robin Lovin points out, Christians are not immune from seeing themselves as those who hold the key to social order (just as others in groups with a comprehensive worldview often do):

> We are always biased to see our own group or our own nation as representative of rational humanity. We should not be surprised that those whose experience differs from ours have different ideas about what natural law requires, and we should not expect that even people who are trying to be rational will come to the same conclusions unless they also share some traditions that shape them to share common values.[5]

---

3. Niebuhr, *Moral Man and Immoral Society*, 257.
4. Lovin, *Introduction to Christian Ethics*, 50.
5. Lovin, *Introduction to Christian Ethics*, 50.

AN ETHIC OF ENGAGEMENT

One of the more fascinating features of Christian communities across the axes of time and geography is the ability to construct, contest and reconstruct the meaning and manifestations of their faith. Peter Brown, one of the world's premier authorities on early Christianity, sees interpretive industriousness and inevitable division as an important survival feature of the faith: "What I do see in late antique Christianity is a constant, constant debate, constant hiving off of small groups, constant chatter. And I think that if Christians had not been so divided Christianity might have gone under . . . It is the sheer capacity for fighting each other that kept Christians going."[6]

Timothy Shah observed a similar process of contestation and division continuing to the present day. Shah also sees this process as a survival feature among contemporary evangelical groups in the Global South. He observes this behavior as both limiting the immediate power of evangelical communities within certain contexts while securing their place within a society in the long-term: "For reasons deeply rooted in its belief and identity, evangelicalism does not constitute a single monolithic movement in the Third World but a multitude of movements that divide and subdivide in an endless ecclesiastical mitosis."[7]

Shah observed that evangelical social movements in different countries adopt perspectives and frame their grievances differently according to the national and cultural context in which they live. Evangelicals around the world may be identified by a more or less common set of theological and ecclesiastical commitments, but their political leanings and manners of engagement may vary widely. That is, where evangelicals in the United States may largely have an affinity for conservative politics, those in Europe or in the Global South may align with the political left, or remain attuned to a specific set of circumstances that escape these polarities.[8]

This "hiving off" and "ecclesiastical mitosis" shows how theological and political perspectives, and the values and principles that flow from them, are in a constant state of renegotiation. Economic pressures, the presence of other religious groups, new technologies, and a host of other influences interact with received traditions in forming how communities respond to their world. As a result, history has revealed a cornucopia of cultural and religious responses within a faith.[9]

---

6. Brown, "Costan Lecture 2014."
7. Shah, "Evangelical Politics in the Third World," 21–30.
8. Shah, "Evangelical Politics in the Third World," 21–30.
9. Johnson and Wu, *Our Global Families*, 85.

The dynamic of cultural change as it relates to mobilization unfolds as an intertextual process. Communities interpret authoritative texts (Scriptures, for example) according to the challenges they face in their historic moment. The behaviors flowing from these interpretations impact the culture of the community. This in turn creates new challenges for the community and starts the dynamic process over again.[10] The more one understands how this dynamic, intertextual process has unfolded over time, the more one may understand the dynamics involved in the formation of values and moral behaviors.

Our current historical predicament is one in which many communities, holding often incommensurable worldviews, must live alongside each other under a common political and social system. In some ways, it reflects the continual mitosis and hiving off observed by Brown and Shah. Disparate perspectives regarding the nature of humanity, the presence and role of God, and the placement of authority continue to divide segments of contemporary society.[11]

With respect to styles of public engagement, American Protestant Christianity has divided itself for more than a century into three main categories. These can be simplified as: (a) mainline denominations characterized by a modernist approach to theology and a Social Gospel orientation to public engagement, (b) fundamentalists, exemplified by theologically conservative denominations and sects that have removed themselves from public life, and (c) neo-evangelicals, populated by theologically conservative Protestants who broke away from fundamentalism in the 1950s in order to remained engaged in civil and political life.[12]

Reinhold Niebuhr's critiques echo through contemporary American Protestantism. Niebuhr criticized Christian liberals for abandoning the message of humanity's imperfection and God's revelatory role in history for the gospel of human progress, in effect discarding the theology of atonement and ignoring the entrenched effects of sin: "Having made reason and history the means of redemption, it had no real place for the doctrine of [Christ's] Redemption.[13]

Niebuhr's general theological perspective about the enduring sinfulness of humanity and its need for redemption provided some common ground with evangelicals such as E. J. Carnell and Billy Graham.[14] Yet,

10. Domingo, "Intertextuality and the Sociology of Religion."
11. Domingo, "Intertextuality and the Sociology of Religion."
12. Marty, *Public Church*, 11–12.
13. Niebuhr and Robertson, *Essays in Applied Christianity*, 124.
14. Harries and Platten, *Reinhold Niebuhr and Contemporary Politics*, 209.

Niebuhr criticized evangelicals for focusing too much on individual conversion as a catalyst for producing a more just society, and not recognizing the need to address the injustice inherent in social structures.[15]

Stanley Hauerwas is a leading voice in the current debate about the nature of Christian ethics and the possibility of public engagement in a pluralistic public square. Hauerwas's idealist position sees the chief role of the Christian in the world as maintaining integrity with respect to the precepts of faith:

> Christian ethics does not provide solutions to moral problems that everyone understands. Christian ethics identifies the human qualities that make it possible for a community to follow Jesus and shows us how those virtues can be sustained. Such a life will make little sense to people who seek other goals, but the aim of Christian witness is neither persuasion nor social transformation.[16]

The heart of Hauerwas's critique of Christian political activism is not far from Niebuhr's complaint in *Moral Man and Immoral Society*. They agree, to a point, that the current political system compels religious actors to violate ideals which are integral to an authentic Christian witness:

> Any consideration of the truth of Christian convictions cannot be divorced from the kind of community the church is and should be. . . . For Christians no theory of justice can substitute for their experience and their discussion of what implications their convictions have regarding how they should care for and treat others within and without their community.[17]

Hauerwas sees this structural political problem as inimical to authenticity: "Put as directly as I can, it is not the task of the church to try to develop social theories or strategies to make America work; rather the task of the church in this country is to become a polity that has the character necessary to survive as a truthful society."[18]

Niebuhr and the realists agree the Christian must maintain their integrity, insofar as that is possible in a fallen world, and an important Christian task is to reach for social transformation. Christian realists like Niebuhr see their efforts as making halting but relentless steps to improve the public

---

15. Niebuhr and Robertson, *Essays in Applied Christianity*, 127.
16. Niebuhr and Robertson, *Essays in Applied Christianity*, 53.
17. Hauerwas, *Community of Character*, 1–3.
18. Hauerwas, *Community of Character*, 3.

order, in full knowledge of their own limitations and need for group security. Lovin describes the Christian realist as seeing

> the human person is both made in the image of God and separated from God by a sinful urge to seek security and power in the self. Realism approaches moral problems by maintaining this balance between human freedom and human limitations, between the transforming power of love and the restraining influence of self-interest. Christianity neither sinks into pessimism that thinks it can do nothing, nor allows itself to imagine, as reformers of all sorts have often done, that it can see the future so clearly as to transform this world into a new one."[19]

Constructing a Christian ethic for public engagement challenges the either/or question that drives believers toward public engagement for the sake of the world's redemption, or away from it for the sake of Christian purity and witness. One of the chief critiques of Hauerwas's position is it offers little practical guidance for Christians working in the political arena, government policy, or a host of other positions where secular engagement is inherent, and where their absence would be felt by the Christian and non-Christian community alike. Christian realists see engagement with the flawed and sinful secular public square as being faithful to the biblical mandate to show God's presence through work for the common good, and to go into all the world.[20]

One of the main idealist critiques of the Niebuhrian realist perspective is that believers find themselves passively or actively endorsing coercion or violence by the state. Niebuhr acknowledges the question of government-sanctioned violence offers a challenge to the Christian realist vision. However, he argues violence is sometimes necessary to prevent evil from triumphing over good, and a Christian life lived in the real world is always tainted with moral culpability at some level: "There is no escape from guilt in history. This is the religious fact that Saint Paul understood so well and that is so frequently not understood by moralistic visions of the Christian faith."[21]

In the mid-1980s, the Yale theologian George Lindbeck observed Christianity was among religions that are "in an awkwardly intermediate stage of having once been culturally established [as in Niebuhr's day], but not yet disestablished."[22] Today, Hauerwas leads the way on the theme of

19. Hauerwas, *Community of Character*, 1–3.
20. 1 Cor 12:7; Mark 16:15.
21. Niebuhr, *Major Works on Religion and Politics*, 222.
22. Lindbeck, *Nature of Doctrine*, 120.

the disestablishment of Christianity. He sees the role of the church in society primarily as a witness. He offered his perspective in a nutshell after the September 11th attacks, delivering a vision of the church as a community increasingly estranged from American culture:

> Christians are not called to be heroes or shoppers. We are called to be holy. We do not think holiness is an individual achievement, but rather a set of practices to sustain a people who refuse to have their lives determined by the fear and denial of death. We believe by so living we offer our non-Christian brothers and sisters an alternative to all politics based on the denial of death. Christians are acutely aware that we seldom are faithful to the gifts God has given us, but we hope the confession of our sins is a sign of hope in a world without hope. This means pacifists do have a response to September 11, 2001. Our response is to continue living in a manner that witnesses to our belief that the world was not changed on September 11, 2001. The world was changed during the celebration of Passover in A.D. 33.[23]

By 2017, the influential conservative writer Rod Dreher pronounced Christianity irrevocably disestablished, and the liberal political order inherently hostile to a faithful Christian life. In *The Benedict Option*, Dreher pointed to a qualified public withdrawal and a contemporary take on monastic discipline as a way for the church to weather the moral decline of civilization. Though Dreher sees the church's salvation in building a stronger sense of idealism, he paints a dark picture:

> The culture war that began with the Sexual Revolution in the 1960s has now ended in defeat for Christian conservatives. The cultural left—which is to say, increasingly the American mainstream—has no intention of living in postwar peace. It is pressing forward with a harsh, relentless occupation, one that is aided by the cluelessness of Christians who don't understand what's happening.[24]

Dreher concedes Christians "cannot afford to vacate the public square entirely." He envisions a "prophetic" role for the church, speaking Christian truth to politicians from across a divide, and perhaps occasionally working with those on both sides of the aisle on certain topics. He sees Christian

---

23. Hauerwas, "September 11, 2001," 425–33.
24. Dreher, *Benedict Option*, 3.

engagement in the public square as potentially "fragile," walking a fine line between cooperation and complicity in creating an immoral public order.[25]

Critics of the trajectory envisioned by Dreher and Hauerwas say their vision of the church leads to increased isolation and a muted witness, with suffering as a by-product of the church's distance from non-Christian culture and politics.[26]

On the other hand, Niebuhr argued for a central presence of Christians in public life, where they could act at some level as a moral compass for the political order. Though Niebuhr was the Christian realist *par excellance*, 21st-century realist theologians have placed him within a long succession of realists, lending a broader historical sweep of their perspective.

Augustine is counted as one of the first Christian realists. In *City of God*, he sets in high relief the religious and political polarization of the fifth-century Roman Empire. At the time Augustine wrote the book, Christians were being blamed for the sack of Rome over their abandonment of traditional Roman religion. For Augustine, the earthly city (i.e., the non-Christian public order) is set in complete dualistic opposition to the city of God (the community of faith and its ideals). Yet, they were not entirely separated by incommensurability when it came to practical matters and the common good. Some of the goods sought by those of the earthly city (peace, justice, human flourishing, etc.) are in fact goods created by God that can be obtained in this world.

Augustine saw the rulers of the earthly city as existing in a state of ignorance, and sometimes opposition, to the form those goods take according to God's design. Nevertheless, he saw that Christians have a role to play. Rather than shunning involvement in the public square, Christians should help bring about a society that produces peace, justice, and other features of the common good. Although a perfect society can never be obtained during the city of God's pilgrimage in the earthly city, Christians can play a role in the penultimate expression of God's intent by building consensus with others around the goods God has for human society, goods that ultimately require a moral orientation toward God's design. The perfect order can only come at the eschaton, but that does not preclude the effort to create consensus around the goods God has to offer in the earthly city:

> In this life, therefore, justice is present in each man when he obeys God, when the mind rules the body, and when the reason governs the vices which oppose it, by subduing or resisting them. Also, it is present when man begs God for the grace to do

25. Dreher, *Benedict Option*, 83.
26. Jenson, "Hauerwas Examined."

meritorious deeds, and for pardon for his offences, and when he duly gives thanks to Him for all the blessings he receives. In that final peace, however, to which this justice should be referred, and for the attainment of which it is to be maintained, our nature will be healed by immortality and incorruption.[27]

Martin Luther also plays a role within the Christian realist tradition. That is, in Luther's view, the personal orientation to the virtues of the Christian life are only attractive to a small portion of society, so the pursuit of Christian government is a foolhardy enterprise. Yet, he recognizes a religious role in the ordering of society:

> To try to rule a whole country or the world by means of the Gospel is like herding together wolves, lions, eagles and sheep in the same pen, letting them mix freely, and saying to them: feed, and be just and peaceable; the stable isn't locked, there's plenty of pasture, and you have no dogs or cudgels to be afraid of. The sheep would certainly keep the peace and let themselves be governed and pastured peaceably, but they would not live long. Therefore care must be taken to keep these two governments distinct, and both must be allowed to continue [their work], the one to make [people] just, the other to create outward peace and prevent evildoing.[28]

Niebuhr saw the tradition of the Hebrew prophets as part of the realist tradition. This is seen in his analysis of the contradictory advice found in the book of Isaiah. Isaiah 31 advises Israel to shun an alliance with Egypt against Assyrian invaders, relying instead only on God's protection:

> Woe to those who go down to Egypt for help, who rely on horses, who trust in the multitude of their chariots, and in the great strength of their horsemen, but do not look to the Holy One of Israel, or seek help from the Lord. Yet he too is wise and can bring disaster; he does not take back his words. He will rise up against that wicked nation, against those who help evildoers. But the Egyptians are mere mortals and not God; their horses are flesh and not spirit.[29]

Niebuhr's perspective on this passage anticipated some of the idealists' arguments against his position. Niebuhr saw an earthly reliance on God alone as an ultimately disastrous approach to the peril faced by the

---

27. Augustinus and Dyson, *City of God against the Pagans*, 961.
28. Luther, *On Secular Authority*, 12.
29. Isa 31:1–3 KJV

Israelites, and a recipe for complacency in the face of grave evil in his day (which was contemporary with the rise of Hitler and atrocities of Stalin). Niebuhr echoes Luther's remarks about the dangers of a Christian approach to earthly life that dismisses the need for coercive power:

> Isaiah's error reoccurs perennially in the history of Christian thought and life. It consists in the belief that God's providence establishes a special immunity from disaster to a nation which makes itself worthy of such immunity by perfect righteousness. Actually, the historical process is not so simply moral. Nations, as well as individuals, may be destroyed not only by violating the laws of life, but also by achieving a defenseless purity, incompatible with the necessities of survival.[30]

Idealists have offered a competing interpretation. John Howard Yoder, for example took the opposite perspective with regard to this passage, asserting a denial of God's ultimate efficaciousness, and a quest for "effectiveness" in the world instead leads to some forms of fruitless social activism, and is tantamount to a kind of "functional atheism."[31]

Niebuhr much prefers the nuanced view of Isaiah 45, which asserts God's sovereignty over all of history as the prevailing factor when it comes to justice: "This prophet, in some respects the profoundest of all prophetic interpreters of historical destiny, insists on the hidden character of God's sovereignty over history, precisely because he is so conscious of the moral inexactness of any specific execution of divine judgment in the actual process of history."[32] In this vein, Niebuhr argues that the fact Jesus the Messiah did not bring about a political solution, as his first followers had hoped, epitomizes the perspective that God is working toward a horizon of perfection, partially through his people but ultimately according to his own schedule and purposes. The kingdom of God Jesus speaks of has arrived in a sense, but at the same time it has not quite arrived. Followers of Christ are caught in the tension between their own historical contingency, and the transcendent truth of the gospel located beyond human reason:

> Men are inclined in every age to resist a truth which discloses the contingent character of their existence and discredits the false answer to this problem of their contingent life in which they are always involved. To make faith the requirement of the ultimate meaning of existence is to recognize the divine mystery as impenetrable by human reason. To find that revelation

30. Niebuhr, *Faith and History*, 224.
31. Yoder, *Politics Of Jesus*, 106, 227.
32. Niebuhr, *Faith and History*, 125.

in an historical drama and person is to understand history as potentially meaningful rather than meaningless. To experience a divine forgiveness reaching out to man in his predicament is to recognize that the human situation, both individually and collectively, is such that man is not only unable to complete his fragmentary life but that, viewed ultimately, there is always false and sinful completion in it. Thus faith is the final expression of man's freedom; but it is an expression which involves the consciousness of an element of corruption in any specific expression of that freedom. It is the expression of his final freedom in the sense that faith achieves a point of transcendence over all the contingent aspects of man's historic existence, individually and collectively. But it must contain a recognition of the contingent and the false element in all his actual knowing. It is thus recognized as a knowledge beyond the capacity of human wisdom, as a gift of "grace." The New Testament insists that the recognition of Jesus as the Christ is possible only by the Holy Spirit.[33]

This perspective has real-life implications for the believer. That is, Christ's followers should not be swayed by the temptation toward an otherworldly perspective and way of life, which leads to complacency and a disregard for the needs of the vulnerable outside the community of faith. Nor in Niebuhr's estimation should the Christian community become so enamored with the rationality of the modern age and the liberal political order that it loses the power of the faith and the promise of perfection. He argued a loss of religious faith was particularly dangerous, since faith in human rationality alone leads to meaninglessness. (One can see Kierkegaard lurking behind the scenes here.) Rather, Christians should embrace the truth in each perspective as they embrace the transcendence of God's role in human history:

> If the truth of faith merely becomes a 'fact' of history, attested by a miracle, or validated by ecclesiastical authority, it no longer touches the soul profoundly. If it is made into a truth of reason which is validated by its coherence with a total system of rational coherence, it also loses its redemptive power. The truth of the Christian Gospel is apprehended at the very limit of all systems of meaning. It is only from that position that it has the power to challenge the complacency of those who have completed life too simply, and the despair of those who can find no meaning in life.[34]

33. Niebuhr, *Faith and History*, 143.
34. Niebuhr, *Faith and History*, 161.

Niebuhr's thought evolved during his lifetime. His critics, particularly those influenced by Anabaptist thought, zeroed in on his acceptance of violence by the state as a theological error. Perhaps one critique of Niebuhr's perspective relevant to today's context is his historical placement in the early mid-20th-century era of dominant Christian culture. The postmodern environment of the 21st century is arguably much different than Niebuhr's world. His life intersected somewhat with the Civil Rights era, but it is hard to say what he would have thought of the ongoing battles in 21st-century legal and cultural life. Even so, Niebuhr's thought about the nature of Christian ethics in public life carries insights relevant to the behavior and effectiveness of Christian public engagement.

Niebuhr wrestled with the idealists' complaint that it is impossible for the Christian community as a group to faithfully participate in the secular order. He also set forth an observation in his book *Moral Man and Immoral Society* that the political behavior of large groups almost always accommodates a predatory stance against competing groups in society.[35] Niebuhr argued this is the case even when members of the group (i.e., the Christian community) consist of honest citizens seeking a moral and ethical individual life. Niebuhr argues this inclination has a bearing on how Christians should approach public life and the pursuit of justice and human rights.[36]

Niebuhr argued group political engagement often means seeking justice exclusive of the welfare of those outside the group. According to Niebuhr, a society of individuals that does not cultivate justice for others is condemned to perennial conflict and a spiral of immorality and injustice. When it comes to contemporary pursuits of religious freedom, seeking religious freedom for one's religious community without a concern for all members of a pluralistic society defeats the overall project of creating a better society, and ultimately defeats the quest by the group to look after its own self-interest.[37]

NIEBUHR AND THE CONTEMPORARY CONTEXT

The search for a 21st-century ethic of engagement leads back to Niebuhr's doorstep. His denominational home was the (German) Evangelical Synod of North America, into which he was ordained in 1915.[38] His pastorate attracted many beyond the German-American community, and his

---

35. Niebuhr, *Moral Man and Immoral Society*, 84.
36. Niebuhr, *Moral Man and Immoral Society*, 258.
37. Niebuhr, *Moral Man and Immoral Society*, 257.
38. Fox, *Reinhold Niebuhr*, 4.

subsequent writings found wide appeal across denominational lines. After his ordination in 1915, he pastored a church in Detroit attended by auto workers. During this time, he developed a public voice in defense of workers, and the oppressed in general. However, he did not entirely accept the Social Gospel of leading theologians such as Walter Rauschenbusch. Rather, he incorporated some elements of that theology with what he would later popularize as Christian Realism. After leaving his Detroit church in 1928, having grown its congregation from dozens of parishioners to hundreds, he became a professor at Union Theological Seminary in New York. He remained at this post for more than three decades.[39]

Niebuhr's Christian Realism saw the need for continued engagement in public life as part of a Christian's duty to be salt and light in the world. He also argued Christianity had much to offer the earthly city in terms of identifying the character of social justice and the role of believers in fulfilling the promises of a liberal political order.

His approach had several attributes. First, it recognized the effect of original sin as affecting all human endeavor, particularly in the realm of large group behavior. For Niebuhr, a peaceful utopia could not be obtained through Christian isolation from the world, nor from a purely secular order devoid of an ethical center. Rather, Christians undertaking activities prescribed by the Christian faith can help serve as a moral and ethical center of an otherwise power-centered social order. Christian realist thought and action is situated between what one might call the Christian expedients, those who attached their public hopes to political figures and social movements with attitudes and agendas far from the tenets of Christianity, and the idealists, who see the political engagement as incommensurable with Christian life and thought.

Christian organizations seeking to engage in religious freedom advocacy do so at an inflection point in history. Religious demographic changes in the United States, for example, show a trend toward greater diversification. A century ago, white Protestantism, and to a lesser extent white Roman Catholicism, were considered the cultural drivers of law and ethics.[40]

Today, some have characterized the current religious demographic trends as "the end of white Christian America."[41] Not only have mainline denominations experienced a dramatic drop in the number of adherents, American evangelicals have also experienced a general aging of

---

39. Fox, *Reinhold Niebuhr*, 27.
40. Lenski, *Religious Factor*, 64.
41. Jones, *End of White Christian America*.

those who identify with the movement and slow growth among younger demographics.[42]

At the same time, the interaction of religious and nonreligious constituencies with competing values and sources of authority has given birth to an increasingly polarized public square.[43] From the late 20th century until about the turn of the millennium, the backdrop of this profoundly polarized moment in history was the *secularization thesis*. This assumption about the course of history arose as a prevailing idea among Western political theorists. The secularization thesis predicted the demise of religion as an authoritative player in the public square. Proponents of the thesis, such as Peter Berger, argued that as modernity advances, the role of faith diminishes. Berger characterized the social and political arenas as places where religion would inevitably recede. Science would replace church teaching as the chief interpreter of reality for the regular citizen. Reason-based political liberalism would replace religious authority in political matters. Indeed, one could see the decline of church attendance across Western Europe as evidence of the march of secularism and the fading role of religious life. Yet, religion did not go gently into history.

Berger recanted his adherence to the secularization thesis, arguing instead for a global resurgence of religion. In his later years, Berger observed public life is marked by plurality, with active and contentious religion as an enduring feature of global culture.[44] Outside of Europe, religion had never gone away as a locus of authority for religious individuals and groups, or as a mobilizing force for democracy. Today, the demographic mix of believers and nonbelievers is becoming more pronounced. The recent Religious Landscape Study by the Pew Forum on Religion and Public Life indicated a dramatic rise in the number of Americans who do not identify with a religious group, with a corresponding decline among Roman Catholics and mainline Protestant denominations. This group of "nones," was marked not only by their lack of adherence to a denomination but also by their secularity (with also a generalized form of spirituality among some in the group). Even with this bump in secularity, the United States remains a deeply religious country. More than 70 percent of the population belongs to a religious group. According to the study, evangelicals experienced a drop of less than 1 percent with regard to its share of the population and increased its net number of adherents by 2 million between 2007 and 2014.[45]

42. Pew Research Center, "Religious Landscape Study."
43. Pew Research Center, "Political Polarization, 1994–2017."
44. Mathewes, "Interview with Peter Berger."
45. Pew Research Center, "America's Changing Religious Landscape."

The question that rises out of the former idyllic secularist visions is how to navigate this pluralism in a way that discourages violent conflict, protects the sector of belief, and leads to greater human flourishing. While Berger's latter hypothesis about religious pluralism is supported by ongoing evidence, the degree of contentiousness that it has brought upon the public square, often with religious freedom at the center of controversy, seems to not have been fully anticipated by movements that now compete for a place of influence in public law and ethics.

Evangelical and Roman Catholic organizations are often at the center of the controversies stemming from the greater religious and ideological diversification. Disputes ranging from the hiring of denominational employees to the tax status of religious organizations to public law about the coverage of birth control have a bearing upon the conscience commitments among adherents of these groups.

The question for religious organizations and individuals seeking greater religious freedom in the courts and in the court of public opinion is: What principles for engagement ought they to follow? Old models that relied on cultural dominance are at odds with the contemporary context.[46] Though evangelicals and Catholics advocating for religious liberty can point to some victories and some losses in the first two decades of the 21st century, a coherent ethic of engagement seems yet to be fully articulated.

Niebuhr's (as well as Augustine's and Luther's) insights about the role of Christians in society speak to the idea that faithful Christians have a role to play within whatever larger cultural context they find themselves in, and despite their own limitations as sinful human beings. Additionally, those who have pointed toward some degree of public retreat have also warned retreat itself may not be enough to save the community from the ever-increasing power of the *Leviathan*-like state on the faith community.[47]

A central concern for both Hauerwas's perspective as well as Niebuhr's is the inextricable draw of the earthly city toward beliefs and actions that may run against Christian teachings. As noted, the effort to withdraw from public engagement may be ultimately impossible in light of obligations that might run against rights of conscience.[48] If one buys Niebuhr's argument that the faithful must remain engaged in public life to protect the Christian community as well as bring about the God-given goods of peace and justice, what does this look like in an age of religious, ethnic, and ideological diversity? Niebuhr was skeptical of social movements and of mobilization

---

46. "End of White Christian America."
47. Dreher, *Benedict Option*, 3.
48. Schmidt, "Tax Refusal as Conscientious Objection To War," 234–46.

on a large scale. However, today's diverse landscape seems to require some type of engagement in this view. Political mobilization may have triggered Niebuhr's distaste for large group behavior. It may also be a sign of what both he and Martin Luther warned against: the death of witness at the hands of those willing to use the tools of power for their own ends. On the other hand, Niebuhr makes a strong case that individuals and small groups have the ability to maintain a religiously coherent approach to social engagement when large groups cannot.

PRINCIPLES OF DYNAMIC ENGAGEMENT

The following case studies are examined through the lenses of social movement theory and the normative debates about the Christian community's public role. The principles of Dynamic Engagement acknowledge the need for faithfulness to one's own tradition as highlighted in the idealist perspective, as well as the compelling arguments for participation in public life made by realists. They also attempt to reflect the current pluralistic, religious, and social environment not fully anticipated by theologians such as Niebuhr. They challenge the approach of Christian expedients, who are tempted to attach their hopes to political groups and politicians who have little concern for Christian ideas of morality and justice for the sake of increasing their own power. The principles are flexible enough to allow the individuals and groups who find them useful to follow their own conscience commitments in the path toward greater faithfulness and effectiveness.

5

American Evangelical Political Mobilization

EVANGELICALS ARE A PERENNIAL force in American politics. Despite some demographic challenges, they are poised to remain a formidable group into the future. Many of today's most visible and contentious battles over religious freedom in the American public square are tied to political and legal battles fought by evangelicals. Some of these battles directly challenge the idea of universal religious freedom in the United States. These hotly contested lines cut across the political debates and campaigns utilized by mobilized ideological groups.[1]

The shape of American evangelical involvement in the political process lends itself to social movement analysis. The following chapter shows how the manner in which evangelicals frame arguments, marshal resources, organize constituencies, and execute mobilization efforts demonstrates their rootedness in the liberal democratic process. At the same time, it brings to the forefront some of the normative questions about Christian public engagement raised by theologians such as Niebuhr and Hauerwas. The examples assessed in this chapter show how evangelicals have at times worked in a pluralistic context for the public good while maintaining the integrity of their tradition, and at times mobilized against other groups in a way that runs counter to their values regarding religious freedom.

1. Stepan, *Arguing Comparative Politics*, 218–25.

This chapter explores how within the American secular legal and political framework religious groups find their public voice. Charles Taylor points out these voices are often tied to political identities as much or more than they are tied to a strictly religious expression.[2] Taylor speaks of the Secular Age as coming in several forms, including the Age of Authenticity, the subjective Age of the World-Picture (à la Heidegger), and the Age of Mobilization. The examples of anti-Muslim mobilization in this chapter show how some forms of religious political mobilization may strain against spiritual principles toward loving one's enemy which are found in Christian Scripture.[3]

One task of this chapter is to show the importance of leadership decisions in Christian advocacy campaigns, which directly impact the ethics of a group's behavior. To demonstrate this, the following examples will delve into the internal and external mechanisms of contemporary religious mobilization to find where ethical strains may occur.

The culture wars have been waged in earnest for more than five decades. Over the past two decades, many American Christians have seen their role in society threatened by a two-front war against secularism and Islam. In recent years, social and political mobilization among evangelicals and Catholics has increasingly turned toward religious freedom as a primary rallying cry.

This study compares the American evangelical campaign for the 1998 International Religious Freedom Act with the ongoing social and political campaign against Islam and Muslims in the United States. This comparison will reveal a degree of symmetry in how evangelicals were mobilized on these issues, as well as divergent trends. That is, as Christian groups pursue universal religious freedom in a pluralistic environment they find success consistent with their own stated values and an increase in religious freedom for themselves and those of other faiths. Conversely, as Christian groups seek to wage a battle for special rights, or against the religious freedom/freedom of conscience for another group, they tend to fail their own tradition's ideas of universal religious liberty and diminish their own religious freedom.

To explore these trajectories, this chapter will delve into the form evangelical mobilization takes with respect to how political grievances are identified and how campaigns to remedy those grievances are carried out. The sources of rhetoric used for this study include sermons and speeches by key mobilizers, published articles and books by activists, and the language of proposed legislation meant to expand or curb religious liberties. It will also examine the process by which mobilization campaigns central to religious freedom were organized and carried out.

2. Taylor, *Secular Age*, 766.
3. Luke 6:27–36.

The primary documents examined in this study also include a range of public comments, newspaper opinion articles, books and literature distributed to constituents, and podcasts and mass media broadcasts used by organizations and leaders to frame their grievances and argue for action among their constituents. This study also examines resources that show how public arguments intersect with the legal framework religious freedom advocates are trying to impact.

American Catholics, evangelicals, Mormons, and other major religious groups have disparate ways they handle the culture wars. The forms these controversies take seem to be expanding with each passing year. As a matter of focus, the cases here dig into two major campaigns launched by evangelicals that impact religious freedom concerns.

EVANGELICAL MOBILIZATION

After the September 11th attacks, evangelicals began to wrestle with a response to Islam and the presence of American Muslims. Some evangelicals did not see Muslims as a menace or Islam as a monolithic, democracy-threatening entity. Rick Warren, the enormously popular and influential pastor of Saddleback Community Church defended his partnerships with Muslims against criticisms from fellow evangelicals and argued for greater religious liberty in a pluralistic context.[4]

Warren was largely the exception to the rule. Influential evangelicals more often took a hard line against American Muslims and the religion of Islam. For example, Tony Perkins, president of the Family Research Center, argued Islam should not enjoy the same religious freedom protections under the Constitution as Christianity:

> I defend religious freedom. However, as the founders understood it, those freedoms, freedom of religion, freedom of speech, all was [sic] under ordered liberty, meaning that it could not tear at the fabric of our society. And those who practice Islam in its entirety, it's not just a religion, it's an economic system, it's a judicial system, and it is a military, a military system, it has Sharia law that you've heard about, and those things will tear and destroy the fabric of a democracy. And so we have to be very clear about our laws and restrain those things that would harm the whole.[5]

---

4. Stetzer, "Rick Warren Interview On Muslims, Evangelism & Missions."
5. Perkins, "David Limbaugh, Michele Bachmann, Todd Starnes," 51:43–52:30.

Perkins failed to address the religious liberty concerns of American Muslims, including blocked efforts to construct mosques, and the spate of bills in local legislatures designed to curb the purported presence of Sharia law around the United States. This is despite data indicating an uptick in government restrictions and social hostilities toward religion in the United States between 2007 and 2014, driven in large part by incidents directed against American Muslims.[6]

With the outbreak of activity by the Islamic State militant group, and the increased flow of immigrants from war-torn areas of the Middle East, Evangelical rhetoric against Islam and Muslims reached ever-higher levels in the 2010s. Like Perkins, evangelicals delivering this rhetoric often conflated the Islam of middle-class American Muslims with the extremism of Al-Qaeda and the Islamic State group, or dismissed moderate Islam as a counterfeit expression of Islam.

This was often used to stoke fear among consumers of evangelical media. For example, on Erik Stakelbeck's Trinity Broadcasting Network program *The Watchman*, he delivered his main argument that radical Islam is a global threat, and Muslims in the United States are a growing source of terrorism.

> Every week comes a new round of arrests and a new round of plots were broken out. Or, as we saw in Chattanooga, they're carried out by home-grown jihadists. If you're more interested in what the Kardashians are doing than what is going on in the world, I know this information may shock you. But if you've been watching the show over the past few months, and have read my book, *ISIS Exposed*, you know we have an epidemic in this country of U.S. Citizens answering the call of ISIS. They're going overseas to join the caliphate, or just staying put right here and plotting attacks against the homeland.[7]

Another influential evangelical leader employing this rhetoric is Franklin Graham, the son of the evangelical icon, Billy Graham. He is the president of the Billy Graham Evangelistic Association as well as the major international disaster relief organization, Samaritan's Purse. In 2018, Samaritan's Purse had an annual revenue of about 700 million dollars.[8] The relief organization is well-known for providing humanitarian relief from tornadoes, hurricanes and other natural disasters around the United States. It also responds to international crises with a number of initiatives, ranging

---

6. Pew Research Center, "Rising Tide of Restrictions On Religion."
7. Stakelbeck, "Watchman," 0:54–1:32.
8. "Form 990, Samaritan's Purse."

from food and shelter to medical care. One notable response by Samaritan's Purse was the deployment of field hospitals in Manhattan's Central Park and in Cremona, Italy during the 2020 coronavirus pandemic.[9] Their relief services are provided "to everyone regardless of race, ethnicity, religion, sexual orientation," Graham said. "We don't discriminate. Period."[10] The organization's popular Operation Christmas Child program provides shoe boxes containing toys and personal care items for children living in poverty around the world.[11]

In addition to his humanitarian and evangelistic work, Franklin Graham is outspoken about current issues in the evangelical world. In 2015, in response to an attack by a lone, "self-radicalized" Islamic extremist who killed four U.S. Marines in Chattanooga, Tennessee, Graham asked American evangelicals to urge political leaders to bar Muslim immigrants from coming to the United States:

> We are under attack by Muslims at home and abroad. We should stop all immigration of Muslims to the U.S. until this threat with Islam has been settled. Every Muslim that comes into this country has the potential to be radicalized—and they do their killing to honor their religion and Muhammad. During World War 2, we didn't allow Japanese to immigrate to America, nor did we allow Germans. Why are we allowing Muslims now? Do you agree? Let your Congressman know that we've got to put a stop to this and close the floodgates.[12]

Research conducted by the nonprofit, nonpartisan RAND Corporation paints a different picture of the sources of jihadist terror attacks in the United States:

- American Muslims are unreceptive to the violent ideologies promoted by al Qaeda and the Islamic State of Iraq and Syria (ISIS). Even those who express support for political violence in some contexts do not show a willingness to engage in violence themselves.
- Of nearly 180 jihadist planners and perpetrators in the United States between 2001 and 2017, 86 were U.S.-born citizens. The others were legal permanent residents or naturalized U.S. citizens, "in other words, people who had long residencies in the United States before arrest."

---

9. Shimron, "Samaritan's Purse Sets Up Emergency Field Hospital."
10. Shimron, "Franklin Graham on His Central Park Field Hospital," para. 7.
11. Samaritan's Purse, "Operation Christmas Child 2019 Special Report."
12. Graham, "Four Innocent Marines," para. 1.

- "The complexity of terrorist motives defies easy diagnosis. Religious beliefs and jihadist ideologies play an important role but are only one component of a constellation of motives. Remote recruiting [i.e., via social media] has increasingly made jihadist ideology a conveyer of individual discontents . . . Personal circumstances also figure heavily in the mix and, in some cases, appear to outweigh ideological grounding. Alienation, anger at perceived prejudice and injustice, avenging personal insult, the quest for identity, a feeling of emptiness . . . all appear in the life stories of jihadists."[13]

A key question emerges in the conflict between evangelical calls for government restraints on American Muslims and restricted immigration from predominantly Muslim countries. That is, to what extent does the evangelical pursuit of religious restrictions for American Muslims promote interreligious conflict and alienation among members of that community? Anti-Muslim rhetoric by American evangelicals seems to stand in sharp contrast to the drive among the same evangelicals for greater religious freedom in previous mobilization campaigns. Even so, the political mechanisms utilized by evangelical leaders in favor of religious freedom and against American Muslims share some parallels in how they originated, and in how mobilization efforts were executed.

There is a dissonance between the rhetoric many leading evangelicals used toward American Muslims and the universal religious freedom agenda that was championed by the evangelical movement in the late 1990s. Echoing the remarks of Perkins, Gen. Jerry Boykin has said Islam "should not be protected by the first Amendment, particularly given that those following the dictates of the Koran are under an obligation to destroy our Constitution and replace it with Sharia law." He also stated that "We need to recognize that Islam itself is not just a religion—it is a totalitarian way of life."[14]

Evangelical religious freedom campaigns and the current stream of anti-Muslim rhetoric have similar trajectories in how they were conceived, how they were introduced to the evangelical community, and how evangelicals were successfully mobilized to achieve political change. Both the anti-Sharia campaign and the evangelical push for passage of the 1998 International Religious Freedom Act (IRFA) have commonalities that reveal characteristics of the evangelical movement.

---

13. Jenkins, *Origins of America's Jihadists*, 1–25.
14. "Jerry Boykin," 0:01–0:07.

IRFA: Framing the Grievance

The passage of IRFA was supported by a wide range of religious and human rights groups. The chief architect of the effort, John Hanford, brought together a broad coalition of supporters for the bill. Hanford had a decade of experience helping pastors and other believers imprisoned by oppressive regimes gain their freedom.[15] At the same time the language of the bill was being crafted, the evangelical movement played a critical role in mobilizing a large, politically active constituency to lend support toward the bill. It also provided key players in drafting the legislation.

The starting point for promoting the campaign among evangelicals was the effort to raise awareness about the persecution of Christians in predominantly Muslim countries.[16] Michael Horowitz, a Jewish human rights activist, prodded evangelical leaders on the plight of Christians in a group of these countries. The credibility Horowitz brought to the issue was an important element in framing religious freedom as the remedy for the persecution of Christians. Since he was Jewish, the campaign could not have been labeled as entirely a political effort by the Christian Right. His familial background also lent the gravitas of the Holocaust experience to the burgeoning movement against global religious oppression.

Horowitz repeatedly challenged Christian activists and leaders such as Nina Shea and Chuck Colson to pay closer attention to the issue. Horowitz convinced evangelical leaders that the persecution of Christians was both pervasive and warranted the active intervention of the American evangelical community. In the words of former senator Bill Armstrong, "a Jew [Horowitz] was responsible, almost single-handedly, for magnifying and focusing the nascent interest of the evangelical community."[17]

Evangelical and nonevangelical Christian organizations concerned with religious persecution, such as Voice of the Martyrs, have highlighted global persecution of Christians for decades. However, Horowitz's activism helped evangelicals discover their political voice in the push to change American foreign policy on this issue.

15. Hertzke, *Freeing God's Children*, 209.

16. Hertzke, *Freeing God's Children*, 175. Horowitz, "New Intolerance between Crescent and Cross."

17. Hertzke, *Freeing God's Children*, 107.

IRFA: Resources

One characteristic of the American evangelical movement is the wide network of churches, para-church organizations and activists. This characteristic is certainly not limited to evangelicals. The same can be said of Roman Catholic and mainline denominations. In *Bowling Alone*, Robert Putnam observed that churches, in general, are large repositories of social capital:

> Churches provide an important incubator for civic skills, civic norms, community interests, and civic recruitment. Religiously active men and women learn to give speeches, run meetings, manage disagreements, and bear administrative responsibility. They befriend others who are in turn likely to recruit them into other forms of community activity. In part for these reasons, churchgoers are substantially more likely to be involved in secular organizations, to vote and participate politically in other ways, and to have deeper informal social connections."[18]

Even so, evangelical, Roman Catholic, and mainline denominations differ from one another in hierarchy of authority (or lack thereof) as well in their approaches to social activism and political engagement. Significant differences in theology abound as well. Defining evangelicalism has been a slippery proposition for scholars, since churches and participants within the movement vary widely in their doctrinal emphases, political activism, and authority structures. Some scholars argue the term "evangelicalism" is no longer useful in light of differences on key issues.[19] Others see a "family resemblance" in how evangelicals pick up ideas from one another, apply them through a historical and theological filter, and bring their responses to the public square.[20] David Bebbington identified four fundamental elements of this family resemblance: conversionism, biblicism, crucicentrism, and activism. A summary of these elements finds evangelicals are concerned with:

A. Personal conversion based upon an individual decision to accept salvation;

B. The Bible as it stands above other documents in terms of faith and Christian living;

C. The crucifixion as the central moment defining humanity's relationship with God;

---

18. Putnam, *Bowling Alone*, 66–67.
19. Dayton and Johnston, *Variety of American Evangelicalism*, 245–51.
20. Dayton and Johnston, *Variety of American Evangelicalism*, 252–69.

D. An activist life that spreads the faith and encourages social reform.[21]

Regarding resources for social reform, Allen Hertzke mentions in *Freeing God's Children* the international religious freedom campaign of the late 1990s drew upon the "thriving network of domestic organizations, both for ministry and social action," and was aided by the explosive growth of evangelical churches in the Global South.[22]

IRFA: Evangelical Mobilization

Horowitz, along with other Jewish activists and opinion leaders such as Abe Rosenthal of the *New York Times* and Rabbi David Saperstein, worked with a broad coalition of human rights activists to help launch the campaign for international religious freedom. A milestone of the campaign was a January 1996 conference organized by Horowitz, Nina Shea, and others that addressed the issue of religious persecution and American foreign policy.[23] In conjunction with the conference, evangelical churches and parachurch organizations promoted the campaign nationally through a "Statement of Conscience," circulated by the National Association of Evangelicals.[24] Mobilization of the evangelical community on this issue included a national campaign to raise awareness among rank-and-file Christians. Evangelical leaders such as James Dobson and D. James Kennedy used their broadcasts and mailing lists to invigorate their audiences in urging Congress to support the legislation. In Washington, conservative evangelical activists worked closely with liberal Jewish activists to strategize about what would eventually become the 1998 International Religious Freedom Act.[25]

At first, the Wolf-Specter bill concentrated on persecution. However, that focus was mitigated by the Jewish participants concerned with the bill's viability for passage. The Wolf-Specter bill was eventually rivaled by the Nickels-Lieberman bill, which placed a higher emphasis on quiet diplomacy, and was seen as more amenable to the Senate.[26] These bills were eventually superseded by IRFA, which accommodated elements of both bills.[27] While support for the bill was wide among evangelicals, the authorship

21. Bebbington, *Evangelicalism in Modern Britain*, 12–17.
22. Hertzke, *Freeing God's Children*, 146.
23. Sider and Knippers, *Toward an Evangelical Public Policy*, 59.
24. Presbyterian Church in America, "Statement of Conscience."
25. Hertzke, *Freeing God's Children*, 128.
26. Hertzke, *Freeing God's Children*, 143.
27. Ratliff, "Congress May Merge Efforts."

of the bill was conducted by a relatively small group led by Hanford, and included William Inboden and Laura Bryant. IRFA was designed to address persecution of all religious groups, and ostensibly promote religious freedom.[28] It established an Ambassador-at-Large for Religious Freedom, the Office of International Religious Freedom, an annual report at the State Department, as well as an independent bipartisan commission. It also called for a Special Adviser for Religious Freedom to be on staff with the National Security Council.[29]

The first Ambassador-at-Large for Religious Freedom was former World Vision president Robert Seiple. The second person to hold the office was Hanford, IRFA's lead author. Under Hanford's leadership the State Department's Office of Religious Freedom was greatly expanded, taking on full responsibility for the agency's annual International Religious Freedom Report.

Evangelical mobilization to support the legislation began with a primary concern about the persecution of Christians. However, the support and participation of nonevangelical groups as well as practical considerations about its viability in Congress ensured the law would seek to protect adherents of any faith.[30] In this case, the pursuit of international religious freedom by evangelicals established a trajectory toward universal religious freedom advocacy and reduced interreligious conflict.

IRFA and other religious freedom legislation has not escaped criticism. For example, Anna Su, an expert on international human rights law at the University of Toronto, argued IRFA served to transform the human right of religious freedom into a justification for continued American power.[31] Indiana University-Bloomington's Winifred Sullivan argues this act of Congress and others related to religious liberty are paradoxical: "They invited a regime under which courts would necessarily have to do the impossible, that is distinguish an exercise of religion, necessarily dividing good religion from bad religion, all the while denying that that was what they were doing."[32]

Since the passage of IRFA, evangelicals, Catholics, and many other groups have continued to monitor and advocate on behalf of international religious freedom for all faiths. Scholars such as Brian Grim, Alfred Stepan, Allen Hertzke, and many others have helped refine and bolster the

28. Hanford, "Has IRFA Succeeded?"
29. *International Religious Freedom Act.*
30. Hertzke, *Freeing God's Children*, 228.
31. Su, *Exporting Freedom*, 4.
32. Sullivan, "Impossibility of Religious Freedom," para. 16.

argument that religious freedom can be considered a first freedom in that other important human rights and a healthy society flow from the freedom of conscience, free religious practice, and the ability to bring core beliefs to the public square.

At the same time, evangelical suspicion of Islam has taken on another form in the first decades of the 21st century. Rather than being a catalyst for pursuing religious freedom for all faiths, evangelicals sought ways to restrict aspects of Muslim religious presence, fearing it would lead to an infringement on their own place in the American public square, and even overturn the U.S. Constitution itself.

ANTI-SHARIA CAMPAIGN

The evangelical campaign against Islamic law in the United States is explicitly concerned with "creeping Sharia," described briefly as the gradual supplanting of the U.S. Constitution with a Muslim legal code.[33] Before tackling the anti-Sharia campaign itself, it would be helpful to review the definition of Sharia, key international concerns, and the existing role of Sharia and other religious jurisprudence in American courts.

The most basic definition of Sharia is: a legal and moral code that governs all aspects of a Muslim's life. The word "Sharia" literally means "path to the watering hole" or, more in the spirit of the definition, "the way to the source of life."[34] It is derived from the *Qur'an*, the *Hadith* (sayings and actions of the prophet), and a tradition of legal opinions by Islamic jurists. Sharia governs a wide range of familial obligations, business dealings, criminal penalties, and religious duties. Underneath this definition is a vibrant debate in the worldwide Islamic community about what constitutes Sharia, how it applies in a secular state, and the questioned authority of laws that were drafted before the modern period.[35]

Critics often point to harsh punishments meted out on those convicted of crimes under some forms of Sharia in some countries. These range from the amputation of a person's hand as punishment for theft, to execution as punishment for apostasy and adultery, conducted according to some interpretations of Islamic jurisprudence. Indeed, the threat of harsh punishments has been the source of deadly violence between Muslims and Christians in Nigeria, where Sharia moved beyond resolving civil disputes

---

33. Sperry, *Infiltration*, xiii.
34. Ali, "Shariah And Citizenship," 1027–68.
35. Johnson and Sergie, "Islam."

among Muslims into the criminal codes of several Nigerian states.[36] Countries such as Saudi Arabia and Iran rely on specific Sunni and Shi'a versions of Sharia for their civil and criminal law. Violent punishments issued in the name of Islamic law are a perennial concern among human rights activists.

Despite the most egregious examples of abuse in the name of Islamic law, there is an ongoing debate among contemporary Muslims around the world about the nature of the law for today. Female Islamic intellectuals promote a progressive interpretation of Sharia that protects the freedom and dignity of women. Other contemporary Muslim thinkers and activists argue for a reform of some Sharia legal codes to consider modern values regarding democracy, human rights, and freedom of conscience.[37]

In the United States, some American Muslims have considered how Sharia could hold a similar place as other religious bodies of law such as Roman Catholic canon law, Halacha, and Jewish *beit din* to help resolve legal disputes between Muslims. They cite the use of Jewish and Catholic law in binding arbitration (an agreement signed by both sides used to resolve a civil dispute, and approved by a civil court) as a precedent in the acceptance of Sharia in family law and inheritance cases among American Muslims.[38] Literature produced by American Muslims on the issue notes the U.S. legal code always takes precedent when the religious law being invoked comes into conflict with the secular civil or criminal penalties. In practice, American courts discard religious rulings that are at odds with U.S. law or the Constitution.[39]

The frequency in which Sharia is used in legal arbitration around the country is difficult to gauge. One Muslim attorney said he has served as counsel in more than one hundred cases that range from family disputes to lawsuits between major international corporations.[40] The anti-Sharia American Public Policy Alliance issued a report in 2010 that outlined fifty cases where Sharia was a factor in U.S. court decisions. These cases dealt primarily with family disputes, including custody and divorce decisions. The report shows how U.S. courts overwhelmingly ruled against the use

---

36. Human Rights Watch, "Nigeria."

37. Samile, *Between Feminism and Islam*, 89. Khan, "Reopening of the Islamic Code," 341.

38. Musaji, "Islamic Sharia and Jewish Halakha Arbitration Courts."

39. *Garrity v. New Jersey*. A portion of this case cites the difference between Constitutional protections against self-incrimination found in the 5th Amendment and what appears in Jewish law. The justices cite the legal superiority of U.S. law when a difference arises with a given religious law.

40. Awad, "True Story of Sharia in American Courts."

of Sharia in cases that involved abuse or the violation of rights by one of the parties.[41]

American Muslim legal scholars are also seeking ways to modernize and reform Sharia. For example, Khaled Abou El Fadl argues that an up-to-date understanding of Sharia can promote diversity, pluralism, and individual rights—including universal religious freedom.[42]

The anti-Sharia campaign faced a credibility issue when it came to the actual beliefs of American Muslims in contrast to the extremism some evangelicals fear. Research by the Pew Forum on Religion and Public Life indicates the American Muslim community overwhelmingly rejects radical Islamist ideologies and agendas, are assimilating well into American society, and do not see a conflict between being a devout Muslim and living in a modern, secular, pluralistic society. However, many in the community say it has become more difficult to be a Muslim in the United States since the September 11th attacks.[43]

Anti-Sharia: Framing the Grievance

Anti-Muslim rhetoric that includes opposing Sharia in U.S. courts and the construction of mosques by American Muslims is widespread in evangelical circles. However, the anti-Sharia campaign originated with a Jewish attorney named David Yerushalemi. As the founder of the Society of Americans for National Existence, Yerushalemi has a history of sounding the alarm over Islamic influence in world affairs. For example, Yerushalemi warned that jihadists, through the specter of the Islamic financing model, were poised to take advantage of the 2008 global financial crisis when the West needed access to liquid funds found in Islamic countries. Yerushalemi was criticized for his views that "Islam is an evil religion," and that blacks "are the most murderous of peoples." Yerushalemi has denied accusations of racism.[44]

Yerushalemi's anti-Sharia activities include drafting model legislation that prohibits the use of Sharia in American courts. The model legislation is designed to prevent the advancement of what Yerushalemi considers the "concerted international effort to insinuate a transnational sectarian law—Sharia—into international treaties regarding blasphemy/hate speech, child custody, marriage/polygamy, international finance, and the like." This

---

41 American Public Policy Alliance, "Representative Civil Legal Cases Involving Shariah Law."

42. Musselman, "American Muslims," 17–24.

43. Pew Research Center, "Muslim Americans."

44. Yerushalemi, "On Race," 7.

includes banning the use of Sharia in private arbitrations, tribal councils, and "*ad hoc* Sharia courts." He also authored a study with Mordechai Kedar that attempted to quantify the association between Sharia and the potential for violence in the American Muslim community.[45]

An important link between Yerushalemi's anti-Sharia advocacy and evangelical circles of influence is his association with Frank Gaffney, founder of the Center for Security Policy, a Washington, DC think tank. Yerushalemi is on the organization's staff. He also worked with Gaffney on a project called *Mapping Shari'a*. The project's study concluded more than 80 percent of American mosques were radicalized, promoting violence against nonbelievers in their sermons and literature. Gaffney promoted the study in conservative media outlets such as *The Washington Times* as proof American Muslims were "using our [American] tolerance of religion to create an infrastructure of mosques here that incubate the Islamic holy war called jihad."[46]

In Gaffney and Yerushalemi's study, "Sharia-adherent" mosques are identified by the study as those frequented by Salafists, measured by "outwardly observable behaviors such as wearing traditional Arabic, Pakistani, or Afghan clothing and growing beards. Sharia-adherent mosques were also identified by the preponderance of women wearing hijabs, the segregation of genders during services, and enforcement of prayer lines."[47]

In *The Washington Times*, Gaffney argued these outward signs of purported Sharia-adherence are "a useful predictor of sympathy for—and in some cases, at least, action on behalf of—jihad, to include both the Islamists' violent or stealthy forms of warfare aimed at supplanting the U.S. Constitution and government."[48] Gaffney's proposed solution was to target nonviolent expressions of Islam in the public square:

> Britain's government has just announced that, pursuant to an update of its counterterrorism program known as '*Prevent*,' it now recognizes nonviolent forms of Islamist extremism can be every bit as dangerous as the violent kinds. We need to do the same—especially since the Muslim Brotherhood and its Sharia-adherents are successfully suing not only mosques, but academia, the media, financial institutions, political groups and

---

45. Yerushalemi and Kedar, "Sharia Adherence Mosque Survey."
46. Gaffney, "Frank Gaffney in The Washington Times," para. 1.
47. Yerushalemi and Kedar, "Sharia Adherence Mosque Survey," 91.
48. Gaffney, "Frank Gaffney in The Washington Times," para. 12.

interfaith 'dialogue' to pursue their previolent yet seditious and therefore anti-constitutional and illegal, agenda.[49]

An important example of the evangelical argument against Sharia is found in a policy briefing published by the Family Research Council (FRC).[50] The FRC is a political spin-off of James Dobson's Focus on the Family organization. It plays an important role in identifying candidates and issues that harmonize with the values of socially conservative evangelical voters. The briefing was written by William Wagner of the Thomas M. Cooley Law School.

Wagner sets forth a line of reasoning that identifies American Muslims as a new enemy alongside "a ubiquitous secular foe" on the legal front of the culture wars. Wagner asserts immigrants from Muslim countries are intent on extending the "Abode of Islam" into the United States, and that social conservatives should thus be concerned with "the issue of Islamic theocracy [that] amasses ominously on our rear flank." He backs this up by quoting a number of Muslim leaders saying they wish Islam to become the dominant religion in the West, and that Sharia should be established locally. Wagner regards Muslim immigrant communities as enclaves where Islamists are trying, through "stealth jihad," to systematically dismantle an "occupied" government's legal system and replace it with an Islamic theocracy.[51]

Wagner argues American Muslims are trying to exploit First Amendment protections of religious freedom to uproot the current American legal framework. In effect, using the U.S. Constitution to destroy the U.S. Constitution. As a result, he says evangelicals are caught between asserting their rights to religious freedom based on the establishment clause, and guarding against the encroachment of Sharia by a group using constitutional protections to undermine the American legal system.

He cites the presence of Sharia courts, Islamic financing, government-sanctioned prayer, and official suppression of Christian religious expression as "building blocks" for an American Islamic theocracy. He argues the difference between a Christian asserting a right to bring their faith-based values into the policy arena and a Muslim who makes a similar claim is the Christian does not wish to eventually form a Christian theocracy.

Wagner argues Islam is in essence a form of competing religious government, which is not protected by the First Amendment. Based on this definition of Islam, he argues Christians should form policy arguments against any recognition of Sharia as a danger to the constitutional system

49. Gaffney, "Frank Gaffney in The Washington Times," para. 14.
50. Wagner, "Islam, Shariah Law, and the American Constitution."
51. Wagner, "Islam, Shariah Law, and the American Constitution," para. 13.

of government. Wagner does not delve into the variety of thought among Muslims in the United States and abroad regarding the definition of Sharia. He also does not consider the perspective of Muslims who have moved to the United States to escape governments that used Sharia as a tool of oppression.

Some evangelicals involved in the anti-Sharia campaign dispute the argument that the majority of American Muslims are potential religious revolutionaries at some level. Legal scholars arguing in evangelical publications, such as John Witte Jr. of Emory University in *Christianity Today*, continue to wrestle with advocating restrictions on Islamic law in the face of a long legal tradition involving the use of canon law and Jewish legal traditions in binding arbitration. Unlike Wagner, Witte doesn't try to define Islam down into a simply a political movement. In the wake of an appeals court decision that struck down an anti-Sharia law in Oklahoma, Witte attempts to define Sharia as a less-evolved species of religious law than its Christian and Jewish counterparts. Witte first recognizes the presence of Christian and Jewish legal institutions in the American legal culture:

> Many Western Christians have religious tribunals to govern their internal affairs, including some family matters. State courts will respect their judgments, even if their cases are appealed to Rome, Canterbury, or Moscow. No one is talking of abolishing these Christian church courts or trimming their power. No one seems to think these Christian tribunals are illegitimate, even when some of them seem to discriminate against women in decisions about ordination and church leadership. Similarly, Jews are given wide authority to operate Jewish law courts to arbitrate marital, financial, and other disputes. Indeed, in New York State by statute, and in several European nations by custom, courts will not issue a civil divorce to an Orthodox Jewish couple unless the Jewish law court, the *beit din*, issues a religious divorce, even though Jewish law systematically discriminates against the wife's right to divorce. If Christians can have their canon laws and consistory courts, and Jews their Halacha and *beit din*, then why can't Muslims use Shari'ah and Islamic courts?[52]

Yet, according to Witte, Islamic law comes to the American legal landscape handicapped by the fact Sharia has not had time to adjust to Western secular legal systems. He also argues a record of struggle by other religious communities in the West has granted these communities certain privileges in the American legal system: "Muslims simply do not have the same history of

---

52. Witte, "Shari'ah's Uphill Climb," para. 16.

persecution Jews have faced in the West ... Over time, and only grudgingly, Western democracies learned to accommodate the core religious beliefs and practices of Jewish communities." Witte goes on to argue before any form of Islamic law can be accepted by courts, the Muslim community needs to reject anti-democratic ideals: "No Western nation will readily grant concessions to a religious community that rejects liberty, equality, and fraternity, or human rights, democracy, and rule of law."[53]

Though Witte goes further than other evangelicals in recognizing the variety of expression in Islam around the world, and the potential place certain types of Sharia may hold alongside Jewish and Christian legal institutions, his solution seems to perpetuate stereotypes about what American Muslims believe about liberty, equality, human rights, etc. It also seems to advocate continued infringements on the Muslim community's domestic religious freedom until they have fought an uphill battle for their religious rights in the West. Or, as one of the online commenters to the article suggested, "Witte seems to be saying, 'No, Sharia is not permissible, except after a long period of semi-injustice.'"[54]

Anti-Sharia: Resources

With regard to rank-and-file churchgoers around the country, many of the same resources that were available to the evangelical IRFA activists are now at the disposal of those involved in the anti-Sharia campaign. This includes a thriving network of churches and pastors. It also includes evangelical publishing houses producing books that warn Christians of the American Muslim threat. Erwin Lutzer's *The Cross in the Shadow of the Crescent: An Informed Response to Islam's War with Christianity*, published by Harvest House, joined a host of other publications by evangelical publishers that have filled the Christian book market. Groups such as the American Center for Law and Justice, founded by Pat Robertson, had previously opposed the construction of an Islamic Center near Ground Zero in New York. The ACLJ also uses evangelical radio and television outlets to warn American evangelicals of Sharia's threat to democracy.[55]

However, there were some political resources enjoyed by the IRFA campaign that proved more problematic for the anti-Sharia push. First, the universal provisions of IRFA made it attractive to a wide range of religious and human rights groups. The anti-Sharia campaign overlapped politically

---

53. Witte, "Shari'ah's Uphill Climb," para. 23.
54. Witte, "Shari'ah's Uphill Climb," para. 1.
55. ACLJ, "Export—Shariah Law Segment."

with the Tea Party movement, and President Donald Trump's supporters in later years, but lacked the wide array of supporters across party and religious lines.[56]

Also, the original promoters of the anti-Sharia campaign, David Yerushalmi and Frank Gaffney, have been discredited to a degree by critics and fellow conservatives. Though Yerushalmi seemingly reached his height of influence with the Sharia campaign, his beliefs regarding race ("blacks are the most violent of all races," etc.), women ("the founding fathers knew what they were doing when they did not give women and black slaves the vote"), and his conspiracy-theory approach has provided fertile ground for critics of the anti-Sharia campaign.[57]

Frank Gaffney has also experienced a backlash against the wide net he cast in seeing Muslim Brotherhood operatives throughout Washington's circles of influence. Gaffney played an influential role in a relevant episode that erupted around Rep. Michele Bachmann. In 2012, Bachmann drafted a letter warning of a possible security threat posed by Secretary of State Hillary Clinton's deputy chief of staff, Huma Abedin. The letter drew a great deal of criticism from both sides of the aisle, including Speaker of the House John Boehner and Sen. John McCain.[58] Gaffney also experienced an embarrassing episode regarding the Conservative Political Action Conference (CPAC) organized by the American Conservative Union (ACU). The ACU's board of directors formally condemned Gaffney over his accusations that leading conservative figure Grover Norquist and Suhail Khan, a senior fellow at the evangelical Institute for Global Engagement, had secret ties to the Muslim Brotherhood.[59]

Anti-Sharia: Mobilization

Like the campaign for the International Religious Freedom Act, a seminal moment in the campaign was a large public event. Though the anti-Sharia campaign was well under way before "The Constitution or Sharia: Preserving Freedom" event was held at Cornerstone Church in suburban Nashville on November 11, 2011, the gathering at the evangelical megachurch helped galvanize and popularize the campaign. Speakers at the event included Gaffney, Yerushalmi, a number of Tea Party activists, as well as

56. "Outcome of 'The Constitution or Sharia: Preserving Freedom' Conference."
57. Murphy, "Meet the White Supremacist Leading the GOP's Anti-Shariah Crusade."
58. Esposito, "'Bachmann Affair."
59. "American Conservative Union Board Resolution."

Lebanese, Coptic Christian, and Nigerian activists warning of the dangers of Sharia. Topics ranged from "The Influence of the Muslim Brotherhood in America" to "Grassroots Organizing against Sharia and Rabat (Including Mega-Mosques)."[60]

One of the most effective voices employed to mobilize evangelicals by the anti-Sharia campaign has been Jerry Boykin. The former army general is just one voice among several influential evangelicals promoting this view of Islam in America. Another influential voice in the campaign has been Paul Sperry, author of *Infiltration: How Muslim Spies and Subversives Have Penetrated Washington*. In this book, Sperry outlined "how Muslims have for years been secretly infiltrating American society, government, and culture, pretending to be peace-loving and patriotic, while supporting violent jihad and working to turn America into an Islamic state."[61] *Infiltration* was published by Thomas Nelson, the world's largest Christian publisher, which has also produced books by evangelical luminaries such as Billy Graham, Max Lucado, and Charles Stanley. Sperry also collaborated with Paul David Gaubatz on *Muslim Mafia: Inside the Secret Underworld that's Conspiring to Islamize America*, a book that alleged the Council on American-Islamic Relations advocacy group was trying, among other things, to plant Muslim spies as staff members in congressional offices.[62]

The anti-Sharia campaign has damaged the religious freedom of American Muslims around the United States through both restrictions in state laws as well as the effort to stop the construction of mosques by American Muslims.[63] A recent study the Pew Forum on Religion and Public Life outlined a number of instances where Christian residents opposed the construction of new mosques. For example, in May 2010, Muslims in Murfreesboro, Tennessee applied for permits to build an Islamic center. Despite protests from some in the community, county officials unanimously approved the plans. Afterward, several residents filed lawsuits against the proposed mosque, echoing the rhetoric from Gaffney, Boykin, Sperry, and others that the mosque was not simply a place of worship, but part of a plot to replace the Constitution with Islamic law.

Notably, Richard Land, head of the Southern Baptist Convention's Ethics and Religious Liberty Commission, refused to sign a letter produced by the Becket Fund for Religious Liberty that supported the construction of

---

60. "Constitution or Sharia," para. 3.
61. Sperry, *Infiltration*, 98.
62. Gaubatz and Sperry, *Muslim Mafia*.
63. Pew Research Center, "Controversies Over Mosques and Islamic Centers"

the Murfreesboro mosque.⁶⁴ Land also opposed the construction of Park51, a large Islamic center near Ground Zero in New York City: "Even though the vast majority of Muslims condemned their actions on September 11, 2001, it still remains a fact that the people who perpetrated the 9/11 attack were Muslims and proclaimed they were doing what they were doing in the name of Islam."⁶⁵

Other evangelical groups were also instrumental in opposing the construction of Park51. The American Center for Law and Justice (ACLJ) backed a lawsuit by a former New York firefighter, arguing, "We're saying no to the group and no to the location. A mosque in the U.S. that's using foreign money from countries with Sharia law is unacceptable, especially in this neighborhood."⁶⁶

Oklahoma was the first state to see the passage of an anti-Sharia bill into state law. However, it was struck down by the 10th Circuit Court of Appeals as unconstitutional. At least 41 bills or state-level constitutional amendments that would specifically restrict Sharia law, or foreign or international law generally, have been submitted in 23 states.⁶⁷ Most have died in committee, or never reach a vote. However, Kansas, Oklahoma, and South Dakota had passed similar bills into law at the time of writing.⁶⁸

After the Oklahoma law was declared unconstitutional, other states (such as Virginia) dropped specific references to Islam and Sharia, and used the umbrella terms "foreign" or "international."⁶⁹ In the case of Arizona, a unique bill was drafted that specifically mentions other religious bodies of law that have a long history of being declared valid for binding arbitration in family and civil matters:

> HB 2582: "A court shall not use, implement, refer to or incorporate a tenet of any body of religious sectarian law into any decision, finding or opinion as controlling or influential authority . . . any decision or ratification of a private agreement that is determined, on the merits, by a judge in this state who relies on any body of religious sectarian law or foreign law is void, is appealable error and is grounds for impeachment and removal from office . . . "Religious sectarian law" means any statute, tenet or body of law evolving within and binding a specific religious

64. Silk, "Islamo-Fearmongering 2012."
65. Land, "Mosque Near Ground Zero is Unacceptable," para. 3.
66. Neroulias, "Quietly, another Mosque Operates in the Shadow of Ground Zero," para. 8.
67. Raftery, "Bans on Court Use of Sharia/International Law."
68. Raftery, "Bans on Court Use of Sharia/International Law."
69. Hieatt, "Bills to Ban Use Of Foreign Laws Rile Groups," para. 7.

sect or tribe. Religious sectarian law includes Sharia law, canon law, Halacha and Karma but does not include any law of the United States or the individual states based on Anglo-American legal tradition and principles on which the United States was founded.[70]

These revised laws affirm the proposition that the pursuit of religious restrictions for one group establishes a trajectory toward religious restrictions for a wide variety of faiths. Also, just as the campaign for international religious freedom grew beyond the purview of its early proponents such as Michael Horowitz, Nina Shea, and Chuck Colson, the anti-Sharia campaign has grown beyond management of the issue by David Yerushalemi and Frank Gaffney. Today, an anti-Sharia cottage industry has arisen that perpetuates ideas and proposes courses of action designed to restrict certain aspects of religious expression by American Muslims.

As indicated above, the anti-Sharia campaign faces credibility issues when it comes to the targets of their campaign to root out radical Muslim influence in the United States (i.e., Gaffney's condemnation by the ACU). As seen in the arguments by Wagner and Witte, the evangelical anti-Sharia campaign also faces conceptual problems when it comes to arguing for religious freedom for everyone except American Muslims. To an outside observer this stance would seem to confirm to religious skeptics "religion is incorrigibly toxic, and that it breeds irrationality, demonization of others, irreconcilable division, and implacable conflict," rather than promoting an organic relationship between full religious freedom and democracy.[71]

Alienating American Muslims may indicate a lost opportunity for the socially conservative evangelical community, since Muslim opinions about contemporary hot topic issues such as gay marriage and abortion track very closely with evangelical attitudes.[72] Polls also show a majority of American Muslims support vouchers for parents who want to send their children to religious schools, government funding for religious institutions providing social services, and even the display of the Ten Commandments in public schools—all which have a common appeal with large segments of the evangelical community.[73]

---

70. "HB 2582," para. 14.
71. Farr, *World of Faith and Freedom*, 45.
72. "Muslims in the American Public Square."
73. "Muslims in the American Public Square."

FEATURES OF THE EVANGELICAL MOVEMENT

Both the IRFA campaign and the anti-Sharia campaign reveal certain contours within the broader evangelical movement. First, both campaigns indicate mobilization within the movement relied heavily on the initiatives of its leaders, rather than a groundswell from its roots. Hertzke refers to a legislative aide once describing evangelicalism as a "grass-tops movement" influenced heavily by opinion leaders and leading organizations.[74] Also, the two campaigns displayed a concern about Islam as a competing religion and a potential source of oppression. Seeing the IRFA and anti-Sharia campaigns together in this context displays a consistent concern with Islam, but an ambivalent commitment to universal religious freedom. The surprising popularity of the anti-Sharia campaign indicates the degree to which the movement tolerates a double standard (even within organizations, like the Family Research Council, which promotes international religious freedom).

Evangelical arguments framing the threat of Sharia and promoting courses of action do not draw upon the content of evangelical Christianity itself. Scripture and theological justifications are almost completely absent when it comes to the framing and mobilization arguments in the anti-Sharia campaign. Some evangelicals who promote pluralistic religious freedom and positive engagement with Muslims tie their efforts to biblical concepts. In a 2009 address to the Islamic Society of North America, Pastor Rick Warren said, "As an evangelical pastor, my deepest faith is in Jesus Christ. But you also need to know that I am committed, not just what I call the 'Good News,' but I am committed to the common good. And as the Scripture says 'Love your neighbor as yourself.' I am commanded to love and I am commanded to respect everybody. Everybody."[75]

However, the anti-Sharia campaign relied heavily on secular arguments that did not draw from evangelical teaching. This demonstrates that members of the evangelical movement can be mobilized to engage in campaigns that are justified by arguments that lie within and outside the content of the faith itself. During the 2012 presidential election, the anti-Sharia campaign became a factor in securing the evangelical constituency for Republican candidates. In short, almost all GOP presidential candidates offered statements against "creeping Sharia" during the 2012 campaign.[76]

International religious freedom, particularly as it relates to Christian communities, continues to hold broad support among evangelicals of all

---

74. Hertzke, *Freeing God's Children*, 195.
75. Vu, "Rick Warren to Muslims," para. 10.
76. Summers, "GOP Litmus Test," para. 2.

types. In *Faith in the Halls of Power*, D. Michael Lindsay credited evangelical participation in the IRFA campaign as a hallmark of the movement's maturation in the world of policy advocacy and human rights. Lindsay also observed the grass-tops phenomenon in the following terms:

> American evangelicalism has gained political momentum as its leaders have built coalitions with others who are interested in similar objectives. This has happened largely at the leadership level, but rank-and-file support has soon followed. Grassroots support within a movement is easier to mobilize when clear boundaries are drawn between allies and adversaries, and evangelicals have excelled at this.[77]

The anti-Sharia campaign put a heavy emphasis on adversarial mobilization, but at the same time threatened to roll back the maturation of the movement regarding human rights that Linsday observed in the IRFA campaign. This could lead to further splintering of the evangelical movement itself. Anti-Muslim rhetoric may also threaten the long-term credibility of some evangelicals who argue for religious freedom as a universal principle in the public square but seek to deny it for competing groups. This contrasts with some Catholic and evangelical leaders who call for a truce between American Christians and Muslims. This includes Robert George, who argues Muslims are the natural allies of American Catholics and evangelicals:

> It is not right for us to make them feel unwelcome or to suggest that their faith disables them from being loyal Americans. It is unjust to stir up fear that they seek to take away our rights or to make them afraid that we seek to take away theirs. And it is foolish to drive them into the arms of the political left when their piety and moral convictions make them natural allies of social conservatives.[78]

Certain patterns emerge in these cases of American Christian mobilization. First, political mobilization is by nature divisive. Each side of the culture war battles tends to portray their political opponents as enemies of morality and personal freedom. Among the consequences of the current political climate, which is energized by modern political mobilization, is the American public is more polarized than ever on party and ideological lines. This is perhaps an unavoidable aspect of the Nietzschean will-to-power ethic inherent in partisan wrangling.[79]

---

77. Lindsay, *Faith in the Halls of Power*, 52.
78. George, "Muslims, Our Natural Allies," para. 5.
79. Pew Research Center, "Political Polarization in the American Public."

Christian groups hoping to secure their place in a pluralistic society are placed in a tough position when it comes to political reform efforts. If religious freedom and freedom of conscience are seen as offering special permission to oppress another group, or merely consist of the state granting special status for religious groups with respect to taxes, compliance with regulations, etc., then the broad assent needed for its long-term survival is endangered.

The concept of religious freedom offers an alternative narrative than a vision of secularism held by some influential thinkers such as John Rawls. That is, the rights of a free conscience lie outside the jurisdiction of the state, and religious and nonreligious actors in society draw from their free conscience and associations to form the values that undergird the behavior of the state. The state tends to consolidate power unto itself, which can only be checked by a domain that lies outside the state. This narrative is fundamental to the formation of modern democracy and the thought of the founding fathers. However, making a compelling case for this narrative is difficult when its proponents are using the tools of the state to battle their opponents over religious claims.

PRINCIPLES OF DYNAMIC ENGAGEMENT

The problematic issues that arise with the anti-Sharia campaigns and anti-Muslim behavior among evangelicals demonstrate the need for consistency within the movement. This includes calls for greater freedom for their own community, while correcting trajectories that create legal restrictions and fomenting social hostilities against others. Seen in conjunction with evangelical mobilization for the 1998 International Religious Freedom Act, it illustrates how Dynamic Engagement can either falter in its pursuits, or be a stabilizing force in a pluralistic context. Here is a review of the Four Cs as they relate to this case:

Conscience: *Effective Christian leaders emphasized within their own communities the central role of the universal free conscience that appears in Scripture, theology, and tradition, and the implications of this in a pluralistic context.*

The current mechanism outlined in social movement theory presents an inward-focused path to how a group identifies an injustice, frames their grievance in a way that resonates with their primary constituency, identifies a political opportunity, and mobilizes members of the larger movement to affect a political change.[80]

80. Snow et al., "Frame Alignment Processes, Micromobilization, and Movement

However, the first principle transcends in-group grievances by providing a justification within the Christian community for universal religious freedom, including those outside of the tradition. It also provides an authentic vision of the Christian justification for conscience rights and religious freedom in the public square. It prepares the ground for public arguments regarding conscience rights and religious liberty using functionally normative tools such as the Universal Declaration of Human Rights.

By using examples from Scripture and Christian history, evangelical advocates for religious liberty can help their own constituents understand the role of a free conscience, and the importance of preserving the free exercise of religion, as well as the approach needed when arguing for religious ideals in a pluralistic secular context. It also lays the groundwork for a more tolerant and welcoming approach with respect to other groups. Beyond pragmatic concerns, this pluralistic understanding of a free conscience helps maintain moral and theological consistency in the public square.

Additionally, as seen in the case studies and supporting examples, a firm understanding of the role a free conscience plays in Christianity coupled with the relational passport to work with others across religious and ideological lines, aids in reducing conflict and increasing influence in the public field and helps maintain a public square that respects the free individual conscience. Looking beyond evangelicalism, Pope Benedict XVI emphasized this principle in a message titled "Religious Freedom, the Path to Peace":

> In a globalized world marked by increasingly multi-ethnic and multi-religious societies, the great religions can serve as an important factor of unity and peace for the human family. On the basis of their religious convictions and their reasoned pursuit of the common good, their followers are called to give responsible expression to their commitment within a context of religious freedom. Amid the variety of religious cultures, there is a need to value those elements which foster civil coexistence, while rejecting whatever is contrary to the dignity of men and women ... The path to take is not the way of relativism or religious syncretism. The Church, in fact, 'proclaims, and is in duty bound to proclaim without fail, Christ who is the way, the truth and the life (John 14:6); in Christ, in whom God reconciled all things to himself, people find the fullness of the religious life.' Yet this in no way excludes dialogue and the common pursuit of truth in different areas of life, since, as Saint Thomas Aquinas would say, "every truth, whoever utters it, comes from the Holy Spirit."[81]

Participation," 464.

81. Benedict XVI, "44th World Day of Peace 2011," para. 34.

Consistency: *Effective Christian public engagement in defense of religious liberty was consistent in its emphasis on freedom and justice across religious and nonreligious boundaries.*

There are logical and ethical gaps between the calls for greater religious liberty for members of the Christian community, and the calls for greater restrictions for members of other religious groups, as seen in the anti-Muslim evangelical campaigns of the past two decades. Evangelical mobilization against the construction of mosques as well as the push for anti-Sharia legislation stands in contrast to the rhetoric demanding religious freedom for Christians in the United States and abroad.

As seen in these case studies, by articulating the theological importance of universal rights of conscience, religious freedom advocates can help remedy the dissonance between their calls for greater freedom for one group, and greater restrictions for another. The evangelical anti-Muslim/anti-Sharia mobilization efforts can be seen as a classic example of Niebuhr's observation that large religious groups have a tendency (in modern terms) to embrace identity politics to the detriment of their own values and credibility in the public square.

Perennial evangelical antipathy toward Muslims is not a foregone conclusion. Some influential Christian leaders discourage stereotyping and activism against American Muslims, including Rick Warren and Texas megachurch pastor Bob Roberts. Internal evangelical debates over the movement's stance with respect to American Muslims has some parallels with the debates within the movement over Roman Catholics in the mid-20th century. A brief look at one slice of evangelical history helps illustrate this.

In the 1950s, Billy Graham was a rising star within the evangelical movement and pioneered an open attitude toward American Catholics. For this (along with his partnerships with mainline denominations), he was criticized by many fundamentalists and neo-evangelicals.[82] At the same time, popular suspicion against Catholics ran high among many Protestants. This suspicion played a role in the formation of the early evangelical movement. One year before Graham's 1957 watershed revival in New York, the head of the National Association of Evangelicals, James D. Murch, published a history of the National Association of Evangelicals. A recurring theme in the book was the suspicion of Catholicism. This included the fear that Catholicism was working to destroy the "distinctive testimony of Protestantism," effect a religious takeover of the U.S. government by the Catholic church, and promote a Catholic presence at state and local government levels.[83]

82. Mitchell, *God in the Garden*.
83. Murch, *Cooperation without Compromise*, 47, 137.

Murch cites these fears as a leading factor in the formation of the National Association of Evangelicals as a counterorganization to efforts backed by the Vatican: "Either Christians who love the Lord are going to take Christ into the political life of the nation or the increasing infiltration of Roman Catholic power will take over."[84]

A generation later, evangelical leaders such as Chuck Colson and Richard Land joined prominent Catholics, including Avery Dulles and Richard John Neuhaus, in signing a document known as "Evangelicals and Catholics Together." Even as some evangelicals criticized the document as flawed in its theology and outlook, the document marked a turning point in the relationship between prominent evangelicals and Catholics in public life.[85] This included an intent to cooperate on common policy interests, such as abortion, family stability, the religious role in civil society, parental choice in education, and the defense of religious freedom abroad, among other issues.

In doing so, the document reflects an understanding that the common threats perceived in both communities, coupled with a thread of theological commonality, compelled evangelicals and Catholics to set aside many differences for their mutual vision of the common good: "The love of Christ compels us and we are therefore resolved to avoid such conflict between our communities and, where such conflict exists, to do what we can to reduce and eliminate it. Beyond that, we are called and we are therefore resolved to explore patterns of working and witnessing together in order to advance the one mission of Christ."[86]

With anti-Muslim sentiment reaching a high-water mark in the United States, some evangelical and Catholic leaders are seeking to build relationships with the American Muslim community.[87] This includes Robert George, who denounced anti-Muslim sentiment and called for "Muslims and Christians alike [to] forget past quarrels and stand together for righteousness, justice, and the dignity of all."[88]

It remains to be seen whether evangelicals will recognize common cause with American Muslims when it comes to public policies that may run against values that the two communities hold in common. Even so, some evangelicals advocating for the freedoms enjoyed by American Christians say these freedoms should as a matter of course and moral obligation extend to Muslims and those of other faiths and no faith. Doing so demonstrates

---

84. Murch, *Cooperation without Compromise*, 140.
85. MacArthur, "Evangelicals and Catholics Together," 7–37.
86. "Evangelicals & Catholics Together," 9.
87. Shellnutt, "Most White Evangelicals."
88. George, "Muslims, Our Natural Allies," para. 4.

a consistent expression of belief in evangelicals' own rhetoric regarding the universality of religious freedom, and builds the community's credibility as a consistent advocate for the common good.

Common Good: *Effective religious freedom initiatives emphasized the role of faith groups serving the common good through participation in civil society.*

The drafting and passage of IRFA is a successful example of an area of concern that gained the most traction with American evangelicals, but also drew upon a coalition of partners to become successful. This coalition included a range of Jewish, Catholic, and Protestant groups working together to increase the common good through legislation. Evangelicals formed the core of the constituency that brought the related bills to the foreground. But it was a cadre of faith groups, concerned about the fate of their co-religionists abroad that provided the most effective catalyst to usher the bills behind IRFA into law. Due in part to IRFA, nongovernmental organizations such as the Institute for Global Engagement were able to advance their own civil society initiatives to increase religious liberty abroad.

The anti-Sharia campaigns, and (for example) the 2016 presidential elections, show the ongoing strength of rank-and-file evangelicals in national politics. However, evangelicals as a group seem to have embraced partisan polarization, and as a result have lost a great deal of credibility among those outside of their own constituency. By increasing their ability to work across religious and social lines, this religious group could help reinvigorate the national conversation over the common good, and move its members away from the type of polarizing politics that have become the norm.

Crossing Over: *Effective religious freedom advocacy groups integrated their work with others across religious and social identity lines.*

A few years after the signing of "Evangelicals and Catholics Together," evangelicals took the lead in mobilizing in favor of legislation that eventually became the 1998 International Religious Freedom Act (IRFA). At first, the legislation was primarily directed at addressing religious persecution of Christians abroad. As the Monica Lewinsky scandal was putting increasing pressure on Bill Clinton's presidency, evangelicals recognized the political opportunity to work for legislation that would please their constituency as the president sought an olive branch for some of his harshest critics.

The success of the initial legislation, the Wolf-Specter Bill, was hampered in the Senate because of its specific focus on Christians and persecution.[89] Rival legislation, the Nickels-Lieberman Bill, also experienced a similar problematic outlook for passage, until evangelicals widened their

---

89. Farr, *World of Faith and Freedom*, 39.

alliance and the scope of the bill to have a more universal outreach.[90] All the social movement resources at the disposal of evangelical leaders were not enough to ensure the passage of IRFA, particularly when support split between the two bills. Success depended upon reaching across ideological and religious lines in crafting a bill that would address the broader issue of religious freedom and the concerns of a wider set of constituencies.[91]

The pluralistic approach inherent in Dynamic Engagement helps mitigate the totalizing impulses characteristic of movements that have adopted a public posture centered on their own self-identity. If the traction of Christian ideas in the marketplace is damaged through inconsistency in their public message, then Christians are in danger of losing credible public engagement. Political mobilization may still retain a role in constructive, pluralistic engagement by Christian groups seeking greater religious freedom. Mobilization itself is a tool which can be used in a variety of ways. The next chapter will examine how Coptic evangelicals struggling for greater religious freedom in Egypt have employed rights-based mobilization to help some of the most vulnerable communities in their country, and secure their long-term place in civil society.

90. Hertzke, *Future of Religious Freedom*, 224–27.
91. Hertzke, *Future of Religious Freedom*, 227.

6

Rights, Development, and Religious Liberty in Egypt

THIS CHAPTER DELVES INTO what religious freedom means in practice for a Christian group living as a minority under significant social hostilities and government pressure. The subject is an evangelical development organization in Egypt that has marshaled the tools of both theology and political mobilization in forming an ethic of effective public engagement. While Egypt continues to experience interreligious violence and social hostilities toward Christians, and Egyptian politics and law favor the Muslim majority, Coptic evangelicals have attained a growing presence in civil society that aligns with their core religious values of loving their neighbor and helping those in need. Through the Coptic Evangelical Organization for Social Services (CEOSS), these Protestant Christians have found a voice in civil society that is disproportionately larger than the size of their population. At the heart of their faith-informed mobilization efforts are strategies that contribute to the common good.

Coptic evangelicals and the CEOSS organization were chosen for study for several reasons. CEOSS is a Protestant/evangelical organization that has a strong reputation in the Global South. As pointed out by Philip Jenkins, the demographic center of gravity for the global Christian community is in the process of moving from Western countries to the Global South.[1] Developing a broadly applicable set of principles regarding religious

---

1. Jenkins, *Next Christendom*, 103.

freedom engagement requires taking stock of groups at work here. At the same time, there are lessons learned about public engagement, particularly in a country with a difficult record of religious oppression, that speak directly to the challenges involved in crafting public responses to political pressures across national contexts. CEOSS and the ideas behind its work shed light on some of the solutions found in the normative debates over Christian public engagement.

CEOSS has operated for decades in a political and social environment that is often hostile to their home community. This case tests the hypothesis put forth by Niebuhr that the larger the religious organization, the more likely it is to veer from its Christian mission. In short, can a Christian group retain a religiously grounded focus on the common good in a political and civil environment hostile to their faith and even their presence? If so, what implications does the Christian model of service to others have for religious freedom in a pluralistic society?

Amid profound social and political hostilities, CEOSS leaders have refined what it means to be an effective Christian presence in a Muslim-majority country. In the process, they have defined the kinds of freedoms they can expect to secure in this context. At the core of CEOSS's programs and initiatives is a mission akin to Lesslie Newbigin's idea that the church should "recognize that they exist for the sake of those who are not members, as sign, instrument, and foretaste of God's redeeming grace for the whole life of society."[2] The following shows how this outward focus on the common good as a Christian ethic has helped preserve CEOSS's ability to remain engaged in Egyptian public life well beyond individual efforts or congregational life.

This chapter examines how CEOSS cultivated its public engagement as a religious organization through its civil society initiatives. It delves into the connection between the in-group religious values that drive Coptic evangelical engagement with Egyptian society, and its public arguments that have led to its continuing growth and success.

In terms of mobilization, the model CEOSS offers has two prongs: mobilization among its Christian supporters, and the pluralistic secular mobilization of the vulnerable groups it assists irrespective of religious affiliation. The development organization's full-time staff is drawn from the Coptic evangelical community.[3] The mission and practice of CEOSS also relies on its home community for financial support, in addition to funds received

---

2. Newbigin, *Gospel in a Pluralist Society*, 233.

3. Hussein, "NGOs and Development Challenges of the 21st Century," 211. In addition to the full-time Christian staff, CEOSS employs about 6,000 Muslim part-time staff members. Also, 70 percent of about 3,000 volunteers working with CEOSS are Muslim.

through international grant-making organizations.⁴ At less than 20,000 adherents, the population of Coptic evangelicals in Egypt is tiny in comparison to the larger Coptic Orthodox population, which itself represents roughly 10 percent of the country's population.⁵ Over the past few decades debates within the Coptic evangelical family, as well as in the leadership of CEOSS, have continually refined the values behind the religious group's public engagement. At the same time, development strategies adopted by CEOSS have deepened the impact of their programs on Egyptian society.

To assess CEOSS's values-based mobilization efforts, this chapter will look at the expressed theological and political perspectives of its leaders, from its founder Samuel Habib, to its current president, Andrea Zaki Stephanous. Emphasis will be placed on Zaki's ideas that underpin the approach CEOSS takes in extending religious freedom through civil-society engagement. It will also take into account the competing ideas of Zaki's predecessor, Rafiq Habib, who expressed ideas in chorus with those of the Muslim Brotherhood prior to the Arab Spring, and whose leadership was ultimately rejected by Coptic evangelicals.

This study relies on field research done in Egypt, including interviews with members of CEOSS staff as well as beneficiaries of the group's programs. These include small-scale farmers in the rural governorate of Qalyubiya, working children in a poor urban district of Cairo, advocates for the disabled in Upper Egypt, and women living in Egypt's poorest villages. The religious profiles of those I spoke to include both Muslims and Coptic Christians, as well as clergy and lay people. Most meetings with these groups were done in the context of focus groups on site in various locations where CEOSS is engaged.

COPTIC ORTHODOX: CHURCH AND STATE

The story of Egypt's Coptic community over the past 125 years can be described as the migration of a community that never left home. That is, a migration from second-class status in the 19th century, to the Egyptian business and cultural mainstream in the 1920s, and then to the margins less than a century later. Until the mid-19th century, Coptic Christians were treated as *dhimmis*, "people of the book," living in an Islamic nation. That is, they were taxed for their exemption from the military, and were excluded from full participation in some areas of public life. The dramatic geopolitical realignments that occurred after World War I allowed Copts to

---

4. Hatina, "In Search of Authenticity," 59.
5. Pew Research Center, "How Many Christians are There in Egypt?"

move into a position of nation-building alongside their Muslim neighbors. Both Muslim and Christian Egyptians stood together in resistance of British control of their country, embodying the slogan "Religion for God, and the motherland for everyone."[6] In the aftermath of the 1919 uprising, feelings of common Egyptian citizenship ran high among Muslims and Christians, particularly in the *Wafd* party, during what is referred to as the liberal period in modern Egyptian history. The Al-Azhar mosque hosted a sermon by the Coptic priest Qummus Sargiyus, and imams spoke in Coptic churches in the name of Egyptian solidarity. Coptic Egyptians and their Muslim *Wafd* party compatriots resisted British proposals to divide parliamentary representation according to religion, which Copts viewed as institutionalizing their political status as a permanent minority. Instead, they evoked a common Pharaonic past among Egyptians of all faiths as grounds for solidarity and full citizenship regardless of religion.[7]

Wafd's rivals disdained the party's inclusive attitudes, accusing it of diluting the Muslim character of Egypt. This attitude prevailed in later decades. It was during this period the Muslim Brotherhood was formed (1928). Copts viewed the Muslim Brotherhood as a direct threat to their empowerment as full civil and political members of Egyptian society.[8]

The Coptic community flourished up until the mid-20th century, and Coptic individuals held cabinet positions and prominent seats in parliament. The status of Coptic Christians shifted dramatically in the 1950s. In the fallout of the revolution of 1952, the pluralistic atmosphere they enjoyed was damaged through a process of inequitable secularization. Prior to the revolution, Muslim family and personal status law was arbitrated by Sharia courts, and Christian families relied on Christian courts. Egyptian secularization abolished the religious courts, and placed Coptic and Muslims alike under a common legal system that drew from Sharia as its foundation for civil affairs. In addition, the abolition of political parties hampered their ability to participate in political life, and the nationalization of many Coptic businesses further set Egypt's Coptic community on the road toward decades of marginalization.[9]

Yet, as the Coptic community was marginalized from civic and political life, development organizations began to emerge. CEOSS founder Samuel Habib had launched literacy programs in Egyptian communities in the mid-1950s, and registered the name Coptic Evangelical Organization for

---

6. Stephanous, *Political Islam, Citizenship, and Minorities*, 120.
7. Wood, "Use of the Pharaonic Past in Egyptian Nationalism," 179–96.
8. Leirvik, *Human Conscience and Muslim-Christian Relations*, 204.
9. Ayalon, "Egypt's Coptic Pandora's Box," 55.

Social Services with the Ministry of Social Affairs in 1960.[10] Over the next two decades, religious revivals invigorated Egypt's Christian communities.[11] A by-product of this revival was the strengthening of Coptic religious identity, and the rise of their distinction from Egyptian Muslims with respect to political and civil life in Egypt.

Deprived of secular party affiliation, Coptic Christianity encompassed both a political and religious identity, a marked contrast to transreligious Egyptian solidarity prior to World War II.[12] Pope Shenouda III used his position as the head of the Coptic Orthodox Church to speak for the rights of his flock, affirming the church hierarchy as the political voice of Egypt's Coptic community.[13] The growing influence of Islamists within the Egyptian political and legal structure during the 1970s and 1980s, and the increasingly political language of Coptic Orthodox leaders, set the government and the Coptic Church on a course toward further polarization, and outbreaks of violence against the Coptic community.

During this period, Coptic Egyptians became increasingly subject to Sharia implemented in Egyptian civil law. The 1971 Egyptian Constitution affirmed the majority presence of Islam in Egyptian society and its laws: "Islam is the religion of the state and Arabic its official language. Islamic law (*Sharia*) is the principal source of legislation."[14] In 1979, the national Court of Cassation (similar to a Supreme Court) attempted to reconcile the secular nature of Egyptian law with the presence of Sharia in the legal system:

> The concept [of public policy] is based on a purely secular doctrine that is to be applied as a general doctrine (*madhhab'cmm*) to which society in its entirety can adhere and which must not be linked to any provision of religious laws. However, this does not exclude that [public policy] is sometimes based on a principle related to religious doctrine, in the case when such a doctrine has become intimately linked with the legal and social order, deep-rooted in the conscience of society (*damir al-mujtama'*), in the sense that the general feelings (*al-shuc'r al-'amm*) are hurt if it is not adhered to. This means that these principles [of public policy] by necessity extend to all citizens, Muslim and non-Muslim alike, irrespective of their religions. This is because the notion of public policy cannot be divided in such a manner that some principles apply to the Christians, and others to Muslims,

---

10. Virtue, *Vision of Hope*.
11. Delhaye, "Contemporary Muslim-Christian Relations in Egypt," 79.
12. Delhaye, "Contemporary Muslim-Christian Relations in Egypt," 79.
13. Scott, *Challenge of Political Islam*, 168.
14. *Constitution of the Arab Republic of Egypt, 1971*, Part 1, Art. 2.

nor can public policy apply only to a person or a religious community. The definition (*taqdir*) [of public policy] is characterized by objectivity, in accordance with what the general majority (*aghlaba'amm*) of individuals of the community believes ... Islamic law is considered an [inalienable] right of the Muslims (*fi haqqal-muslimin*), and is therefore part of public policy, due to its strong link to the legal and social foundations which are deep-rooted in the conscience of society.[15]

In practice, non-Islamic law was most often used in cases of marriage and divorce only when the husband and wife were of the same non-Muslim sect. In all other cases, Islamic law (as it is enshrined in Egypt's general law) was applied by default. Many legal issues that were once handled in Christian courts, ranging from personal status (including religious conversion) to inheritance, were placed in the jurisdiction of sharia for non-Muslim Egyptians.[16] This created a host of complications. For example, a spouse could convert to Islam or a different form of Christianity to have the case moved out of a Christian court, where divorce is difficult, to the Sharia court, where divorce is much easier to obtain. This particularly favored those converting to Islam. Those converting from one type of Christianity to another must have done so before beginning litigation, but one party could convert to Islam at any time in the process to move the case to a Sharia court. Additionally, conversion to Islam is allowed, but conversion away from Islam (considered apostasy) is not. Conversion from Islam, though not criminally punishable, nullifies marriages, prevents the convert from getting married in the future, and bars inheritance among other legal repercussions.[17]

The use of Sharia in secular law, and the growing issue of Islamism in Egyptian society further alienated the Coptic community and deprived Coptic Orthodox Christians of a political and legal voice. Their only recourse was to draw closer to the church as a source of solidarity, and the church hierarchy as their chief voice in public affairs. Pope Shenouda had been a vocal opponent of Article 2 of the 1971 constitution that held Islam as the religion of the state and Sharia as the principal source of legislation. He had a series of conflicts with President Sadat, particularly over the Camp David accords and the growing presence of Islamism in Egypt.

From the late 1970s to the early 1980s, violence erupted with increasing frequency between Copts and Muslims. It boiled over in June 1981, when Copts and Muslims clashed for several days over a plot of land in Cairo

15. Agrama, *Questioning Secularism*, 93.
16. Berger, "Public Policy and Islamic Law," 88–136.
17. Berger, "Public Policy and Islamic Law," 99.

where Copts intended to build a church. The conflict left five Copts and four Muslims dead. Coptic leaders, including Pope Shenouda, complained security forces stood by without interfering in the conflict as a punishment for Shenouda's rejectionist stance toward Egyptian policies.[18]

Shenouda was sent into in-country exile one month before Sadat was assassinated by Islamists in October 1981. He remained in exile until released by President Mubarak in 1985. Upon returning to public life, Shenouda shifted from being a vocal opponent of the regime's national policies, to one of its most prominent supporters. This left many Copts dissatisfied. He also used his authority to dissuade Copts from retaliating against sectarian strife that was seen as stirred up by members of Mubarak's government.[19]

Shenouda made a strong appeal for justice following the New Year's midnight prayer service bombing at the Two Saints Church in Alexandria on New Year's Eve, 2010. Twenty-three Copts were killed and 97 injured by the bombing. Some blamed the government for providing inadequate security.[20] Others placed the bombing's organization and execution within the Egyptian interior ministry itself. The attack was followed by a series of violent clashes between Copts and security forces. The Tahrir Square protests that led to the 2011 revolution a few weeks later upturned the process of identifying and prosecuting those responsible for the bombing, despite periodic protests in the following years. (Shenouda had discouraged Copts from joining the protests in Tahrir Square.)[21] Unarmed Coptic Christians clashed with Egyptian security forces in October 2011. During the demonstration, Egyptian security fired live ammunition into the crowd, and ran over Coptic protesters with military vehicles. Two dozen Copts were killed.[22]

After Shenouda's death in 2012, the new pope, Tawadros II, vowed to reform the way Copts engaged in public life. This included shifting the role of political leadership back to lay members of the community, rather than have the pope continue the role of both the religious and political leader of Egypt's Coptic Orthodox citizens. "The most important thing," he said, "is for the church to go back and live consistently within the spiritual boundaries because this is its main work, spiritual work."[23]

18. Tarek, "Pope Shenouda III."
19. Sedra, "Class Cleavages and Ethnic Conflict," 219–35.
20. "Deadly Blast at Egyptian Church."
21. Khalifa, *Egypt's Lost Spring*, 142.
22. Kirkpatrick and Afify, "Top Egyptian Finance Minister Quits."
23. Kirkpatrick, "Coptic Church Chooses Pope Who Rejects Politics," A4.

The Coptic Orthodox Church's response to increased marginalization in the latter half of the 20th century follows the rights-grievance model in a number of respects. Their specific grievances were linked to an overall complaint their religious rights and their ability to participate freely in public life were eroded due to the Egyptian government's response to pressure from Islamist groups. Integral to their overall grievance were ongoing social hostilities against Copts, including rioting, arson, kidnappings, and other violence.

To pursue a remedy to these grievances, the Coptic community relied on solidarity among its members and the voice of the church in the person of Pope Shenouda. For a time, his voice carried the grievances of Coptic community to both the Egyptian government and the international stage. However, Shenouda's postexile shift to government support marked a loss for the Coptic Orthodox Church's ability to advocate for itself. After his death, the new head of the Coptic Orthodox Church devolved his political role to lower levels of the church hierarchy in order to address the deficit in citizen-level engagement. This major adjustment in public engagement could mitigate the government's ability to tame the opposition through, for example, the exile of its leader. Today, the community remains under heavy pressure from the Egyptian government and is frequently a target for violent social hostilities.[24]

When it comes to the formation and protection of identity, mobilization among the Coptic Orthodox members is a complex prospect. Asserting grievances through an emphasis on their status as a minority community, a strategy often used in the West, places them in danger of being identified as *de facto dhimmis* by their opponents. That is, attempting to leverage their minority identity may entrench the idea that they are second-class citizens in this particular context. Rather, their rhetoric focuses on their place as full citizens that deserve equal protection under the law, and relief from the social hostilities that have plagued the community for decades.[25]

COPTIC EVANGELICALS: PURSUING AN ALTERNATIVE PATH

The Protestant community in Egypt, and Coptic evangelicals in particular, have pursued a markedly different course than the Coptic Orthodox Church and Pope Shenouda. For this group, identity still takes a central role in political participation. However, their cultivation of resources for mobilization

24. Pew Research Center, "Religious Hostilities Reach Six-Year High."
25. Younan, "Coptic Christians Of Egypt."

and how they manage domains where they lack resources speak to a model of engagement that is both innovative and effective in achieving many of their stated goals.

Coptic evangelicals have their roots in the 19th-century Presbyterian missionary movement. In 1854, a group of missionaries from the American Midwest arrived in Egypt. They were part of a large movement of American and British evangelicals fanning out across the globe with the hope of spreading the gospel to every country. The missionaries who came to Egypt in the 1850s were members of the United Presbyterian Church of North America. The denomination, based in Pittsburgh, had roots among descendants of Scottish immigrants to the United States. It was staunchly abolitionist during the American Civil War and worked with freed slaves afterward. In the United States their work with "freedmen's missions" helped diversify the movement beyond its rural Scottish roots.[26] In Egypt, the lasting institutions of the Presbyterian missionary efforts are seen today in the Coptic Evangelical Church, CEOSS, as well as the American University in Cairo.[27]

In Egypt, Presbyterian missionaries experienced a period of adjustment in finding a receptive audience for their call to conversion. Upon arriving in Egypt, they found the lower Nile region, including the city centers of Cairo and Alexandria, were nearly completely Muslim. Social, legal, and religious restrictions made evangelizing among Muslims particularly difficult. There were many Coptic Orthodox Christians in this area, but they were mostly well-educated government workers with little interest in switching their religious affiliation.[28]

The missionaries then directed their resources to Upper Egypt, with its larger population of rural *fellahin* Coptic Christians. The missionaries travelled up and down the Nile in riverboats, and became known as "Riverboat Missionaries" to the locals. By the turn of the century, the Presbyterian missionaries had established fifty congregations serving more than 6,500 Coptic evangelicals, and had begun moving the care of the Egyptian church to local leaders.[29]

By the end of the Suez Crisis in 1956, most foreign missionaries had left the country. Two years later, the Coptic Evangelical Church was recognized as an independent Presbyterian synod. One former missionary defined the new, more equal relationship between the American and the Egyptian

---

26. Sharkey, *American Evangelicals in Egypt*, 15.
27. Sharkey, *American Evangelicals in Egypt*, 149.
28. Sharkey, *American Evangelicals in Egypt*, 20.
29. Gilman, "Peddling the Promise Along the Nile," 19.

church: "They are not now our children. They are our sister churches in Christ and join us in being witnesses to the whole world."[30]

CEOSS had its roots in the late 1940s as a village literacy program run by Presbyterian missionaries. Reverend Samuel Habib established his ministry in 1952. Habib's services soon expanded to include a variety of programs. These early development efforts ranged from agricultural education to small business development.[31] Today, CEOSS has grown into a large and influential NGO with a wide array of services that serve about 2.5 million in twelve of the country's 27 governorates.

Among their biggest projects is the Horus Eye Hospital in Minya, Upper Egypt.[32] The hospital was established in 2010 to address the high rates of cataracts and other treatable eye diseases in a region of Egypt that has few advanced medical facilities. In 2011, the hospital examined more than 2,000 patients, and performed more than 300 surgeries.[33] CEOSS also promotes the education of girls through scholarships and transportation. This is a concern in Upper Egypt where roughly 50 percent of girls ages 10 to 14 cannot read and write.[34]

CEOSS has been noted as a particularly effective advocate for women.[35] The organization takes a holistic approach to the welfare of women and girls in rural areas by engaging a number of issues with local authorities and community leaders. This includes discouraging early and forced marriages, female genital cutting (FGC), and other practices. Several observers have praised CEOSS for helping resolve issues of FGC and other practices through their participatory approach.[36] According to one independent report, five communities voluntarily stopped FGC through initiatives organized by CEOSS.[37]

In terms of economic development, CEOSS works in urban areas, such as Cairo, as well as rural regions to improve the livelihoods of the population it serves. Programs include establishing a job-seekers database, vocational training, interviewing and resume writing, and help for young entrepreneurs

---

30. Sharkey, *American Evangelicals in Egypt*, 202.
31. "PC(USA) Mission History in Egypt."
32. CEOSS, مستشفى حورس.
33. CEOSS, *Annual Report: 2011*.
34. Center for Development and Population Activities, "Community Ownership Spurs Girls' Education In Egypt."
35. Hadi, "Community of Women Empowered," 113.
36. Yount, "Symbolic Gender Politics," 1063–90.
37. Abdel-Tawab and Sahar. "Critical Analysis of Interventions," 17.

starting businesses.[38] CEOSS has an active micro-credit program. In 2011, they disbursed nearly 57,000 small loans to nearly 40,000 active clients. Sixty-four percent of the loans were to poor women and households headed by women. CEOSS claims a repayment rate of 98.7 percent.[39]

These are just a few examples of development programs CEOSS is using to improve the lives of the poor and disadvantaged in Egypt. By all accounts, the organization has a solid reputation for delivering the services they promise. For example, Habitat for Humanity celebrated the completion of a large housing project in cooperation with CEOSS, praising the organization in its press release about the successful partnership: "CEOSS is an experienced and effective development organization. In both Christian and Muslim communities, CEOSS staff work to develop local leadership, determine needs and facilitate programs that lead to better health, education and economic development."[40]

CEOSS's key point of public engagement has been through development programs aimed at Egypt's poor and disadvantaged since its inception in the 1950s. The organization reviews their overall development strategies every five years. Since the 1990s, CEOSS has evolved their approach to helping Egypt's poor and vulnerable from institutional support, to fostering self-dependence, to a participatory strategy. In 2005, CEOSS adopted a rights-based development approach to help increase the scalability of its development projects and deepen the ownership of its programs among its beneficiaries.

Rights-based development has a variety of definitions among development organizations around the world. For CEOSS, it involves educating local NGOs and associations about what they can do to improve their lives through both public resources and self-determination. CEOSS conducts programs that help the poor and vulnerable write proposals, communicate effectively, conduct local elections, and establish long-term public engagement.[41]

CEOSS employs a modified version of the rights-grievance approach, shifting the emphasis away from the protection of their personal identity to solutions for grievances held among other vulnerable groups. Rights-based development is the largest among a portfolio of CEOSS's public engagement initiatives. The majority of their human and capital resources are focused on

---

38. CEOSS, *Annual Report: 2011*, 20.
39. CEOSS, *Annual Report: 2011*, 24–25.
40. "HFH Egypt Celebrates Completion Of 6,000 Houses," para. 10.
41. Ratliff, interview with Rafik Nagy and Suzanne Fouad.

these programs, and it forms the core of their outreach beyond the Coptic evangelical community.[42]

As noted below, Coptic evangelicals have common experience with other Christian minority communities who have experienced violence and persecution in Egypt. They have also continually worked to resolve problems that cut across cultural and religious lines in their country. Through rights-based development they have been able to dramatically increase their freedom to exercise what they see as the Christian calling to help their neighbor. Religious freedom in this context, where it is intertwined with the ability to increase the common good, is strengthened as their capacity to address the common good grows.

Their rights-based framework has several stages. First, the poor often need immediate help that cannot wait for a long process of establishing committees and securing rights. This includes addressing issues of dangerous or inadequate housing, safe drinking water, or other issues that directly affect the health and safety of the group involved. Second, as local committees outline their priorities, CEOSS uses their long experience and deep connections with leaders at all levels of government to help create a relationship between the rights owners and those who bear the duty of meeting those rights (i.e., government entities). Developing a mechanism for open communication between the rights holders and sponsors is critical for CEOSS's overall approach to creating productive relationships between citizens and those in government. Through elected committees and local nonprofit associations, rights owners move into a position where they hold duty-bearers accountable for their rights. In this way, CEOSS continues to foster dialogue and development between vulnerable communities and various levels of the Egyptian government.

AT-RISK YOUTH

One example of the work CEOSS is doing can be seen among working children in the El Salam neighborhood of Cairo. These children often begin working at a very young age, sometimes as early as six years old. They commonly experience various forms of abuse by their employers and miss educational opportunities.[43]

One boy, 17-year-old Hamed, worked as an assistant in a pharmaceutical factory. He said his regular shift was twelve hours, and if the next boy didn't show up for his shift, he would work another twelve hours without

---

42. "Annual Report 2013."
43. United States Department Of Labor, "Child Labor and Forced Labor Reports."

relief. He said he regularly endured physical and verbal abuse by his overseers at the company. Yet, he needed to work in order to help sustain his family in one of Cairo's poorest neighborhoods. Hamed stumbled upon a small neighborhood association that was trying to help working children like him. The program offered by this small charity was funded and the staff trained by CEOSS. Their strategy for helping thousands of children like Hamed involved educating working children about their rights, and helping them secure those rights from the companies and government agencies bearing a duty to uphold those rights.

Hamed felt empowered. He felt he no longer had to suffer long hours and abuse. The first thing he did was stand up to his bosses at the company. As a result, he lost his job. Still a young teen, he began driving a tuk-tuk to earn money, and kept working various jobs while deepening his involvement with the local children's organization.[44] With the help of CEOSS and the neighborhood association, he soon moved from Cairo's child workforce to its student population. Growing up, he did not see much opportunity or use for education. Now, he says he enjoys learning. He still works, now at a restaurant, with better hours and working conditions. He also has time for his studies. Through the training he received from CEOSS and their affiliated local association, Hamed is also helping improve the lives of other working children here. The rights-based program advanced by CEOSS enabled Hamed and his peers to advocate for the rights of hundreds of their peers in this neighborhood.

Ayman Ali Maher, a local committee leader, said he has seen many improvements among children like Hamed. This includes increased morale among working youth, and more widespread relief from abuse. The children have also been steered away from dangerous work and have learned negotiation and cooperation skills. Children's committees, including Hamed's, have been able to develop their ability to articulate their needs and grievances and pursue their rights to education and a better livelihood. Though many children still work, their lives have improved. They have also been able to participate in advising the constitutional committee about enshrining the rights of children in national law.[45] In this case, the children from CEOSS-sponsored development groups helped construct Article 80 in the 2014 Constitution, which helps protect the employment and education rights of minors.[46]

---

44. A tuk-tuk is a small, three-wheeled vehicle used as a taxi.
45. Ratliff, Interview with Egyptian children and children's rights advocates.
46. *Constitution of the Arab Republic of Egypt 2014.*

Small-Scale Farmers

Another example is found among small-scale farmers in the Qalyubia governorate, just north of Cairo. CEOSS currently helps about 13,000 farmers across three governorates, including about 4,200 women farmers. The majority of Egyptian crops are grown by farmers who cultivate a few acres. Historically, these farmers lost much of their income to middlemen who would purchase their products in order to resell them to the general public. These intermediaries were dictating the types of crops the farmers would grow (primarily grains) and facilitated the use of expensive artificial fertilizers.[47] As CEOSS began the process of rights-based development, they instructed the farmers in the use of composted fertilizer, rather than burning or discarding manure and other organic waste. They also provided contacts with public distributors who would buy their products directly, and educated farmers in how to become more strategic in the types of crops they grew. The farmers interviewed in this study indicated they doubled their income within a few years as a result of these efforts. At the same time, they improved their farming practices overall by shifting from grains to potatoes, onions, and peanuts, and by dealing directly with companies distributing their produce.[48]

During this process, CEOSS trained farmers in forming local committees of elected representatives. These committees set and pursued priorities with representatives of the Ministry of Agriculture. For the Qalyubia famers, this included the right to government assistance in clearing irrigation canals that were in disrepair, and improving the overall irrigation infrastructure. Through the rights-based approach, the farmers were able to organize themselves, set their own priorities, and pursue those priorities with respect to the local government. The approach has proven popular with both the farmers and local government representatives tasked with looking after agricultural improvement in the area. The levels of involvement increased as the agricultural committees learned more about the process of engagement. As the CEOSS-trained committees and organizations matured, these groups were able to contribute their own preferred rights language to Article 29 of the 2014 Egyptian Constitution. These articles are designed to establish and protect the rights of farmers and agricultural workers.[49] "This was the

---

47. Murphy, *Changing Perspectives*, 19
48. Ratliff, interviews with Egyptian farmers and government officials.
49. *Constitution of the Arab Republic of Egypt 2014.*

first democracy that we practiced in our life," said one farmer, "and we feel successful."[50]

Similar stories are found in the other domains CEOSS has engaged, including the disabled looking for employment and women in need of better health care. In each case, immediate needs were coupled with organizing efforts among those seeking a remedy to their grievances as a means to a better life. In their training and organizing efforts, CEOSS points to both Egyptian law and international human rights conventions as tools for those seeking to improve their situation.

Their ethic of engagement and method of mobilization is borne out of a dynamic based on their identification as members of multiple communities: as Christians, as members of a small religious minority, and as Egyptian citizens. Through this multi-dimensional perspective, CEOSS has been able to weather multiple regime changes, frequent social hostilities, and hostile government officials on its way to becoming one of Egypt's largest and most respected development organizations. For CEOSS, the pursuit of greater religious freedom includes the freedom to serve their neighbors, Christian, Muslim, and secular alike.

ETHICS OF ENGAGEMENT

The work CEOSS is doing among Egypt's most vulnerable is an example of using social movement organization by a religious group to pursue secular human rights in a manner that engenders broad appeal. It presents an important counterpoint to other Christian movements and organizations that are directly engaging the political process to secure rights for their own community, exclusive of those beyond their in-group. CEOSS is looking after rights across demographics that make up Egyptian society, transcending religion or subculture. Behind their decade-long project in rights-based development is nearly seven decades of providing social services. During this time, CEOSS's presence in Egyptian civil society has continued to grow in size and reputation, even as Egypt has undergone dramatic political, social, and economic upheavals. Their footprint as one of Egypt's preeminent NGOs stands in sharp contrast to the small population of their home community of Coptic evangelicals.

Since the Arab Spring, Coptic Christians in Egypt have suffered increasing persecution and violent social hostilities. This includes blasphemy charges, religious attacks, arrests, and kidnappings. They have also seen their churches and homes destroyed by arson and mob violence. Coptic

50. Ratliff, interviews with Egyptian farmers and local government officials.

evangelicals are a small minority in Egypt's historic Christian community. Yet, they have suffered similar violence and persecution as their Coptic Orthodox brethren. In 2015, this has included arrests of evangelical youth on charges of insulting Islam, mob attacks on Coptic evangelicals meeting in homes, and gunfire directed at Coptic evangelical churches.[51]

CEOSS is also involved in a wide variety of civil society initiatives typical of development organizations (micro-loans, poverty eradication, vocational training, etc.) Their rights-based approach, in conjunction with their other initiatives and partnerships with Islamic and secular NGOs, has created a deep civil society presence for CEOSS. This presence has provided a buffer against opposition the group has received with respect to their religious identity. Their emphasis on looking after the needs of a cross-section of Egyptian society, and not limiting themselves to the unique concerns of their own group, has proven an effective strategy in strengthening their survival in an otherwise hostile environment.

CEOSS's civil society efforts are part of a twin strategy for governmental and societal engagement. First, the leaders of the organization believe violent extremism can be reduced by addressing needs related to poverty, disenfranchisement, unemployment, and other pressing social issues. They believe actively helping to relieve these pressures will prevent some Egyptians from falling into extremism.[52] Second, CEOSS remains closely engaged across different strata of government, from local councils to national leaders. By establishing relationships and keeping communication channels open, they are able to make a strong case for their unity with other Egyptians across demographic lines, alongside a conduit for communicating their own community's concerns among government leaders.

For example, prior to the Arab Spring, the head of CEOSS would meet regularly with President Mubarak to inform him personally of the group's activities. These meetings served to counteract the negative reports from religiously biased security officials that would otherwise threaten the organization's ability to remain active.[53] After the 2011 revolution, President Morsi expressed his appreciation of CEOSS during an Egyptian NGO forum.[54] Top-level support continues under President Abdel Fattah al-Sisi,

---

51. Ibrahim, "'Incensed' Muslims Surround Christian Home"; "Masked Men Fire at the Evangelical Church in Fayoum"; El-Fekki, "3 Copts Face Charges."

52. Al-Salam, "Muslim-Christian Forum in Alexandria."

53. Springborg, *Mubarak's Egypt*, 155.

54. "President Morsi Visits CEOSS Pavilion."

who recently included CEOSS among nine of Egypt's largest organizations addressing Egyptian development issues.[55]

Opponents of Egypt's Coptic Christians can be found in government and among certain religious and political groups. These opponents attempt to perpetuate *de facto dhimmitude* for the Coptic community. This manifests itself in a variety of ways, including employment and educational discrimination, and restrictions on church construction and maintenance.[56] CEOSS combats this by making a public case for the national Egyptian character of their community and organization. They reinforce their case by developing economically sustainable initiatives that improve the lives of vulnerable Egyptians, regardless of religion, gender, or social class, while avoiding proselytism. Their style of engagement includes communicating the Christian nature of their activities (i.e., the church's concern and obligation to the poor), as well as the beneficial role they play in protecting the rights of those across Egyptian society.[57]

Though persecution, discrimination, and occasional violence toward Egypt's Coptic citizens persist, CEOSS's national profile as a contributor to the common good continues to grow. Their rights-based development work across a range of vulnerable Egyptian groups helps make the case to their compatriots and government leaders that the Coptic evangelical community is interested in improving the lives of every suffering Egyptian, regardless of faith. Their historical success may point to a horizon where they may one day achieve relief from social hostilities and political oppression.

A rights-based approach recognizes many development goals are intertwined with a human right, such as those defined in the *Universal Declaration of Human Rights*.[58] CEOSS identifies rights-based outcomes as "participation in decision-making, providing better opportunities for developing human capabilities, and releasing humanity from confining boundaries and increasing community self-reliance."[59] In addition to programs that, for example, improve education or provide better medical care, CEOSS also engages elected local governing bodies, public ministries, private companies, and Egyptian media to help secure the rights to the service areas they pursue. In each program, they train leaders and organize self-sustaining committees and organizations capable of continuing their pursuit of rights

---

55. State Information Service, Arab Republic of Egypt, "Sisi Probes Civil Society's Role in Achieving Development."
56. "Egypt Eases Restrictions on Repairing Churches."
57. Khalīl, "Pope Shenouda Leaves Hospital After Medical Checkups."
58. Kuruvilla et al., "Millennium Development Goals and Human Rights," 141–77.
59. CEOSS, "Local Development," para. 1.

beyond the direct assistance of CEOSS.⁶⁰ Rights-based development not only alleviates poverty or resolves an issue such as illiteracy or poor health care, it also empowers those benefiting from the program to have a greater say in their own affairs. This includes participation in local government as citizens, better governance, improved laws that promote development and human rights, and so on.

MODES OF ENGAGEMENT

The process of setting forth an alternative path toward public engagement has generated some contention among Coptic evangelicals. In recent decades, the two chief contenders over the driving narrative behind Coptic evangelical engagement were CEOSS directors Rafiq Habib and his successor, Andrea Zaki Stephanous.

Rafiq Habib

Rafiq Habib is the son of CEOSS founder Samuel Habib, and a former director of the organization. During his tenure, he developed increasingly closer ties to the Muslim Brotherhood via the *al-Wasat* party, and subsequently the Freedom and Justice Party (FJP) associated with the group. Habib was influenced by anti-Orientalist literature, including Edward Said, who spoke to a deep dissatisfaction among many Arabs with the culture and forms of government formed in the West and in place in the Middle East.

For Habib, the grievances held by his community had common cause with Arab cultures across the region suffering from colonialism, Western hegemony, and the influx of non-Islamic foreign culture. According to Habib, the proper form of resistance to Westernization and domination was to construct a Christian narrative that resembled the Muslim Brotherhood's resistance to the West. This narrative rejected foreign religious and political elements in favor of a native Arab/Islamic approach, including the acceptance of Islamic culture as the dominant character of Arab culture and society.

In a nutshell, Habib envisioned the Christian community in Egypt as existing within a communal Islamic state. The structure of this society relied heavily on NGOs to provide most of the social support, which in effect limited the direct role of government in the lives of citizens. Habib saw the Egyptian government as deeply exploitative of its citizens, and the nationalization of institutions such as health care, education, and welfare as

60. CEOSS, "التنمية المحلية"

how the government has bankrupted the Egyptian community.⁶¹ He blamed the large, intrusive government structure on the influence of Western colonialism. He located the source of his society's ills in Western interference in Arab-Islamic culture. The remedy Habib saw was a return to a model of society found in Islamic civilization, while stopping short of advocating Islam itself as a religion. "*Umma* [Islamic communal society] is for us as civil society is for the West," Habib wrote. "We believe that the *umma* has a very important role to play in bringing about our renaissance. The *umma*, not the state, will be the catalyst of progress. The functions of the state must be restricted, while civil society must play a much more important role."⁶² He rejected both the Western model of a democratic nation-state, as well as an Islamist religious state, in favor of a middle ground that limits the role of government in the society's cultural institutions.

Habib's model differs from the Western approach to democracy, individual rights, and freedom of conscience in three essential aspects. First, it elevates the interest of the group over that of the individual in order to foster "social altruism." Second, it calls for supervision over "intellectual conduct" to prevent deviation from the sacred values of the nation or causing offense to the religious and cultural sensitivities. And third, it rejects the notion of a global melting pot of cultural interactions, particularly with the foreign and corrupt West. As Habib put it, "Different cultures should be open in different ways. You can have scientific, economic and diplomatic cooperation. You can exchange ideas. But you cannot exchange values."⁶³

His ideas and political affinities helped place Habib in a leadership position in Muslim Brotherhood political parties. The short-lived Muslim Brotherhood government was the high-water mark for Habib's influence on the Egyptian national stage. He ascended to prominent leadership positions in Muslim Brotherhood parties, particularly the FSJ. But this period also marked a nadir for him among his fellow Coptic evangelicals. He retained a directorship at CEOSS, but his ideas and political roles were roundly condemned by his community. This included his father and founder of CEOSS, Samuel Habib, who condemned his son's views in the *Cairo Times*.⁶⁴ Other Coptic evangelicals sought his banishment from their community, arguing his ideas gave ammunition to their Islamist opponents and caused greater

---

61. Hatina, "In Search of Authenticity," 49–65.
62. 'Ila et al., "We are a Civil Party with an Islamic Identity," 31.
63. 'Ila et al., "We are a Civil Party with an Islamic Identity," 57.
64. 'Ila et al., "We are a Civil Party with an Islamic Identity."

strife between Coptic Orthodox and evangelicals, as well as between Copts and Egyptian Muslims.[65]

Andrea Zaki Stephanous

For the current director of CEOSS, the role of the Christian in addressing grievances and seeking public influence goes far beyond the confines of protecting one's own religious identity group. Andrea Zaki Stephanous has outlined an ethic of engagement he calls "Dynamic Citizenship." He defines this as:

> an inclusive process that reaches beyond equality to justice by relating political rights to economic, social and cultural realities. Dynamic Citizenship promotes pluralism via multiple commitments and institutionalizations of identity. Being democratic in nature, it transcends religious, ethnic and gender loyalties. It is connected to the nation-state but also transcends borders.[66]

CEOSS has many resources at its disposal to address these grievances. This includes decades of accrued social capital in Egyptian political and civil society, as well as human and material infrastructure in place to conduct their programs. Along with resources traditionally associated with social movement organizations are resources internal to the group that provide the engine for continued engagement. These resources flow from a theology that focuses on the role of the believer to address societal problems beyond the walls of their own community. Zaki sees the civil society role of CEOSS as consistent with an understanding of Christianity that seeks to address poverty, oppression, injustice, and other causes of distress found among their neighbors.[67] If the dynamic citizenship of CEOSS has a precedent, Zaki argues, it is found in the cooperation between Egyptian Christians and Muslims in the 1930s, where the reigning ethos of Egyptian citizenship was common struggle.[68] Over the decades, consistent government support was often hard-won from regime to regime, and occurred despite social and government pressures on minority religious communities, particularly Coptic Christians.

At the heart of Zaki's approach is fostering pluralism in a manner that steers away from direct religious or ideological conflicts. Zaki argues

---

65. 'Ila et al., "We are a Civil Party with an Islamic Identity," 62.
66. Stephanous, *Political Islam, Citizenship, and Minorities*, 194.
67. Stephanous, *Political Islam, Citizenship, and Minorities*, 190.
68. Gershoni and Jankowski, *Egypt, Islam, and the Arabs*, 43.

polemics against other belief systems often slide into contempt for the believers of a competing faith, which often leads to violence: "All of this leads to rejection of 'the other', provoking sectarian strife and creating a huge gap in the community, isolating and confining some Christians in the Middle East to their own communities, rather than being open and integrating into society. This in return leads to intensified violent sectarianism, as experienced during the past year."[69]

Zaki refers to rioting in 2013, when Muslim Brotherhood supporters left Coptic churches and properties destroyed across Egypt, including property owned by CEOSS in the city of Minya. Yet, for CEOSS, the answer was not retreat. Instead, Zaki outlined an incarnational approach to continued engagement in the face of religious and political opposition. He observes that ideas that seek to remove the spiritual community from the larger society is a poor example for today's Christian communities that have a divine calling to preserve and transform society.[70] He also sees the 19th-century evangelical missionary ethic as teaching a form of puritanism that also set Christians on a trajectory of isolation: "When evangelicals escape from their social role, they escape from their role as light and salt of the world as God desired."[71]

Zaki envisions the incarnational role in society as a partnership between Christians and those outside the church. That is, just as God entered the world as Christ in order to establish a church to accomplish his purposes, so too are Christians called to enter society as representatives of Christ to further the objectives laid out in Scripture: "Spirituality, represented in a clear relationship between God and the community, is reflected in creative actions that seek development of the group's mission and vision," he argued. "The establishment of schools and hospitals, community development, the realization of human dignity and improvement of the standard of living, are matters not less spiritual than worship, but instead are within the mission and calling of the church of God."[72]

The idea that public engagement brings the presence of God into the world resembles ideas found in the Social Gospel movement of the early 20th century.[73] However, Zaki sets his vision apart from the Social Gospel by tying his core idea to the Arab cultural context, and setting forth a specifically 21st-century concept of interreligious pluralism. He sees Arab

69 Stephanous, "Middle-Eastern Evangelical Perspective," 331.
70. Renard, *Islam and Christianity*, 176.
71. Stephanous, "Middle-Eastern Evangelical Perspective," 331.
72. Stephanous, "Middle-Eastern Evangelical Perspective," 336.
73. Rauschenbusch, *Christianizing the Social Order*, 52.

identity as inherently pluralistic in terms of religious affiliation. He also sees a focus on the common good of fellow Arabs as driving the Christian community to incarnational engagement. This stands in contrast to the Social Gospel movement, which has its roots in the Protestant response to Western secularism. That is, its context was not seen as religiously pluralistic:

> The idea of pluralistic history is crucial; it introduces a new element to the concept of Arabism. Arabism is not limited only to Islam; it includes other religions and cultures in the Middle East as each one contributed to Arabism as we see it today. Pluralism in terms of history, culture and religion could lead us to new concepts for identity formation in the Arab world.[74]

Though Zaki sees a common Arab identity as a catalyst for Christian engagement across religious lines, he is careful to distinguish this idea from the historical development of Pan-Arabism, and its successor Pan-Islamism. He observes these historical movements as devastating for Christians in the Middle East:

> Pan-Arabism, its Islamic undertones undeniable despite its professedly secular call, was highly problematic for the Christians as a frame of reference. The confiscation of extensive Coptic property and the nationalization of Christian-controlled businesses deprived the Coptic elite of its public influence, as did the abolition of political parties, the main avenue of political participation. Prior to 1952, Copts occupied posts in major ministries in the prime-minister's office, and as the head of the Parliament ... A collision could have been avoided had the Egyptian political leadership perceived the danger of using religious symbols, language and concepts to deal with national problems.[75]

He argues the government's use of religion, specifically Islam, as a tool of legitimization led to the current environment of disunity among Egyptians. Zaki argues this environment hampers the kind of broad dynamic citizenship critical for religious adherents of a variety of faiths to feel a common identity with those outside their group. Instead, religious groups become political havens for those of a similar faith, and the locus of identity group mobilization: "Thus, religious belonging increasingly becomes the unique or principal means of defining oneself, i.e., something that divides citizens rather than something that unites them."[76] Defiantly asserting an

---

74. Stephanous, *Political Islam, Citizenship and Minorities*, 156.
75. Stephanous, *Political Islam, Citizenship and Minorities*, 120.
76. Stephanous, *Political Islam, Citizenship and Minorities*, 123.

alternative to this trend recovers the dynamic aspect of citizenship and offers hope for national unity amid pluralism.

Zaki says any defensible political theology outlines a strong social role for the church. This role recognizes the equal citizenship of those from all religious persuasions. The religious approach to public life can also help strengthen solidarity across faith traditions and social demographics through robust participation in civil society. In this way, religion lends strength to the unity of a pluralistic state. The alternative is politics rooted in identity struggle, in which the state will be ripped apart over religious and ideological differences:

> The ultimate goal of the church is that people will live in peace with God and with others. To achieve this goal, the church must have relationships with individuals as well as an established role in society. This does not mean that the church approaches public life with the idea that it will use ideology and the tools of mobilization to increase its own power. Rather, it has a social role and it should understand the boundary between the political role and the social one. The Church must not extend the social role into the political one.[77]

CONCLUSION

In the case of CEOSS, there is a clear connection between the theology and values expressed within the organization and the ability to mobilize for public change across a variety of constituencies. To be sure, Christians of all kinds face steep hurdles when it comes to full religious freedom in Egypt. For example, changing one's legal status from Muslim to Christian in Egypt is effectively impossible. Coptic Christians experience violence, and the Egyptian court system favors Islam over Christianity.[78] Even so, through CEOSS, Coptic evangelicals have found an avenue for their public religious expression through mobilization for the poor and vulnerable. Here are three key points to this approach.

First, Coptic evangelical political independence has been a critical factor in maintaining a relationship with those at the highest levels of political power. From the Mubarak regime, to the 2011 Muslim Brotherhood government, to the current government, CEOSS has been able to assure those holding office they are working toward the common good, and are not part

---

77. Stephanous, *Political Islam, Citizenship and Minorities*, 134.
78. Tadros, *Motherland Lost*, 50.

of a political opposition. A notable exception to this is the political aspirations of Rafiq Habib, who sought a solution for the plight of his community that was tightly woven into the politics of religious identity.[79] However, he was roundly criticized across the Coptic evangelical community for his political ideas and his association with the Muslim Brotherhood. After the fall of the Muslim Brotherhood government, it is likely the status and credibility of CEOSS as a politically independent NGO depended upon the distance the Coptic evangelical community placed between itself and Habib's political activities.

Today, CEOSS continues to grow as one of Egypt's most prominent development organizations, due to its concentration on service to the public. In cases where their work has crossed over into Egyptian public policy, it was as a catalyst for obtaining the rights among a variety of vulnerable groups, rather than exclusively strengthening the political position of their own identity group. In this way, they have also maintained a form of religious independence. That is, by working for the common good of all Egyptians, regardless of religious affiliation, they have avoided the pitfalls of identity politics. The grievances framed by CEOSS in their mobilization efforts are those representing a spectrum of vulnerable communities. In contrast, the Coptic Orthodox community has seen a historical arc of combining their religious, ethnic, and political identity, and pursuing their grievances through politics, only to see their freedom and influence weakened by the majority opposition.

Second, Coptic evangelicals have bolstered their ability to mobilize within their community by internally framing their work in civil society as a theological imperative to help those in need. Zaki's concept of "Dynamic Citizenship" embodies the idea the Christian maintains a complex set of identities, including believer, citizen, neighbor, and family member. Their identity as a believing community directly influences how they behave as members of the public. Through the work of CEOSS, they can express their role as Christians publicly through acts of service.

Third, CEOSS's mobilization efforts address secular needs in a manner that gazes outward toward the common good of all Egyptians versus gaining converts or strengthening the political power of their own community. Among those outside their community, their work is seen as a critical exercise in improving the lives of those who would otherwise have little public voice. The rights-based development approach also creates a manner of engagement that points toward self-reliance among the communities they assist. This mitigates any criticism that CEOSS coalesces power by creating a

---

79. Rowe, "Building Coptic Civil Society," 111–26.

system of dependence. On the contrary, their training and advocacy agenda is directed toward having vulnerable communities create and pursue their own priorities related to obtaining their rights.

Though Coptic evangelicals are a very small minority within a minority, CEOSS is one of Egypt's largest development organizations. Its reach goes far beyond the congregational level, where Newbigin and Niebuhr saw the greatest possibility for public Christian behavior that remained faithful to Christian principles. Through focused leadership and community participation, CEOSS has retained its outward emphasis toward the good of their neighbor through civil society projects. At the same time, they have engaged the political process by developing relationships with those in the highest levels of government, while being careful not to seek political power for themselves.

The case of Rafiq Habib is the exception that proves the rule. His embrace of politics, particularly that of the ascendant Muslim Brotherhood, was roundly condemned by his home community. The fall of the Muslim Brotherhood from Egyptian halls of power strengthened the argument against Coptic evangelicals seeking political power.

Rather, CEOSS's most effective engagement with the political sphere has been through communication channels with political leaders across a succession of regimes in concert with their effort to secure the rights of the vulnerable communities they serve. CEOSS seems to have mitigated Niebuhr's concern that as a Christian group grows, the more likely it is to veer into the quest for power, and away from its mission and principles. In doing so, they have preserved their ability to thrive in a national context that otherwise presents high barriers to religious freedom.

PRINCIPLES OF DYNAMIC ENGAGEMENT

Several factors emerge from CEOSS's experience with rights-based development and their overall role as a Coptic evangelical organization. In light of lessons learned from the other cases, they offer evidence supporting Dynamic Engagement, which ties the religious freedom of this group with their ability to contribute to the common good.

Conscience: *Effective Christian leaders emphasized within their own communities the central role of the universal free conscience that appears in Scripture, theology, and tradition, and the implications of this in a pluralistic context.*

CEOSS draws heavily from the Coptic evangelical community for its own staff, and emphasizes within its own literature the dignity of each individual, regardless of their religion, gender, disability, or class. Simultaneously, they avoid proselytization in favor of building relationships in a pluralistic context in which they are a small minority. There is a close connection between the ideas taught by CEOSS leaders regarding the free conscience and the moral agency of each individual, and their method of rights-based development.

A central feature of CEOSS's ethos is the biblical principle of loving one's neighbor. CEOSS animates this principle through their rights-based development approach that seeks to build up their most vulnerable neighbors within the framework of universal human rights norms. At the same time, Coptic evangelicals working within CEOSS have a strong sense that the work they are doing has a deeply spiritual component: they are loving God and keeping his commandments through their development work.

Consistency: *Effective Christian public engagement in defense of religious liberty was consistent in its emphasis on freedom and justice across religious and nonreligious boundaries.*

CEOSS provides an exemplary case of a Christian group working across many strata of Egyptian society for greater freedoms and lasting social justice. Though greater religious freedom and reduced social hostilities are often elusive in this country and the region, their work has given them a voice for religious freedom that is backed up by decades of concern for their neighbors, regardless of faith or social station.

Common Good: *Effective Religious freedom initiatives emphasized the role of faith groups serving the common good through participation in civil society.*

The bottom-up approach illustrates the importance of civil society engagement for increasing the common good as well as its importance regarding the long-term prospects of religious liberty. In this respect, the efforts of Coptic evangelicals in Egyptian society could prove instructive for advocates in the United States and other countries.

Crossing Over: *Effective religious freedom advocacy groups integrated their work with others across religious and social identity lines.*

One of the remarkable aspects of Coptic evangelical social engagement is their central focus on the role they can play in civil society. Their rights-based approach has given them the ability to organize groups across a broad spectrum of Egyptian society. In this approach, their concerns run much deeper than the immediate religious concerns of their community. Rather, they are seen as advocates of farmers, rural women, people with disabilities, and others. This is in conjunction with their own call for fewer government restrictions and an easing of social hostilities. Their attention is focused on organizing civil groups that endeavor to clearly identify rights issues, elect representatives, and foster the development of programs that help vulnerable groups become better educated about how to improve their circumstances. This includes everything from better crop management to techniques that improve women's health. Through this process, the local groups, aided by CEOSS, identify the rights they are entitled to by international convention or by Egyptian law. CEOSS and their partners also contributed to the rights articulated in the new Egyptian constitution. Over time they have facilitated tangible improvements in the lives of the people they work with. As a result, they have been able to cultivate relationships at all levels of Egyptian society, and put to rest arguments that greater religious involvement in the nation's public life necessarily means greater conflict.

7

The Institute for Global Engagement and Vietnam

RELIGIOUS NGOs HAVE UNDERGONE significant changes over the past few decades. This includes the rise of international faith-based NGOs that project significant influence in the areas of development and human rights advocacy. Religious freedom advocacy is part of this wave. The Institute for Global Engagement (IGE) is an important example of an international religious NGO attempting to make a global impact. IGE is an example of a parachurch organization acting across national borders, helping to shape the relationship between religious communities and national governments. IGE's leadership describes their organization as a "think-and-do" tank that pays close attention to the cultural and political contexts in which it operates, while pressing for full citizenship and freedom of conscience and religious liberty for people of all faiths.[1]

Situating IGE within the evangelical movement and its associated organizations reveals how the contours of engagement have changed in the 21st century. In the middle of the last century, evangelical missions working internationally concentrated on conversion, exemplified by the work of Billy Graham and other evangelists. This emphasis on conversion reflected the divergent trajectories taken by fundamentalist and modernist churches in the West during the 20th century. Fundamentalism, the parent movement of today's evangelicalism, rejected the "Social Gospel" that emerged

1. "About IGE."

as the focus of modernist Christian organizations, and largely focused on preaching, church planting, and discipleship.[2] They saw their task as reorienting society toward a right relationship with God, one individual at a time. Evangelicals rejected "statecraft as soulcraft."[3] This fell in line with the historical evangelical attitude that considered the church, independent of the state and operating free of government interference, as responsible for the formation of a virtuous citizenry. It was a counterpoint to the idea the state was the primary agent for the formation of character in its citizens.

This early focus on conversion by mostly western evangelicals was succinctly described by James Murch in 1956:

> Evangelicals are, therefore, convinced that the preaching of the Gospel is the essential task of missions and must always remain so. They do not object to programs for the solution of agricultural, social, political and industrial problems, but they believe that each country, race and generation must solve its own problems in the light of God's Word through the native churches. Their chief aim is the personal conversion of men to a new life in Christ, to complete surrender to God's will as revealed in His Word and to new relations of love to their fellow man.[4]

As the decades progressed, a debate emerged among evangelicals about the need for denominational and parachurch organizations to expand beyond conversion efforts to the social issues that affected their international audiences. In 1974, the watershed International Conference of World Evangelization in Lausanne, Switzerland emphasized the primary place for evangelism, but addressed the need for greater attention to the social needs of those being evangelized:

> We express penitence both for our neglect and for having sometimes regarded evangelism and social concern as mutually exclusive. Although reconciliation with other people is not reconciliation with God, nor is social action evangelism, nor is political liberation salvation, nevertheless we affirm that evangelism and socio-political involvement are both part of our Christian duty.[5]

One attribute of modern evangelicalism is its variety of expression and presence of internal debate. This includes debate over the role of

---

2. Shin, "America's New Internationalists?"
3. Shah, "For the Sake of Conscience," 136–37.
4. Murch, *Cooperation without Compromise*, 97–98.
5. "Lausanne Covenant," para. 6.

proselytism, particularly when it is emphasized to the exclusion of social change as an expression of Christian love for one's neighbor. While many large and influential evangelical organizations continued to focus on evangelism, a submovement emerged that sought change by addressing social structures of injustice and political reform, particularly on the international stage. Perhaps the largest organization in this group is World Vision. The organization's president, Richard Stearns, wrote in his book, *The Hole in Our Gospel*: "This gospel—the whole Gospel—means much more than the personal salvation of individuals. It means a *social revolution*."[6]

The Institute for Global Engagement (IGE) falls squarely into this submovement. True to the larger historical evangelical movement, IGE emphasizes the role of religious freedom in allowing faith to form good citizens. At the same time, it defends its lack of emphasis on conversion while remaining within the larger, conversion-oriented evangelical movement.

Chris Seiple was IGE's president from 2003 until 2015.[7] During his tenure, Seiple was the driving force behind IGE's advocacy initiatives. He was also its chief intellectual, forming the theological and political ideas that would undergird IGE's strategy to increase religious freedom around the world. Seiple outlined this position in *Christianity Today*:

> CT: *What is IGE about biblically?*
> Seiple: It is trying to promote and protect a freedom that is given by the Author of life. You can think about it as preevangelization, but I see us as a nonproselytizing, evangelical organization. In 2 Corinthians 5, Paul asks us to be ambassadors. An ambassador is someone who has been trained to engage a culture and its politics to advance the interests of his state. Well, our state is the kingdom. And you advance or build that kingdom by loving people in a language and logic they understand. The local church cannot create discipled ambassadors, cannot serve society as salt across all sectors, unless it is free to do so.[8]

In the first decade of the 21st century, Vietnam's hope for greater international integration was hindered by domestic crackdowns on its minority religious populations.[9] The government of this Southeast Asian nation had set a trajectory leading toward normalized trade with the United States. However, Vietnam's treatment of its Protestant and Catholic groups alarmed the U.S. government and American co-religionists. The conflicts had a long

---

6. Stearns, *Hole in Our Gospel*, 7 (emphasis original).
7. "Chris Seiple, President Emeritus."
8. Galli, "Chris Seiple on Relational Diplomacy," 31.
9. "S. Rept. 109–321."

history. The region's rulers have experienced tensions with Christian minorities living in the country for centuries.[10] In the first decade of the new millennium, the country's economic future relied in part on resolving this deeply rooted cycle of suspicion and violence.

Members of the U.S. Congress sought improvements in Vietnam's human rights record before granting the Communist country normalized trade status.[11] At the same time, the newly founded IGE stepped in as an advocate and guide to help Vietnam resolve the entrenched conflict between Vietnam's religious communities and its government.[12]

IGE drew intellectual resources from a nexus of its founders' evangelical faith, experience in American international affairs, and a history of the organization's founders in work with poor and oppressed communities. By their own account, IGE needed to speak the language of all three of these domains to effectively pursue religious freedom for Vietnam's Christians.[13] How these strands were pulled together speaks to how the organization articulated its religious and humanitarian values. In terms of social movement analysis, IGE's efforts involved identifying a central grievance: violence and mistreatment of religious communities by the Vietnamese government. They also needed to frame the grievance for their audience. This entailed arguing for their style of engagement, dubbed "relational diplomacy," in terms that resonated with an evangelical constituency. Prior to launching their mobilization initiatives, they needed to marshal resources to address the grievance. This includes raising funds for travel and other programmatic activities, as well as developing a network of contacts in the Vietnamese government, U.S. State Department, and in religious communities. They mobilized these resources in a multifaceted campaign to bring about a positive change in how Vietnamese minorities fared with respect to the Communist government.[14]

As an evangelical organization venturing into diplomatic waters, framing the issue was a complex task. They had to simultaneously articulate an identity that resonated with their core religious constituency and form an approach that would also defuse suspicions within the Vietnamese government. Mobilization entailed marshalling the human and fiscal resources necessary for education and outreach between IGE and the Vietnamese government. To accomplish this, IGE's leadership relied on the "top-down,

10. Shortland, *Persecutions of Annam*, 375.
11. H.R. 5602—114th Congress (2015–2016)."
12. Vu, "Institute in Vietnam."
13. Seiple, "Theology, Strategy & Engagement."
14. Benford and Snow, "Framing Processes and Social Movements," 611–39.

bottom-up" approach as a central resource in their ability to frame the rights issues they attempted to address. Though concerns about Vietnam's treatment of its religious minorities continue, IGE counts their Vietnam program as one of their leading successful and ongoing initiatives.[15]

Seiple argued a free religious citizenry was good for Vietnam's stability and prosperity, and that IGE held a particular vision in how to bring this about. *Christianity Today* highlighted this vision and IGE's role:

> For a Communist country that five years ago was breaking up prayer meetings and shooting into crowds, this is extraordinary. The freedom of people "to choose or not choose their religion" has been a part of the Vietnamese Constitution for some time, but the government is only now getting around to enforcing that ideal—thanks to forceful op-eds, government sanctions, and the patient, relational work of IGE . . . "It has two dimensions," [Seiple] said. "One, religious freedom is legally protected. Two, it is culturally owned. Culturally owned means the people who live there understand that this is in their self-interest, and they contextualize the principle [of religious freedom] to a preexisting principle that's already in their culture . . . Seiple gave an example from Vietnam. Government officials have been reluctant to allow seminaries to be built. His response to them has been, "Seminary is security." He argues that if they don't encourage the church to have theologically trained Christians who can educate their flocks, those flocks are open to being hijacked by extremists who can create social unrest. The argument makes sense to officials and allows churches to work their spiritually liberating influence on society quietly . . . The Cold War model of many organizations has been covert support for oppressed Christians combined with outsider advocacy. In the early years of the 21st century, IGE is flipping this model on its head: open support for Christians and insider advocacy.[16]

One Vietnamese leader, Professor Do Quang Hung, described his perspective about IGE's role as a "think-and-do" organization:

> Over time, I realized two critical features of IGE. First, IGE is not an ordinary institution in both status and prestige in the sense that it not only serves as a scholarly linkage among research institutions, but I found IGE's status to be truly global and in possession of rich experience that they work very effectively and efficiently . . . The second feature that impressed me a

15. Vu, "Institute in Vietnam."
16. Galli, "New Day in Vietnam," 27.

great deal and increasingly helped strengthen our cooperation with IGE is that they appear to be highly pragmatic and have a thorough understanding of Vietnam. I believe this is very important. In my work, I have collaborated with many institutions in various countries around the world, and some among those may not understand Vietnam well enough. These organizations may propose plans or projects that are not practical. This is not the case with IGE. IGE is unique in that it both has high status and effective operation, which I admire.[17]

BACKDROP FOR ENGAGEMENT

The United States responded to Vietnam's pattern of religious oppression through diplomatic tools. This includes assigning Vietnam the status of "Country of Particular Concern" (CPC) in 2004.[18] These and other tools tying international relations and trade agreements to human rights improvements placed Vietnam in a difficult position. They needed to either effectively (or even ostensibly) make progress on entrenched conflicts between the state and the country's religious groups or lose out on economic opportunities critical to Vietnam's economic development.[19]

At the same time these issues crystalized for the Vietnamese government, the newly founded IGE was seeking ways to engage Vietnam regarding its religious freedom concerns. Immediately prior to IGE's founding, Robert Seiple, IGE's first president and Chris Seiple's father, had been the first U.S. Ambassador-at-Large for Religious Freedom.[20] Prior to his diplomatic post, Robert Seiple had been president of World Vision, which itself was preceded by his tenure as president of Eastern College and Eastern Baptist Theological Seminary in Pennsylvania.[21]

Robert Seiple had a personal interest in Vietnam. He flew 300 combat missions as a bombardier in an A-6 Intruder during the Vietnam war between 1966 and 1969. His experience in Vietnam stuck with him throughout his career as an educator, humanitarian executive, and diplomat. Among the first initiatives he launched after leaving the State Department in 2000 was founding IGE with a primary outreach to Vietnam.

17. Hung, "Importance of Partnership," 1:24–2:50.
18. *Annual Report on International Religious Freedom.*
19. *Annual Report on International Religious Freedom.*
20. Miller, "De-Seiple-Ing World Vision."
21. Chandler, "New World Vision President Named."

In the earliest days of the organization, IGE was run from World Vision's offices in Washington, DC. It later moved to Eastern College, and then to its present home in Arlington, Virginia.[22] Though IGE cultivated programs around the world covering a number of areas of emphasis, the religious freedom program in Vietnam emerged as a flagship program for the organization.

Although the officially atheist Vietnamese form of government has its roots in the Communist ideologies of its Soviet and Chinese counterparts, the country is made up of a plurality of religious communities and a range of ethnic groups. This includes Mahayana Buddhists, Roman Catholics, evangelical Protestants, and even a small Muslim community.[23] The story of how Vietnam's Communist government has evolved over the past four decades is tied closely to how the government has dealt with its religious minorities. This includes phases of accommodation and control, integration and suppression.[24]

There are certain themes that recur in the history of Christianity in Vietnam. First, the adoption of Christianity challenged the traditional practices tied to the veneration of ancestors, even in cases where the new faith did not always demand the believers cease civic rituals respecting ancestors.[25] Second, Christianity offered, and continues to offer, a number of avenues for engaging modernity in a way acceptable to Christian believers.[26] Third, the centuries-long track record for Christians in the region is one of suppression and persecution, marked by instances of relative religious freedom.[27] Fourth, periods of religious toleration for Vietnamese Christians seem to be tied directly to the practical, economic, and political concerns of the country's rulers.[28] For about a decade after the turn of the millennium, trade relations with the West, particularly the United States, came with stipulations to reduce religious restrictions and violations of human rights. These could only be resolved by easing religious oppression against Vietnamese religious minorities.[29]

Roman Catholicism has a long history in Vietnam. Catholic missionaries first entered the region of what is today the country of Vietnam in the

---

22. "Institute for Global Engagement: Brandywine Forum."
23. Bouquet, "Vietnamese Party-State and Religious Pluralism Since 1986," 90–108.
24. Dutton, *Tây Son Uprising*.
25. Keith, *Catholic Vietnam*, 184.
26. Ng, *New Way*, 51.
27. Keith, *Catholic Vietnam*, 248.
28. Dutton, *Tây Son Uprising*, 178.
29. Keith, *Catholic Vietnam*, 248.

early 1500s. By 1600, a permanent mission had been established in Đại Việt. Jesuit missionaries continued to expand their efforts in the area, establishing churches, schools, and relationships with local rulers.[30] The Jesuits entered a religious milieu accustomed to a variety of faiths existing alongside each other. These included traditional folk beliefs, Confucianism, Daoism, and Mahayana Buddhism. In this context, Christianity was not initially seen as a threat. As in many missionary contexts, Christianity was most readily adopted by those at the economic and social margins of society.[31]

Over the next few centuries, through individuals like Alexandre De Rhodes and organizations such as the *Société des Missions Etrangères de Paris* (SMEP), Christianity continued to grow in Vietnam, despite occasional crackdowns by hostile governments.[32] A 1784 census placed the Christian population of the area around 350,000 to 400,000 among a population of 5.5 to 10 million.[33] As the population of Christianity increased it came into conflict with traditional practices. During this period, Christians were ordered by their missionary and local church leaders to tear down altars to their ancestors, and discontinue giving money to support festivals and community rituals associated with ancestor worship and folk beliefs.[34]

From the 17th to the 19th centuries, Đại Việt was marked by political rivalries across the northern and southern regions. Uprisings, such as the Tây Sơn rebellion in the late 18th century, saw alternating periods of persecution and religious freedom as juntas displaced regimes, and were subsequently repulsed. In the early 1800s, the Christian population was sufficiently large, and its legitimacy was strengthened through a multigenerational heritage of their faith in the region. Area rulers found it increasingly difficult to alienate them through techniques of suppression. Also, Christian missionaries were also seen as a vital connection to the outside world, which competing forces used at times for access to arms and economic opportunities. At other times, the loyalty of the Christian population was questioned due to their disavowal of traditional beliefs regarding a spiritual connection to their ancestors and the king.[35]

By the 19th century, the Catholic population constituted a formidable subgroup with ties to French missionaries and burgeoning colonial powers. Life for Vietnamese Christians became worse under the Nguyen dynasty,

30. Dutton, *Tây Son Uprising*, 176.
31. Dutton, *Tây Son Uprising*, 173.
32. Keith, *Catholic Vietnam*, 41.
33. Dutton, *Tây Son Uprising*, 124.
34. Dutton, *Tây Son Uprising*, 186.
35. Ramsey, "Extortion and Exploitation in the Nguyễn Campaign," 314–15.

which had wrested power in the Tây Sơn rebellion.[36] Intensified pressure boiled over in the 1830s and 1840s, when tensions between the northern and southern areas of Vietnam, as well as cultural and ethnic strains on the kingdom, erupted into violence. Between 1833 and 1838, hundreds of local Catholics, seven missionaries, and 20 priests were executed by the Vietnamese king Minh Mang. The king had engaged in a campaign to homogenize religion and culture under his rule. Christians were seen as an impediment to this program, compounded by the sense they were loyal to a growing imperial power.[37]

Reports of the execution of missionaries and the widespread violence against the local Christian community outraged French citizens. As a result, French support of missionary work was strengthened, manifested in a stronger naval presence in the area. These events helped precipitate a full invasion of Vietnam by French imperial forces in 1858.[38] It is notable that French imperial influence and money flowing through the Catholic missions played a role in the regime's persecution of Christians during this period.

In 1862, Vietnamese Catholics celebrated the Treaty of Saigon, which guaranteed them freedom from official harassment. However, social hostilities remained high against Christian communities and leaders. Catholics experienced frequent rioting and plundering of their villages toward the end of Nguyen rule of the region. Catholic leaders complained to Western sources that government officials tasked with protecting them were often complicit in the rioting or did nothing to stop the violence.[39] Article Nine of the Second Treaty of Saigon (1874), which included reinforced commitments to religious freedom and government protection under the threat of French imperial power, provided further relief for Vietnam's Catholic community.[40] Subsequent agreements followed as France strengthened its control over the region in the following decades.[41] Yet, treaties did not resolve the tensions between Vietnam's Catholic and non-Catholic populations.

During World War I, new rifts emerged between priests and French imperial officials over the recall of missionaries and pullback of resources. This pitted the missionary effort in Southeast Asia against the war effort in Europe. Prior to the war, another rift had emerged between Vietnamese

---

36. Keith, *Catholic Vietnam*, 4.
37. Ramsay, "Extortion and Exploitation in the Nguyễn Campaign," 311.
38. Ramsay, "Extortion and Exploitation in the Nguyễn Campaign," 312.
39. Shortland, *Persecutions of Annam*, 425–27.
40. Shortland, *Persecutions of Annam*, 428.
41. Shortland, *Persecutions of Annam*, 420.

priests and the French missionaries and government. Many Vietnamese priests were arrested for their participation in anti-French resistance movements planning to overthrow imperial rule.[42]

In the 1920s and 1930s, the Vatican responded to calls for a transition away from mission-centered Catholic life in Vietnam by supporting an independent national church.[43] This was accompanied by renewed enthusiasm for Vietnam's political independence from France. An effort was launched to create an entirely Vietnamese Catholic Church hierarchy during the First Indochina War (1946–54), which followed on the heels of World War II.[44]

During the French Indochina War, several Catholic bishops organized their own militias to provide a defense against both French and Communist forces.[45] For example, in the southern Ben Tre province, a French army officer named Captain Leroy organized a group of Catholic brigades. These became the Unified Mobile Christian Defense Units, a paramilitary force that eventually controlled the whole province following the departure of French forces. In the central region of Annam, the area's bishop was given both spiritual and political authority in the region from the king of Annam. Catholics tended to cluster in their own villages, and the "prince-bishop" raised his own taxes and formed his own militias. These autonomous bishops initially cooperated with the Communist Viet Minh forces in a common effort to resist a return of French control after World War II. This alliance eventually failed, and Catholic regions led by the bishop remained autonomous Catholic pockets that resisted both French and Communist control.

After the Geneva Accords of 1954, more than 600,000 Vietnamese Catholics (roughly half of the north's Catholic population) fled to the south, and the church was stripped of its autonomy and ability to control geographic areas. Catholics were told they could continue to worship as they pleased as long as they did not criticize socialism, refuse manual labor, or threaten the state in any way. By the mid-1960s, southern Vietnam's population was approximately 10 percent Catholic (about 1.6 million people).[46]

Protestantism in Vietnam is a much more recent phenomenon. One of the most significant developments came in 1911, when the Christian and Missionary Alliance denomination launched an effort to evangelize the region. Today, roughly one-quarter of Vietnam's 400,000 Protestants (or *Tin Lành*) come from this denomination. Baptist and other missionary groups

42. Keith, *Catholic Vietnam*, 5.
43. Keith, *Catholic Vietnam*, 12.
44. Keith, *Catholic Vietnam*, 13.
45. Spector, "Phat Diem," 44.
46. Liên, "Catholic Question in North Vietnam," 440.

became more active in the subsequent decades until the 1960s.[47] Most Protestants are found among the ethnic minorities on the Central Highlands. These Montagnard believers are generally very conservative theologically, and often experience friction from their neighbors over their rejection of ritual altars and community ceremonies honoring the dead.[48] The term "Montagnard," or *Degar*, refers to a variety of tribes that live in Vietnam's south and Central Highlands. Like the Hmong, many of the Degar are Christian, a result of missionary efforts during the first six decades of the 20th century. Because of their ethnic distinction and their Christian faith, they are often looked upon with suspicion by the government and their majority Kinh neighbors. As a result, they have experienced persecution, social hostilities, and religious restrictions.[49]

Living alongside the Montagnard communities are Hmong Christians. Linguistic analysis seems to indicate the Hmong ethnic group has lived in southern China and Southeast Asia for about 2,000 years, with more recent migrations into Thailand, Vietnam, and Laos.[50] Traditional Hmong religion can be categorized as a form of animism.[51] This includes beliefs in the spirit world, mediated by the rituals and activities of shamans. Their traditional beliefs place an emphasis on ritual respect for ancestors, reincarnation, and the connection of all things in the material world to an underlying spiritual fabric.[52]

Hmong beliefs include eschatological hopes for the return of a mythical king who will lead the Hmong people to a spiritual and earthly restoration of power. This eschatological expectation has played a role in the conversion of many Hmong to Protestant Christianity.[53] Parallels between end-times evangelical teachings and the expectations of a restored Hmong monarchy, as well as a non-Communist means of adapting to modernity, have contributed to the adoption Christianity by many in this group.[54]

The introduction of Protestant, evangelical Christianity to the Hmong began with the radio broadcasts of the Far East Broadcasting Company missionary organization. FEBC programming targeted refugee communities in the south, delivering sermons in the Hmong language. The sermons included

---

47. Rivers, "Baptists Celebrate 50 Years in Vietnam with Hugs, Tears."
48. Ng, *New Way*, 51.
49. Jones et al., *Repression of Montagnards*, 402–16.
50. Ratliff, "Vocabulary of Environment and Subsistence," 160.
51. Ngo, "Protestant Conversion and Social Conflict," 274–92.
52. Ngo, "Protestant Conversion and Social Conflict," 279.
53. Ngo, "Protestant Conversion and Social Conflict," 280.
54. Ng, *New Way*, 95.

evangelical millenarian expectations of the second coming of Christ. These radio broadcasts were picked up by Hmong living in the Central Highlands, who listened with interest to the broadcasts delivered in their own language, rather than the Kinh Vietnamese language that dominated official government radio broadcasts.[55]

The dynamics involved in the Hmong adoption of Christianity depended on several factors. First, the parallels between evangelical eschatology regarding the second coming and Hmong legend provided an avenue for traditional believers to consider the newly introduced faith. Second, Protestant evangelical Christianity offered an avenue toward modernity for the Hmong. That is, the religion provided an alternative to the assimilationist program of the Vietnamese government. Christianity allowed Hmong adherents to join a modern global community without losing their identity to neighboring majority ethnic groups or the secular Communist government. Among other things, the Hmong found in Christianity a competing narrative to Vietnamese Communism that tied them into a global community of fellow believers.

One aspect of Hmong lived culture is its ongoing distinction from the majority Vietnamese (Kinh) ethnic group. The Hmong are considered by the government and Vietnamese majority to be a backward people. They point to the animistic beliefs as well as their agriculture techniques as a lack of cultural sophistication. Many government programs were designed to assimilate the ethnic group into national culture. This included promoting everything from modern cultivation of crops to primary education the "Vietnamese Way." The drive to sway Hmong to the Vietnamese Way was an effort to convince an ethnic group with a strong sense of identity and a tradition of self-preservation to forsake their culture and the ways of their ancestors in favor of their "cultured despisers."[56] Those who adopted Christianity were able to accomplish a modern adaptation to a world system that could compete with Communism ideologically, as well as plug them into a network of religious denominations and organizations beyond the borders of Vietnam.[57]

The Vietnamese government's reaction to Hmong Christian activity has often been harsh. In February 2003, the government launched a suppression campaign, shutting down 354 out of 412 house churches, and "disappearing" 56 pastors.[58] Among those caught in the campaign were four

55. Ng, *New Way*, 166.
56. Michaud, "Montagnards and the State in Northern Vietnam," 340.
57. Ngo, "Protestant Conversion and Social Conflict," 292.
58. "H.R.1587," Section 2.

Hmong Christians operating a house church. They were sentenced to 24 to 36 months in prison for "disturbing public order." According to Freedom House, interviews with their families revealed that government officials also threatened heavy fines unless they abandoned Christianity and rebuilt shrines to their ancestors.[59] In another case that year, an ethnic Hmong Communist party member named Vang Seo Giao, who had converted to Christianity, was beaten to death and his body thrown in a river after he refused to renounce Christianity and rebuild an ancestral altar.[60]

In June 2012, two Hmong churches were destroyed by government officials.[61] In March 2013, the Hmong deacon of a legally registered evangelical church died in police custody. Officials said he had committed suicide by putting his hand in an electrical socket. However, family members released photos of his body, which displayed evidence of beatings and torture.[62]

RESOURCES & POLITICAL OPPORTUNITY

The persecution of Vietnamese Christians provided the impetus for IGE's interest in the country. In 2003, Robert Seiple's son, Chris, took over as president of the organization, and served as its leader until 2015. Chris Seiple (hereafter "Seiple") is a former Marine infantry officer, and holds a PhD from the Fletcher School of Law and Diplomacy at Tufts University.[63] Under his leadership, IGE expanded its portfolio of issues and greatly increased its staff and reputation. Contributions to IGE grew from less than $900,000 per year to more than $4.5 million during his tenure.[64]

When IGE began reaching out to Vietnam two years prior to Seiple's tenure, its government was attempting to quell rising protests among the country's Catholics and Protestants. This entailed heavy-handed tactics, including arrests, church burnings, and beatings.[65] These crackdowns were among a number of factors that generated opposition to greater economic cooperation between Vietnam and the United States, even as the U.S.-Vietnam Bilateral Trade Agreement was signed in December 2001 by President

---

59. "Vietnam Sentences Four Hmong Christians to Prison," para. 9.
60. *Annual Report on International Religious Freedom, 2004.*
61. *Violations of Religious Freedom in Vietnam.*
62. Minh, "Thêm Một Người Chết Tại Đồn Công An Tỉnh Dak Nông."
63. "Chris Seiple, President Emeritus."
64. *Form 990: Institute for Global Engagement* (2003); *Form 990: Institute for Global Engagement* (2014).
65. Young, "Testimony."

Bush.⁶⁶ For example, according to the Jackson-Vanik amendment to the Trade Act of 1974, nonmarket countries with a record of human rights abuses would be denied most-favored-nation trading status with the United States. Also, religious abuses in Vietnam were frequently tracked and reported on by human rights groups and major evangelical media outlets, such as *Christianity Today*.⁶⁷

Vietnam initially denied entry for Robert Seiple in 2001. However, as that country sought closer economic ties with the U.S., IGE was granted increasing access to government officials dealing with religious communities in Vietnam, as well as the religious communities themselves. It was a sign Vietnam was interested in addressing the human rights issues that could jeopardize their trade agreements. IGE attempted to make the most of this political opportunity, utilizing the "top-down, bottom-up" mobilization approach to religious freedom advocacy. As a result, IGE was able to build capacity among government officials to implement better policies toward Vietnam's religious minorities. Also, IGE was able to listen to the perspectives of Vietnam's Christians, help them develop their own theological and political understandings, and provide opportunities for them to make their case to the government in a productive way.⁶⁸

IGE'S RESOURCES

One of the most important resources for IGE, and any religious NGO, is its recognizable identification with its core faith group. From the outset, IGE has identified itself as an evangelical organization. This identification speaks to the group's ability to raise funds from members of the movement, tap into the network of contacts across the movement's churches and organizations, and focus their message on a set of values and rhetorical themes that resonate with the movement.⁶⁹

The evangelical movement encompasses many groups with a variety of agendas, and millions of individuals. In IGE's early days, founder Robert Seiple outlined a set of Christian characteristics and principles that would shape how the organization engages its mission. This early example of rhetorical framing by IGE reflects many aspects of Bebbington's criteria for

---

66. *Agreement between the United States of America and the Socialist Republic of Vietnam on Trade Relations.*
67. Callahan, "Vietnam's 'Appalling' Persecution."
68. "Vietnamese Delegation Visits U.S. to Build Friendships."
69. Schneider, "Comparing Stewardship across Faith-Based Organizations," 521.

"evangelical," particularly as it relates to the dynamic between the evangelical hallmarks of biblicism and activism:

1. Know Him: "Know your maker . . . Know your faith at its richest and deepest best, and enough about your neighbor's faith to respect it."
2. Know Yourself: "Understand your strengths and weaknesses . . . Cultivate the characteristics of the biblical metaphors for global engagement: the streetwise common sense of the snake, the gentle humility of the dove, the wise statesmanship of the ambassador . . . Act incarnationally and establish the worth of the gospel so that the truth might be revealed."
3. Know His World: "This is God's world . . . We 'plant and water; he brings the increase . . .'"
4. Know history—political and cultural, yours and theirs. Know all the questions, not just the answers. Understand geographical complexity and local nuance.
5. Pray over the land: "Pray for discernment to take place, for wisdom to reveal itself . . ."
6. Find partners: "Who has been trustworthy, credible, persevering and relevant? Build relationships that endure . . ."
7. Act comprehensively: "Put yourself in everybody else's shoes. Develop a policy and a supporting strategy around objectives formed in faith. And remember: global engagement has a face. A difference is made, a plan is enacted, a transformation takes place one life at a time . . . a life already made in the image of God."[70]

IGE leadership has closely associated its mission with spiritual principles. A common feature of evangelical NGOs is their inclination to frame their purposes for action around biblical themes and historic Christian ideals.[71] IGE resembles other theologically conservative Christian organizations in this respect. IGE also employs robust secular arguments for religious freedom and other issues in order to mobilize support and convince secular leaders to adjust their policies toward religious minorities (including non-Christian minorities).

As president of IGE, Chris Seiple set forth a vision for IGE that combined an inward spiritual perspective with an assessment of the outward Christian role in postmodern society. He has stated the central purpose of

---

70. Seiple, *Ambassadors of Hope*, 209–10.
71. Schneider, "Comparing Stewardship across Faith-Based Organizations," 517–39.

IGE is: "To make Christ visible and Christians relevant on the cruel edges of the world."[72] Central to this vision were a number of key starting points, not all of them necessarily theological. Seiple's secular and religious arguments are woven together in a seamless perspective that seeks to improve lives in a practical sense, as well as honor the Christian's spiritual role in the world.

Seiple sought to be both evangelical and pluralistic, emphasizing the crucial role of religious freedom for all faiths in building a just and peaceful society. He argued, "We as Christians are called to love our neighbor, to love them in a language and logic that they understand, or it's not love. And to show up and to shut up and listen, and to discern how God is moving in that context."[73]

Seiple identified the current era's looming question as "how we are going to live with our deepest differences?"[74] He saw religious freedom advocacy and partnerships as a means to address this question. According to Seiple, religious freedom in public life strengthens both religious and secular goals that cannot be unraveled from each other. That is, religious freedom helps reduce sectarian strife. It also speaks to a strong sense of human dignity at the core of a flourishing, free society. Seiple argued freedom of conscience is an intrinsic good in that it is a gift from God, and is the means by which human beings may encounter God of their own free will. The two sides of the argument are integral to his secular defense and definition of religious freedom:

> We believe that humans, as a function of their innate dignity, possess the inherent freedom to believe in whatever they want, religious or otherwise, as well as practice and share those beliefs in private and public settings. Humans should experience this freedom as equal citizens under the rule of law, where governments also ensure that this freedom is not used to harm fellow citizens. They have the right to bring those beliefs respectfully to the discussion of society's governance, and global affairs. Put differently, sustainable religious freedom is the legally protected and culturally accepted opportunity to choose, change, share, or reject beliefs of any kind, including religious ones, and to bring those beliefs to public discussions.[75]

Through this structure, IGE leaders framed the organization's mission within an evangelical understanding of Christian theology and the

---

72. Seiple, "Building Religious Freedom," 97.
73. "IGE's Work," 5:27–5:40.
74. "IGE's Work," 6:04–6:12.
75. "IGE's Work," 7:15–8:02.

pragmatic needs served by a society that observes the rights of a free conscience. Evangelical NGOs frequently use scriptural references and biblical illustrations to convey their sense of mission, in contrast to the toned-down religious language of Christian organizations associated with mainline Protestant denominations.[76] It is also a feature of the rhetoric IGE deploys to provide a rationale for their programs and inspire their constituents.

Yet, IGE differs in one important respect with respect to the primary mission associated with many other nonprofit evangelical organizations: they leave conversionism aside in favor of building relationships. Here, Seiple outlines how limiting evangelism efforts serves to expand global religious freedom and allow citizens to decide their faith for themselves:

> We love our fellow Christians by helping to inspire and equip them to understand and engage this world strategically—with shrewdness and without guile—so that they themselves reveal the love of Jesus Christ. We also love them and our non-Christian brothers and sisters by helping to develop environments in which they can seek truth freely and without coercion. In short, the Institute is an evangelical—but nonproselytizing—organization. It is our great hope that our non-Christian friends worldwide, given the true opportunity for religious freedom, will choose and experience the transformative power of Christ's love. Achieving that end, we confess with gratitude and awe, is His job, not ours. Our task is to love God by loving His people and working to build healthy societies in which they are liberated and empowered to respond to Him.[77]

Articulating the mission of IGE as an evangelical, but nonproselytizing, organization is an important stage of the mobilization process. For organizations such as IGE, expressing the organization's message in a way that elicits action can be seen as operating on two fronts. First, organizations rely on a core base where various forms of support and mobilization occur.[78] For IGE, this includes a certain level of reliance upon fellow evangelicals for approval of its mission to help facilitate fundraising, recruit staff and volunteers, and develop partnerships in other initiatives. Like other faith-based advocacy and development organizations, they need to cultivate the arguments for their existence within their core base of support.[79] They use Scripture and biblical illustrations to frame the vision of IGE and legitimize

---

76. Kniss and Campbell, "Effect of Religious Orientation," 100–1.
77. "From the President," para. 17.
78. Schneider, "Comparing Stewardship across Faith-Based Organizations," 517–39.
79. Jeavons, "Stewardship Revisited," 108.

the organization's mission. This lends credibility to their stewardship of evangelical ideals. In the case of the religious communities it hopes to serve, articulating a spiritual core provides a passport to engagement.[80]

Second, IGE's mission relies upon its ability to speak to the secular needs of the government it wishes to persuade, as well as the governmental and nongovernmental organizations it hopes to work with. Secular arguments for action are critical to IGE's success in achieving aims associated with these nonreligious entities.

Their approach is not without criticism among American evangelicals. Bob Roberts, Jr. pastor of Northwood Church in the Dallas-Fort Worth area, has a close relationship with the IGE, including his time as chairman of IGE's board. They have worked together on IGE's flagship Vietnam projects, as well as projects across the Muslim world.[81] Roberts and IGE have focused on peacemaking between Muslims and Christians in the United States and abroad.[82] However, Roberts has been a frequent target of evangelicals warning against Sharia law in American courts, particularly for his church-sponsored interfaith peacemaking events that include members of local mosques. Even so, Roberts's base of support among like-minded evangelicals appears strong, revealing the nonmonolithic nature of the American evangelical movement.[83]

IGE has largely avoided popular evangelical criticism regarding their work in Muslim-majority countries, perhaps due to the specialized nature of their work overseas and an international focus on religious freedom that enjoys broad support in the overall movement. Their religious framing directed at home constituents, and their secular arguments for religious freedom directed at governments such as Vietnam's, appear as two rhetorical species sprouting from the single root. This does not necessarily indicate a disparity between the secular and religious arguments made by IGE. Rather, it can be seen as a product of the dynamic relationship between inwardly focused definitions and outwardly focused actions toward the goal of strengthening global religious freedom.

---

80. Kniss and Campbell, "Effect of Religious Orientation," 108.
81. "Northwood Church Hosts Vietnam Delegation."
82. Roberts, "Wycliffe School for Global Engagement."
83. Kennedy, "There's No Room for Hate."

MOBILIZATION AND ENGAGEMENT

Since the mid-1980s, Vietnam has moved from a Soviet-style economy toward a form of market economy.[84] At the same time, human rights concerns are often bundled with economic agreements.[85] Vietnam's effort to join the World Trade Organization (WTO) began in 1995 and continued until their acceptance in 2007. IGE engaged the Vietnam government to alleviate religious freedom concerns during the last four years of the 12-year process (after initially being denied entry). Their efforts were a component of the process that led to Vietnam's acceptance into the WTO.[86] Membership in the global organization includes a host of benefits that facilitate trade between countries and reduce economic volatility. This includes reduced tariffs, peaceful dispute resolution, and free trade agreements between members, among other benefits.[87]

The following timeline offers a look at the interplay between the Vietnamese government's behaviors toward it's religious minorities, its diplomatic outreach outside the country, and the efforts of IGE to improve religious freedom. It shows the relationship between the political opportunities that arose with respect to Vietnam's rising international economic interests, ongoing oppression of Vietnam's religious minorities, and IGE's initiatives in favor of greater religious freedom in the country.

---

84. Alpert, *Vietnamese Economy and its Transformation*, 152.
85. Alpert, *Vietnamese Economy and its Transformation*, 216.
86. Seiple, "IGE In Vietnam."
87. Amadeo, "Three Reasons Why WTO Membership is so Important."

IGE IN VIETNAM: 2001–2010

Year	IGE Engagement in Vietnam[88]	U.S. government and diplomatic developments	Events in Vietnam
2001	IGE applies for a visa request to visit Vietnam during a crackdown on Christian communities in the Central Highlands.	The United States Commission for International Religious Freedom (USCIRF) recommends the State Department designate Vietnam as a "Country of Particular Concern." The State Department catalogues abuses in Vietnam in its annual report on international religious freedom, but redesignates only Burma, China, Iran, Iraq, and Sudan with CPC status.[89] December: U.S. and Vietnam enter into a bilateral trade agreement.[90]	Vietnam conducts a six-month crackdown against Christian communities in the Central Highlands, closing and burning churches, arresting and torturing leaders, and killing Christian villagers.[91]
2002	IGE's request for visa is denied.	USCIRF again recommends CPC status for Vietnam. State Dept. redesignates the same five countries with CPC status.[92] Vietnam's deputy prime minister visits the U.S., urging closer economic ties. President Bush and Congress extend a waiver of the Jackson-Vanik trade provision, which would have affected trade with Vietnam amid continuing human rights concerns.[93]	Vietnam renews crackdown on Montagnard Christians, arresting leaders, breaking up religious gatherings, cutting electricity in villages, confiscating land, and removing Bibles and religious publications.[94]

88. From Seiple, "IGE in Vietnam," unless otherwise noted.
89. Farr, "Designation of Countries of Particular Concern."
90. "VN-US Economic & Trade Relations."
91. "Case Study."
92. Mufford, *Religious Freedom in Vietnam*, 2.
93. "Timeline."
94. "New Crackdown on Montagnards in Vietnam."

2003	IGE founder Robert Seiple is granted a visa request, and meets with a government religious affairs official regarding religious freedom issues	November: The first U.S. naval vessel to visit Vietnam since 1975, the USS Vandergrift, makes a port call in Ho Chi Minh City.[95]	December: Protestant Christians are arrested and beaten by Vietnamese security officers for distributing religious leaflets in Ho Chih Minh City.[96]
2004	May: IGE hosts a Vietnamese religious affairs official in DC. The official remarks: "You are the first Americans who did not give us a list and tell us what to do."[97]	September: U.S. sanctions Vietnam for religious freedom violations. Vietnam is designated a "Country of Particular Concern" in the State Department's International Religious Freedom report.	November: Vietnam issues new religious freedom ordinances.
2005	June: IGE visits Central Highlands, becoming the first American NGO to do so since the 2001 crackdowns and 2004 sanctions.	May: U.S. and Vietnam agree to a plan to remove sanctions over religious persecution June 2005: Vietnam's Prime Minister visits the U.S. November: Vietnam remains listed as a "Country of Particular Concern" in the State Department's International Religious Freedom Report.	March: Vietnam issues guidelines for regulating religious groups

95. "Christian Tract Distribution in Vietnam Brings Arrests."
96. "Timeline."
97. Seiple, "IGE in Vietnam."

| 2006 | February: IGE sponsors exchange of pastors, scholars and government leaders between Washington and Hanoi, facilitating off-the-record discussions.

July: Seiple advocates before the Senate Finance committee that Vietnam should be removed from the State Deptartment's CPC list, and U.S. should establish Permanent Normal Trade Relations with Vietnam (PNTR) as an integral part of a plan to address religious freedom and human rights concerns.

September: IGE hosts a conference in Vietnam focusing on Religion and the Rule of Law, and signs a memorandum of understanding regarding ongoing initiatives between Vietnamese government and religious leaders. | The State Department removes Vietnam from its CPC lists shortly before President Bush's visit to the APEC summit in Hanoi. U.S. Congress approves "Permanent Normal Trade Relations" (PNTR) with Vietnam. | Vietnam pushes for greater integration with the global economic community. A party congress emphasizes economic reforms. Hanoi hosts APEC summit, which includes President Bush. Efforts are aimed at lowering tariffs, normalizing trade and increasing employment. |
|---|---|---|---|

2007	IGE conducts a second conference on religion and rule of law in Hanoi. IGE leaders meet with Vietnam's president in Hanoi and Washington, DC.	June: President Nguyen Minh Triet visits the United States, the first official visit in more than 30 years. U.S. signs agreements that will help pave the way to more free trade between the countries.[98]	January: Vietnam joins the World Trade Organization (WTO)
			May 2007: Nine Buddhist monks from a banned sect are sentenced from two to six years in prison for peacefully protesting their community's treatment by the Vietnamese government.[99]
			November: Several pro-democracy activists are jailed, including two American citizens. They were later charged with terrorism.[100]
			Baptist and Mennonite movements are officially recognized by the Vietnamese government.[101]

98. "Bush, Vietnam President Hold Historic Meeting."
99. "Vietnam: Religious Freedom Denied."
100. "Pro-Democracy Activists to Be Charged with Terrorism in Vietnam."
101. "Hanoi Officially Recognises Baptists and Mennonites."

2008	Vietnam's Prime Minister visits the United States, IGE hosts a meeting with American religious leaders. IGE also sponsors the attendance of a group of Vietnamese government leaders at a conference in Beijing on religion and rule of law.[102]	President Bush meets with Vietnam's prime minister, U.S. begins process of political-military cooperation.[103]	Protestants in the Central Highlands stage demonstrations to demand the release of religious prisoners of conscience and the return of confiscated church land. Dozens are arrested and police forcefully seal off Christian villages. Catholics hold prayer vigils in Hanoi to urge the government to return confiscated church land.[104]
2009	IGE hosts scholars from the Vietnamese government's Institute for Religious Studies on a study tour covering Protestantism in America.	U.S. becomes Vietnam's largest export market, and Vietnam's largest source of direct external investment. US humanitarian aid surpasses $100 million.[105]	After 20 years in Vietnam, Assemblies of God churches (with about 40,000 adherents) receive official permission to operate.[106]

102. "20 Years of Vietnam-US Relations."
103. "Timeline," 350–53.
104. "Timeline," 350–53.
105. Manini, *U.S.-Vietnam Relations in 2010*.
106. "Assemblies of God Receive Permit Covering 40 Provinces."

| 2010 | IGE aids in the effort to have Vietnamese churches communicate with each other more effectively. IGE staff appears in interviews on VTV4, highlighting IGE's work and the importance of religious freedom. IGE inaugurates a "Protestantism Roundtable" with government officials and Protestant leaders. The roundtable discussed Vietnamese Protestant churches from 1911–1975. It also delved into government efforts to train officials and religious leaders on Vietnam's religious freedom legal framework.[107] | Vietnam chairs the Association of Southeast Asian Nations (ASEAN). The Obama administration indicates it wants to take the U.S. relationship with the country to the "next level" in terms of diplomatic cooperation in the region. U.S. criticizes Vietnam for continued human rights abuses in the wake of some improvements with respect to dissent and religious freedom.[108] | The government allows a large public Christmas celebration. Religious oppression steps up as government propaganda campaigns and "public criticism" ceremonies launched against Catholic and Montagnard Protestants, which includes coerced official denunciations of Christianity among hundreds of households representing thousands of adherents.[109] |

CONCLUSION

The case of IGE's engagement in religious freedom advocacy demonstrates the need for interdisciplinary models of engagement that reach beyond the standard social movement theory. That is, IGE's strategies parallel the processes outlined in the mobilization theories but seem to transcend the rights-grievance model in other ways. Their top-down, bottom-up approach, and their programmatic strategies to address the concerns of both

---

107. Institute For Global Engagement, "Vietnam."
108. Manyin, "U.S.-Vietnam Relations in 2010," 3.
109. "Montagnard Christians in Vietnam."

the oppressors and the oppressed departs from the classic social movement grievance narrative. In doing so, they have forged a path forward to address the plight of Vietnamese Christians by also addressing the suspicions and concerns of the government. This involved constructing an approach that involved a more holistic assessment of the factors at work in Vietnam. IGE's continual engagement over nearly two decades has not stopped centuries-long friction between the Vietnam government and the country's religious minorities. Even so, IGE's continual engagement efforts have shown some significant fruit.

In his book, *The Art of Not Being Governed*, James Scott argued the rugged mountainous country that stretches from Vietnam's Central Highlands to Burma (and beyond) is peopled by a cornucopia of ethnic groups that have spent generations evading subjugation by the state. They have retained self-governance, their own language and customs, and an identity distinct from those living in the lowlands. Even so, advancements in logistics and communications technology are allowing the state to more effectively project power into this region and establish clear lines of control.

State-resistant religious minorities in the Central Highlands are now experiencing a clear trajectory that will result in the end of their multi-generational resistance to government rule. As practical resistance to rule diminishes, these groups are finding ways to insulate their identities and ideologies from the state. Scott observed Christianity is a key component of this continued resistance.[110]

The case of Christianity among Hmong evangelicals demonstrates that resistance to the state is not the same thing as resistance to modernity. Christianity has a growing track record of being an avenue toward modernity for believers in groups like this—an avenue that runs as a parallel path that does not include assimilation into what the Communist rulers require of the minority.

A major feature of the vision IGE sees is the nature of the relationship between the Vietnamese government and traditionally state-resistant Christian groups, from the rural Hmong to urban Catholics. The narrative they put forward is that the centuries-long story of religion-state conflict can end, and the choice between anarchy and state hegemony is a false dilemma. Rather, they argue minority communities free to pursue their faith without state interference will aid in their country's stability and productivity. In this way, they transcend the grievance model that applies pressure for a political change.[111]

---

110. Scott, *Art of Not Being Governed*, 319.
111. Grim and Finke, *Price of Freedom Denied*, loc. 4999 of 5125.

In this respect, IGE's work in Vietnam and other countries has several layers. First, they are attempting to make the case that governments should respect the freedoms of minority religious groups as a pragmatic strategy. Second, they are forming their own method of mobilization that not only respects their own religious identity, but seeks to understand all of the factors involved in a given context, including an open understanding of the concerns of the government involved in the oppression.

Harassment of Christians in Vietnam continues to this day.[112] Seiple argues IGE played an important role in moving the persecution of Christians from a form of government policy to isolated incidents of harassment, particularly through its relational diplomacy with Vietnamese leaders.[113] Even so, the question remains open as to whether the "systematic, egregious and ongoing" persecution of Christians in Vietnam by the state will come to a definitive end in the near term.[114]

The ability to promote religious freedom in restrictive environments such as Vietnam is based on a theory of change that is still being worked about by those continuing work similar to that of IGE in Vietnam. This theory of change is based upon an organization's ability to build trust and working relationships across sectors of the government and within a pluralistic society.[115] Seiple tied the pragmatic effort to build trust within the Vietnamese government with the principle of honesty, citing Christian Scripture.[116] The Vietnamese were sometimes disappointed when some American delegations would say one thing, mostly positive, to them in Vietnam, and then say something else, mostly negative, in Washington. IGE emphasized honesty and consistency, even on difficult or sensitive topics. "It is the only way to build trust, in any culture," Seiple said, "Perhaps more importantly, we said the same things back in Washington, D.C [to American officials and policy makers]."[117]

Building trust was central among Seiple's goals at all points of engagement: "Every trip, every activity was something that was closely coordinated with the Vietnamese as a function of trust. And each time we achieved

---

112. Turton and Seangly, "Montagnards Flee to Thailand."
113. Seiple correspondence with Walter Ratliff.
114. "Vietnam: USCIRF Testifies on Capitol Hill," para. 2.
115. Seiple, "Building Religious Freedom," 97–102.
116. "All you need to say is simply 'Yes' or 'No'; anything beyond this comes from the evil one" (Matt 5:37 NIV).
117. Seiple correspondence with Walter Ratliff.

something, [Hien Vu, IGE's Vietnam program manager] and I would intentionally think through what is the next envelope to press."[118]

IGE's evangelical identity "was a point of suspicion for everyone," Seiple said of their dealing with the Vietnamese government, State Department diplomats, and partners in nonreligious partner organizations. There were several ways IGE addressed this challenge. An attitude of honesty and consistency in their rhetoric was a big part of this, he said.[119]

Another component of their work entailed a holistic understanding of the issues surrounding the lived experiences of religious minorities in Vietnam. "No one actually lives in the development of human rights 'sectors' assigned by western academics," Seiple observed. He emphasized need for a strong sense of identity as an important part of developing relationships in a "top down/bottom up" strategy: "Sociologically and secularly, if you do not know who you are, you don't know where you are going. People in other cultures pick up on that right away. Because we were so clear in our point of moral departure, and resulting love for the Vietnamese, and because we kept our word, we were trusted . . . accelerating our work in practical ways, cutting much red tape," Seiple said. As a result, IGE was able to help establish greater communications and monitoring of religious harassment, "There's no issue we can't talk about. We even established a 'hotline' to the ministry of Public Security, which controls everything, to ensure a dialogue where both sides were being heard, even if we disagreed."[120]

He said a solid understanding of the economic and geo-political forces that place smaller nations like Vietnam under pressure helped create a convincing case for greater religious freedom: "There has always been a China camp and an American camp among Vietnamese elites. It was harder to make the case to the China camp in a purely economic context, but it has been easier when you add the geo-political dimension. No one in Vietnam wants to be invaded for an 18th time."[121]

IGE's example confirms in part Niebuhr's argument that it is easier for smaller religious organizations to articulate an ethical, orthodox vision for political action that avoids the ills that come with large-scale mobilization. A critical component of this is the ability of the organization's leadership to form a distinct theological and practical approach without the pressures and compromises that come with mobilizing large numbers for a mass political

---

118. Seiple correspondence with Walter Ratliff.
119. Seiple correspondence with Walter Ratliff.
120. Seiple correspondence with Walter Ratliff.
121. Seiple correspondence with Walter Ratliff.

cause. IGE was able to remain agile in its approaches and form personal relationships with a relatively small team of people and see effective results.

There is, however, the other side of the coin: their argument is for religious freedom for religious minorities in Vietnam. This requires changing the minds and actions of large numbers of private citizens and government actors. The top-down, bottom-up approach attempts to instill a durability of vision across the private and public sectors. If successful in the long-term, this could demonstrate the strengths that theologically and ethically grounded leadership can have in political mobilization. A companion to this observation is the argument presented to the Vietnamese government (and others around the world) by Chris Seiple, Brian Grim, and other leading advocates for religious freedom on the international stage. That argument states religious believers in a country are not inherently inclined toward rebellion, sectarianism, and violence. Rather, religious freedom liberates the ethical and contributory aspects of the religious groups within a society. This in turn creates greater stability and productivity for the nation.[122]

PRINCIPLES OF DYNAMIC ENGAGEMENT

IGE's unique and persistent approach in Vietnam provides a clear example of a faith-centered NGO engaging in religious freedom advocacy across national, ideological, and cultural lines. Their example helps provide a template for future efforts by other organizations. What follows are examples of how the Four C's of Dynamic Engagement are illustrated by IGE's approach.

Conscience: *Effective Christian leaders emphasized within their own communities the central role of the universal free conscience that appears in Scripture, theology, and tradition, and the implications of this in a pluralistic context.*

During his tenure at IGE, Chris Seiple used his platform in the domain of international religious freedom advocacy to outline an ethic of engagement that fits within the evangelical tradition. This included a theological grounding in the role of a free conscience, and the Christian's role in working toward a world of greater religious freedom. As an evangelical organization, IGE developed a Scripture-based theological outlook that reinforced its placement within evangelicalism. At the same time, this outlook has a distinctive approach designed to make room for dialogue and practical cooperation with those of other religious traditions.[123]

---

122. "Seven Ways Religious Freedom Contributes to Sustainable Development."
123. "IGE Co-Convenes "Peace, Security & Co-Existence" Conference in Myanmar."

This approach is set within the context of its role as an international NGO advocating for religious freedom around the world. Their lessons learned include the idea that building relationships across the spectrum of authorities and communities helps bring the players into a space where practical solutions can be crafted to reduce conflict and build respect. Seiple also argued NGOs can help contribute to a common moral framework agreed upon by those at the negotiating table—a framework that respects the identities of those involved, but also recognizes the legitimacy and value of those who hold a different identity or ideology. IGE also counts among its lessons learned that it is not enough to point out Western notions of the freedom of conscience and religious liberty as a philosophical truth and a right outside the state's jurisdiction. Rather, IGE asserts part of being a wise advocate and religious representative is to also speak to the concerns of those in power. In this way, appeals to evidence that religious liberty pays valuable dividends in the country's economic health, internal and external security, and role on the world's stage can be more persuasive than philosophical appeals or a rights-grievance approach. As Seiple notes:

> In places like Dien Bien and Xinjiang, we have suggested that religious freedom is the best counterterrorism strategy, that seminary is security, that religious freedom—when properly rooted at the intersection of culture and the transparent rule of law—is preemptive peace. The premise is simple: if religion has been a part of the problem—if religion has been used to organize and rebel against the state, and/or used for terrorism—then it has to be a part of the solution. The best of faith can defeat the worst of religion, if given the chance. The more religious leaders who know how to live out the best of their faith, the more likely it will be that their congregations will seek to serve the local community by living out the Golden Rule. More theologically sound leaders mean better citizens, and better citizens mean more stability and prosperity.[124]

Consistency: *Effective Christian public engagement in defense of religious liberty was consistent in its emphasis on freedom and justice across religious and nonreligious boundaries.*

In the case of Vietnam, IGE's top-down, bottom-up approach entailed building an ongoing working relationship with Communist government leaders. This yielded a greater understanding of the precise concerns of government leaders about the populations they were seeking to manage. In many cases, IGE's high-level relationships also revealed a lack of

---

124. Seiple, "International Good Faith," 1–8.

understanding within the Vietnamese government regarding international human rights norms related to religious freedom and other human rights. This has led to regular training sessions to help government and academic leaders better understand the issues and how to resolve them.

IGE's commitment to religious freedom in Vietnam has shown how an evangelical organization can learn sophisticated diplomatic language, conflict resolution skills, and policy development techniques that equip them to engage the issue of religious liberty abroad. Working with Vietnam's Communist government as well as the variety of religious groups in the country has also expanded their capacity to identify aggravating circumstances that lead to oppression. In doing so, they demonstrate how a religious organization rooted in a specific tradition can play a role in advocating for universal rights of conscience and freedom of religion.

Common Good: *Effective Religious freedom initiatives emphasized the role of faith groups serving the common good through participation in civil society.*

IGE demonstrated their civil society approach through their top-down, bottom-up technique. The group recognized the recurring oppression of the Vietnamese government against religious groups, including both Protestant and Catholic groups that had a long history in the region. For IGE, the task involved working with government officials as well as the religious community to foster greater trust between religious minorities and political leaders. They also continue to educate government officials on international norms regarding human rights (as well as rights of religious freedom already enshrined in Vietnamese law), as well as the value of those standards.

Seiple noted that, prior to their involvement, religious organizations had not emphasized direct engagement with the Vietnamese government, which has proven important for practical improvements among Vietnam's oppressed religious minorities. Seiple emphasized the need to listen to the government's concerns regarding the country's religious communities. This included fears of violent extremism. The government was also concerned about the need for some religious populations to modernize their agricultural practices and other factors in order to improve their economic prospects.

From the top down, IGE's work had connections to Vietnam's economic and diplomatic interests in resolving the human rights concerns of those in the United States and the international community, particularly as they related to the prospects of a normalized trade status with the U.S. From the bottom up, IGE listened to those who suffered, and catalogued the accounts of government oppression and social hostilities experienced by Vietnam's Christian communities. They also worked with the government and religious groups in the country to allow for the construction of seminaries, and trained those affected in making their own case for human rights, including religious freedom.

Crossing Over: *Effective religious freedom advocacy groups integrated their work with others across religious and social identity lines.*

As in the case of IRFA, a political opportunity provided the opportunity to pursue change. In this case, the country of Vietnam was hoping to solve a series of economic issues by pursuing normalized trading status with the United States. The challenge for the Communist government included the painful memory regarding the American experience in the Vietnam War, the ongoing record of religious persecution by the Vietnamese government, and the antipathy among Vietnamese Communists in the government to address the concerns of the country's religious communities.

IGE adopted a unique strategy that departed from the "name and shame" tactics utilized by other organizations and enshrined in U.S. diplomacy under the 1998 International Religious Freedom Act. Instead, IGE worked to develop a relationship with Vietnam's government to seek innovative solutions to the country's religious freedom challenges.

8

Principles of Dynamic Engagement

CHRISTIAN COMMUNITIES HAVE A deep history in the formation of the functional norms that underlie universal human rights.[1] At the same time, some American Christian groups have also become entrenched in perennial culture wars, a symptom of an ever-thinning consensus and damaged civil discourse. Today, Christian denominations, NGOs, and parachurch organizations find themselves at a juncture as to what path they will take with respect to the state and to other groups in society. Within this context, the case studies presented here examined how religious networks and organizations approach issues related to religious freedom and advocacy.

History shows religious groups' commitments to protect their community at times do not align with a concern for the common good. However, some highlighted in this project are working toward the horizon of a more just and equitable social order. Leaders of the Coptic Evangelical Organization for Social Services and the Institute for Global Engagement argue the freedom to exercise their faith in public life is linked to the well-being of all in society. They also argue greater religious freedom helps disrupt cycles of conflict, rather than exacerbate the divisiveness that comes with identity politics.[2]

Certain principles have emerged in this project that speak to engagement efforts that reflect ideals formed in the Christian tradition, as well as efforts that demonstrate their effectiveness in the marketplace of ideas.

1. Tutu, "First Word," 3.
2. Grim and Finke, *Price of Freedom Denied*, 205.

These principles can be thought of as contributing to the conversation about the possibility of religious public engagement, as well as the pragmatic concerns that would accompany this engagement.

Coupling Christian ideals with what it takes to remain effectively engaged from a practical standpoint may, on its face, seem to correspond to the 20th-century Christian realism of Reinhold Niebuhr and others. However, there are certain aspects that depart from classical (or Niebuhrian) Christian realism. First, Niebuhr and the Christian realists of the last century assumed a continued dominant role of the white mainline Protestant church in American society. This doesn't reflect the current pluralistic context. Second, the type of globalization that has occurred in the past few decades, catalyzed by the rise of the internet and the information revolution, could not have been fully anticipated in the early-to-mid-20th century. The disestablishment of white Protestant Christianity in American public life and the new forms of communication that shaped the age of globalization have generated different challenges for those who wish to retain their religious distinctiveness while remaining connected with the issues of the day.[3]

In the old scenario, the church sometimes acted as the chief endorser and sometimes the chief critic of the state and those in power. In the theology of John Howard Yoder and Stanley Hauerwas, Christian realism came uncomfortably close to the Constantinianism they identify as tearing away the faithfulness of the church in exchange for proximity to power. The Constantinianism Yoder, Hauerwas, and others warned against included the church's validation of the state's use of coercive force, as well as the church's role in bolstering the secular authority of the state.[4]

The current political and social climate has changed dramatically since Reinhold Niebuhr's death in 1971. White mainline Protestantism has faced a continual decline in numbers and influence over the past 60 years.[5] Evangelicals have largely retained their numerical strength, but see some significant social and demographic challenges ahead. The relationship with the Trump presidency notwithstanding, evangelicals have not obtained the political and cultural clout once held by their mainline Protestant siblings. Rather, legal and social developments have fractured the American moral consensus, producing a variety of visions in the public square about the role of government and the nature of public policy. At the moment, these visions are often aligned along deeply partisan, political, and religious lines.[6] This

---

3. Jones and Cox, *America's Changing Religious Identity*, 10.
4. Hauerwas, *Approaching the End*, 135.
5. Hauerwas, *Approaching the End*, 36.
6. DeGirolami, "Religious Accommodation, Religious Tradition, and Political

points to Peter Berger's insight that secularism doesn't lead to a new consensus based on reason, but rather to a plurality of religious and nonreligious voices in the public square that compete for power and influence.[7] The new world order is a chorus, but with its members often simultaneously singing very different tunes.

In this present state, the Christian realists no longer have the platform as the conscience of the state ostensibly enjoyed by Niebuhr and his peers. As a result, Constantinianism is mitigated by the disestablishment of Protestantism in the American public square. At the same time, Christians in the United States and around the world fear the effects of a rising tide of religious restrictions, and the effects that might result from disengagement from public life.

The case studies found in this project point toward a set of principles that recognize the plurality that exists within Protestantism itself. The observations are meant to be ecumenical in the sense that they do not offer an endorsement of any theological camp. Rather, they offer perspectives that can be accessed across the theological spectrum.

Though some contemporary debates might seem exotic to Reinhold Niebuhr if he were alive today, his observations about human nature and religious group behavior remain salient. Niebuhr's argument in *Moral Man and Immoral* Society can be expressed as saying (in part) the larger a Christian organization grows beyond the congregational level, the more likely it is to foster injustices that often accompany the will to power associated with identity group conflicts. He considers group behavior, including (and perhaps especially) Christian group behavior, susceptible to the "natural impulse" of consolidating power unto itself.[8]

At the individual level up to small groups, Niebuhr argued selfish impulses are mitigated by the human conscience, which can transcend one's own pursuit of well-being in favor of the well-being of others. Yet, the transcendent concern for those outside one's own group diminishes the larger the group gets, and is placed in political competition with other large groups. In his estimation, the selfish impulses will win out. Christian groups that profess an interest in the common good of society are not immune from this phenomenon.[9]

Niebuhr's arguments ring true in some cases. For example, legal campaigns stemming from anti-Sharia mobilization have increased social

---

Polarization," 1127–56.

7. Berger, "Secularization Falsified," para. 5.
8. Niebuhr, *Moral Man and Immoral Society*, 48.
9. Niebuhr, *Moral Man and Immoral Society*, 25

hostilities for Muslims in the United States, threatening religious liberty for a broad set of American religious groups. Yet, Niebuhr's sociological effect does not seem to be universal, as seen among Coptic evangelicals in Egypt. Granted, some Coptic evangelicals and orthodox leaders, including Rafiq Habib, modelled their response to political Islam along the same rhetorical contours as the Muslim Brotherhood. This led to a stronger sense of disempowerment and alienation among their people. Coptic evangelical leaders such as Andrea Zaki Stephanous have worked to overcome this.

Yet, the drive for universality and inclusiveness is found in many efforts. This includes the drive to pass the 1998 International Religious Freedom Act, which combined the work of a small cadre of advocates under the leadership of John Hanford with the political strength of a large evangelical constituency. These and other examples temper Niebuhr's pessimism. The Coptic evangelical ability to advocate for the rights and freedoms of their group in concert with their efforts to look after the rights and freedoms of other groups points to a form of engagement that strengthens the common good and produces a strong argument for religious freedom in civil society.

American evangelicals and other Protestant groups live in a highly charged political environment, with increasing polarization on the horizon.[10] There are also relevant social and economic trends at work. Income inequality is growing both nationally and on the world's stage.[11] Also, the center of gravity for the religious world is shifting from Europe and the United States to the Global South. The "Next Christendom," as Philip Jenkins calls it, will be made up of a wide variety of cultures and ethnicities around the world, with their own sets of local concerns and theological nuances.[12]

The current mechanism of political mobilization presents an inward-focused path that demonstrates how a group identifies an injustice, frames their grievance in a way that resonates with their primary constituency, identifies a political opportunity, and activates members of the larger movement to bring about political reform that benefits the group.[13] For Christian religious liberty practitioners, there is something missing from this arc of activism: engagement across group boundaries. As seen in this project's case studies, long-term effectiveness includes concern about religious liberty and conscience rights across societal lines.

10. Pew Research Center, "Political Polarization in the American Public."
11. Dabla-Norris, et al., "Causes and Consequences of Income Inequality," 9.
12. Jenkins, *Next Christendom*.
13. Snow et al., "Frame Alignment Processes, Micromobilization, and Movement Participation," 464.

There are several fields that address factors that have arisen from the evidence presented here, including social psychology, as well as organizational and communications theory. One factor from the field of social psychology is "epistemic motivation," defined as the willingness of an individual or group to use their analytical and emotional resources to find and hold well-informed conclusions about the world, particularly observations that reach beyond their own cultural or ideological context.[14] Research into epistemic motivation has shown that a high degree of willingness for one or both parties to know the concerns, values, and norms of those across the negotiating table increases the chances a productive agreement can be formed between the parties. High epistemic motivation corresponds to better chances of negotiating a win-win conclusion.[15] This is particularly true when those engaged in a complex intercultural negotiation effectively communicate their own preferences and priorities, as well as have a clear understanding of (and willingness to understand) the factors influencing their counterparts. If understanding gained through this pluralistic approach is effectively communicated to members in the movement, it may reduce the negative effects of "cognitive encumbrance" by introducing adaptability into the movement's understanding of themselves and their place in the world.

According to Job van der Schalk, et al., high epistemic motivation can lead to a greater overall understanding of how a variety of cultures operate and how to process new information related to the intercultural understanding among experienced practitioners. This contributes to a higher cultural intelligence, which in turn facilitates greater effectiveness in a cross-cultural or cross-political context.[16] In light of the shift of Christian demographics to the Global South and the rise of competing religious and nonreligious groups in the West, it follows that Western Christian organizations would feel compelled to cultivate the kind of cultural intelligence that will help them meet the challenges ahead. It is important to note the psychological propensity toward epistemic motivation is not the domain of one party or political inclination. Epistemic motivation is no more likely to be associated with those who consider themselves politically liberal than conservative.[17]

One result of increased cultural intelligence driven by the engine of epistemic motivation is those engaged in cross-cultural negotiations have greater motivation to reach creative, integrated solutions that have a wide benefit. The research in this area indicates those who actively seek a deeper

14. De Dreu, et al. "Group Creativity and Innovation."
15. van der Schalk et al., "More (Complex), the Better?," 356.
16. van der Schalk et al., "More (Complex), the Better?," 362.
17. Federico et al., "Ideological Asymmetry," 381–98.

understanding of their partners and adversaries from other cultures build their capacity for effectively engaging other new cultures.[18]

A benefit of cultural intelligence is the ability to communicate well across cultural and political contexts. Effective dialogue among the players has been an important component in successful cases cited in this project, ranging from the passage of the 1998 International Religious Freedom Act, to rights-based development in Egypt, to religious freedom advocacy in Vietnam. Engagement across cultural and political boundaries, and the creative solutions that can flow from this engagement, expands the horizon beyond the capacities of a classical rights-grievance approach that focuses on mobilization of an identity base.

PRINCIPLES OF DYNAMIC ENGAGEMENT

The following principles of engagement were drawn from the evidence gathered in each of the case studies, and interpreted through an interdisciplinary lens employing social movement theory and the perspectives presented by thought leaders such as Reinhold Niebuhr and Stanley Hauerwas. These theologians have been generally critical of Protestant social movements in the public square, albeit in different ways. For Hauerwas, getting too close to secular power structures endangers an authentic Christian witness due to the irreconcilable differences between the nonviolent, noncoercive nature of the Gospel, and political participation that legitimates ways of life "made possible by violence and sustained by coercion."[19] On the other hand, Niebuhr has observed the larger a Christian organization or social movement becomes, the more likely it is to demonstrate a will toward self-preservation at the expense of others.[20]

A closer look at the modes of religious engagement in these contexts shows the important role of leadership in shaping a group's engagement. That is, the framing of messages and the choice of partnerships among those with influential platforms can have a decisive impact on whether Christian groups can remain consistent in their message and effectively advocate for religious liberty. The Four Cs of Dynamic Engagement articulate some of the lessons learned in this analysis:

Conscience: *Effective Christian leaders emphasized within their own communities the central role of the universal free conscience that appears in*

---

18. Imai and Gelfand, "Culturally Intelligent Negotiator," 83–98.
19. Hauerwas, *With the Grain of the Universe*, 86.
20. Niebuhr, *Moral Man and Immoral Society*, 9.

Scripture, theology, and tradition, and the implications of this in a pluralistic context.

This principle provides a justification within the Christian community for universal religious freedom to those outside of the tradition (set against the tendency to defend religious liberty merely for one's own group). It also provides an authentic vision of the Christian justification for conscience rights and religious freedom in the public square. It prepares the ground for public arguments regarding conscience rights and religious liberty using functionally normative tools such as the *Universal Declaration of Human Rights*.

Evangelicals place a premium on scriptural resources that tie into the pressing questions of the day.[21] In this case, there are ample scriptural justifications for the universally free conscience and religious freedom. However, as seen in the case of anti-Sharia and anti-Muslim mobilization among evangelicals, religious principles rooted in Scripture rarely make an appearance in their efforts to thwart the religious liberties of those of other faiths. Rather, evangelical mobilization was rooted in generating suspicion of American Muslims, portraying their religion as violent and anti-American. This contrasts with biblical principles outlined in the Old and New Testaments. For example, a fundamental idea behind a free conscience is found in the book of Job, in which the story hinges on Job's ability to rise above blessings or punishments in freely choosing to respect God and resist evil. It also stands in contrast to the Sermon on the Mount, where Jesus' listeners are exhorted to look after their own conscience and examine their own failings before condemning others.

Early church teachers such as Tertullian reinforced similar ideas regarding the freedom of conscience in Christian tradition: "It is a fundamental right, a privilege of nature, that every man should worship according to his own convictions . . . It is assuredly no part of religion to compel religion—to which free will and not force should lead us."[22]

From the 1960s onward, the leaders of CEOSS have utilized Scripture to develop the theological foundation for their work. The organization's founder, Samuel Habib, drew from biblical sources including Jesus' parable of the good Samaritan (Luke 10:25–37), in which a foreigner with a foreign religion is held up as an exemplar of good ethics, to cultivate human rights and development work across religious lines.[23]

---

21. Juzwik, "American Evangelical Biblicism as Literate Practice," 335–49.
22. Donaldson and Roberts, *Ante-Nicene Christian Library*, 11:47.
23. Virtue, *Vision of Hope*, 58.

These and other examples in Scripture and history lay the groundwork for a relational approach to other groups. Beyond pragmatic concerns, this pluralistic understanding of a free conscience displays a moral and theological consistency among Christians in the public square. Their example shows that a firm understanding of the role a free conscience plays in Christian tradition coupled with the relational passport to work with others across religious and ideological lines reduces conflict and increases influence.

Consistency: *Effective Christian public engagement in defense of religious liberty was consistent in its emphasis on freedom and justice across religious and nonreligious boundaries.*

Religious liberty advocates can showcase the strong tradition of a free conscience within their own community as well as make the public case they are consistent in the promotion of these rights for all. This includes public rhetoric that includes the fundamental role of a free conscience in their own faith tradition, as well as their interest in universal rights found in secular norms.

Evangelical mobilization against the construction of mosques, for example, as well as the push for anti-Sharia legislation stands in contrast to the rhetoric demanding religious freedom for Christians in the United States and abroad. Articulating the theological importance of a universal right of conscience, American evangelical religious freedom advocates can help remedy the dissonance between their calls for greater freedom for themselves, and greater restrictions for others. If they do so, they have an opportunity to counter Niebuhr's pessimistic predictions about large group behavior.

Antipathy toward Muslims is not a foregone conclusion. There are some influential evangelical leaders who discourage anti-Muslim bias. Leaders such as Rick Warren and Bob Roberts do not seem to have the ear of the larger evangelical community to the degree of others who have stoked anti-Muslim sentiment, such as Robert Jeffress and Jerry Falwell Jr. Even so, there a precedent for shifting evangelical conflict to common action with those outside their faith.

For example, evangelical suspicion of Roman Catholicism ran high in the 1950s during the birth of the neo-evangelical movement. The formation of the movement itself was tied to a conservative Protestant desire to counter Catholic influence in the public square.[24] Some founding leaders in the evangelical movement, such as James Murch, saw evangelical political mobilization as a way to resist a Catholic "takeover" of the United States, a sentiment in the same genus as the contemporary evangelical fear of a Muslim

---

24. Murch, *Cooperation without Compromise*, 47, 137.

takeover.²⁵ At the same time, evangelist Billy Graham developed relationships with Catholics, as well as mainline Protestants.²⁶ However, it wasn't until the 1990s the evangelical movement's relationship with the Catholic church shifted to one of mutual support and cooperation. The solidification of this relationship was manifested in the document, *Evangelicals and Catholics Together*.²⁷ Though some evangelicals criticized the document as flawed, it delivered evidence of how the movement was able to self-correct in moving from an oppositional stance to one of partnership on public issues where they have a common stake. Meanwhile, even as anti-Muslim sentiment remains at a fever pitch among many evangelicals, some continue to seek productive relationships and plant the seeds of future cooperation.²⁸

An ethically consistent approach to advocating for the freedoms enjoyed by American Christians includes advocacy to extend those freedoms to Muslims, as well as those of other faiths and no faith. To do so demonstrates belief in evangelicals' own rhetoric regarding the universality of religious liberty.

Common Good: *Effective religious freedom initiatives emphasized the role of faith groups serving the common good through participation in civil society.*

One of the strongest practical arguments for religious freedom revolves around the role religious groups play in the domain of civil society. This principle highlights the level of influence independent religious groups may have when they are unencumbered and independent from the state. It also highlights the unique role religious groups play in creating a more just and peaceful pluralistic society when they apply theological resources pertaining to reconciliation, human rights, and restorative justice. As the case studies demonstrate, contributions to the common good from religious groups have proven their value. The wide range of civil society services and societal engagement speak to the potential for free religious groups to contribute to peace and human flourishing in a pluralistic context.

Christian groups have a long track record of participation in initiatives that intersect with human rights, health and welfare, and economic development. The evangelical organization World Vision is one of the world's largest charities with an annual budget in excess of 1 billion dollars.²⁹ The organization's most well-known program is its child sponsorship program.

---

25. Murch, *Cooperation without Compromise*, 140.
26. Mitchell, *God in the Garden*.
27. MacArthur, "Evangelicals and Catholics Together," 7–37.
28. Shellnutt, "Most White Evangelicals"; George, "Muslims, Our Natural Allies."
29. "Rating for World Vision."

It also delivers services in the areas of development, humanitarian relief, and human rights advocacy. Their work is recognized by some developed countries as effective in providing a holistic approach to humanitarian aid and rights development. The Canadian government's International Development Agency endorsed the role of religious NGOs in relief and development based in part on World Vision's track record of effectiveness in areas not addressed by secular NGOs:

> Christian NGOs believe that spirituality, belief systems, values and religion play an important role in the development process. CIDA also recognises that there is a spiritual dimension to the development process and accepts that Christian NGOs and their southern partners often integrate this dimension into their relief and development programming.[30]

According to research by Dan Philpott, religious NGOs possess a unique set of resources when it comes to advocating for the common good. This includes a recurring theme regarding the value of truth recovery when it comes to past government abuses or sectarian conflict, as well as articulating a theology of reconciliation and an emphasis on human rights. Philpott argues the more independent religious groups are from the state, the greater positive influence they have in this domain. He argues their autonomy is particularly effective in transitional justice contexts where societies are emerging from oppression and human rights abuses. This contrasts with government entities or secular organizations that focus instead on retribution, or a top-down political role in preventing future conflict.[31]

There are many examples where the bottom-up approach combined with a faith-based perspective has proved effective in moving an entrenched social conflict to a period of transitional justice, and eventually to peaceful intergroup relationships. For example, from Central America to Northern Ireland, the Mennonite Central Committee has put into practice their theologically based perspective on healing between social groups and reducing inequality. Their programs are designed to consider the religious, social, and economic frameworks of a given area of conflict. They promote new perspectives in the contexts they are working in, which help establish relationships between groups and foster alternatives to violent conflict. The Mennonites' comprehensive approach complemented, for example, United Nations initiatives that focused on senior leaders and legal accountability. Similar examples arose in other contexts. During the Somali Civil War, the Mennonite group worried that the U.N.'s armed humanitarian assistance

30. Tripp, "Gender and Development from a Christian Perspective," 62–68.
31. Philpott, "When Faith Meets History," 190.

that focused on warlords would not provide the lasting peace and improved human rights that peace-oriented initiatives offered.[32] There are many other examples across a host of religious NGOs, including Catholic and Protestant religious organizations. Some concentrate on grassroots reconciliation and human rights development, and others (such as the community of Sant' Egidio) engage actors at all levels of government and society to mediate conflict and build trust between communities.[33]

The cases presented in this project also exemplify the unique role of religious groups as sources of societal norms. This includes values of peace and reconciliation, and a well of ideas regarding the dignity of the human being and the importance of protecting human rights. It has been noted that these ideas, which help create and reinforce functional norms of peace and reconciliation in the societies they engage with, are sometimes at odds with governments that wish for greater control of their citizens, and even secular rights organizations that may have a greater focus on retributive justice.[34]

CEOSS provides a prime example of a group working toward greater religious liberty within the context of promoting the role of civil society in a country wracked by upheavals. Through their deep civil involvement, they advocate for farmers, rural women, people with disabilities, and others, in conjunction with their own call for fewer government restrictions and an easing of social hostilities. CEOSS also increases the presence of civil society organizations in Egypt by sponsoring, training, and launching smaller groups focused on a particular need. Through their efforts, they are deepening the role of civil organizations as both a support for vulnerable groups in the absence of government programs, and creating a mechanism for vulnerable groups to address their own concerns. In doing so, they are helping make religious and nonreligious civil society organizations an integral part of Egypt's public life, along with building the social and political infrastructure to address religious freedom concerns.

IGE emphasizes their top-down, bottom-up approach in showing the value of civil society organizations in the countries where they work. In the case of Vietnam, they have long-standing consultative and educational programs for government officials. These help Vietnamese officials gain a greater understanding of international norms regarding human rights, including religious liberty, with respect to their country's religious minorities. These efforts also reinforce the understanding of Vietnam's own laws and international commitments in this domain. IGE also works at the community level

---

32. Boesenecker and Vinjamuri, "Lost in Translation?," 345–65.
33. Boesenecker and Vinjamuri, "Lost in Translation?," 355.
34. Bartoli, "Forgiveness and Reconciliation in Mozambique," 362–81.

to gain a greater understanding of the social and governmental challenges faced by these communities. In doing so, they build the capacity to foster trust and facilitate real-world solutions that lead to stability.

IGE President Chris Seiple noted that, prior to their involvement, religious organizations had not emphasized direct engagement with the Vietnamese government, which would prove important for any practical improvements for Vietnam's oppressed religious minorities. Seiple emphasized the need to listen to the government's concerns about the country's religious communities. This included fears of violent extremism. The government was also concerned about the need for some religious populations to modernize their agricultural practices and other factors to improve their economic prospects.

IGE engaged in conferences and educational programs designed to build the capacity for the respect of human rights within the Vietnamese government. These efforts were tied to Vietnam's economic and diplomatic interests in resolving the human rights concerns of those in the United States and the international community, particularly as they related to the prospects of a normalized trade status with the U.S. From the bottom-up, IGE listened to and catalogued the accounts of government oppression and social hostilities experienced by Vietnam's Christian communities. They also worked with government and religious groups in the country to allow for the construction of seminaries, and trained them in making their own case for religious freedom and other human rights. Seeking the rights of Catholics, Protestants, and other religious minorities in that country remains difficult.[35] Even so, IGE is keeping channels open, and keeping open future possibilities for greater religious freedom through their ongoing role as an engaged civil society organization. In this way, they display some parallels to CEOSS, which is on a trajectory toward deep and lasting engagement as a trusted civil society organization.

Groups seeking religious freedom have the opportunity to utilize ample evidence that they have much to contribute toward the common good through a civil society role. This includes building peaceful relationships across religious and identity lines and doing what it can to reduce social instability. They also have the ability to address issues across a range of domains in a holistic manner.

Crossing Over: *Effective religious freedom advocacy groups integrated their work with others across religious and social identity lines.*

Evangelicals played a leading role in mobilizing popular support for legislation that became the 1998 International Religious Freedom Act.

---

35. "International Religious Freedom Report 2002: Vietnam."

Though evangelicals were the key popular force, its passage through Congress and signature by the president required cooperation with those beyond their usual political and religious allies. Episcopals, Jews, evangelicals, Catholics, and adherents of other faiths, helped craft a final bill designed to promote religious freedom, and also broaden the language to address the universal concerns connected to conscience rights worldwide.[36]

IGE's religious freedom advocacy in Vietnam also demonstrated the efficacy of working across ideological, political, and religious lines. A political opportunity presented itself as Vietnam was searching for a solution to the trade restrictions connected to their human rights record. Government oppression of religious minorities was among the obstacles standing in the way of normalized trade. IGE worked to develop a relationship with Communist government leaders to find an innovative path that would serve to ease restrictions and oppression experienced by Vietnam's Christian communities, and simultaneously assist in giving Vietnam the visible progress in human rights needed to make normalized trade relations more palatable for the American government. Long after trade was normalized between Vietnam and the West, IGE continued to work in the country to advance religious liberty.

IGE's form of engagement cultivated an ongoing relationship with government leaders and helped yield a greater understanding of the precise concerns of government leaders about the populations they were using oppression to manage. Their high-level relationships sometimes revealed a lack of understanding among government officials of international human rights norms and their value, particularly as pertained to religious freedom and human rights. This led to frequent training sessions to help government and academic leaders better understand the issues, how they are seen with respect by the international community, and how to resolve them.

Though serious issues remain in Vietnam, IGE's presence as a mediator and educator has poised the organization to remain an effective influence and conduit of communication across political and ideological lines. Their commitment to religious freedom in Vietnam has shown how an evangelical organization can learn sophisticated diplomatic language, conflict resolution skills, and policy development techniques that address issues on the international stage. Engaging Vietnam's Communist government and religious groups has also expanded their capacity to find ways to identify underlying issues that may aggravate local circumstances that lead to oppression.

---

36. Hertzke, *Future of Religious Freedom*, 224–27.

This principle is also exemplified by CEOSS. The organization's approach includes bringing religious leaders of all persuasions to the table for practical, problem-solving discussions. At the same time, the rights-based development approach contributes to the moral underpinnings and functional norms behind the rights they are seeking. They demonstrate through their actions faith-informed values regarding human dignity and the need to care for others.

CONCLUSION

A frequent touchstone in the debates among believers over the role of the faith community in secular society are Augustine's observations in the *City of God*. Augustine posited that a temporal city of God (a regime fully aligned with God's standards of love and justice) is never fully achievable on earth. The city of God's relationship with the earthly city is complex. Those whose passions are tied to the earthly city are sometimes within the church itself. Conversely, those who seek the goods of the city of God are sometimes outside the Christian faith. Because of this, it is possible to have a republic of a certain kind that respects justice and has a place for Christians to pursue the common good. Those whose allegiance is to the city of God have a life that exists on two axes: they have a vertical relationship devoted to God, and a horizontal relationship that compels them to love their neighbor. In this framework, loving one's neighbor means seeking their welfare, which includes a free pursuit of spiritual matters. It also means working with them to devise practical solutions to common problems, as well as increase societal goods identified as desirable and beneficial.[37]

In Augustine's time, Christianity was on its way to political establishment. We are living in much different times than those of Augustine, Luther, and Niebuhr. As seen in this discussion, Hauerwas presents strong arguments against continuing the assumption that Christians may still engage the public square with moral integrity, even in the face of disestablishment.

A contemporary perspective takes into account the lack of moral consensus and a church in conversation with others in a pluralistic environment. The principles here present an alternative to the rights-grievance approach that institutionalizes Augustine's chief complaint of human self-centeredness at the core of the earthly city. Alasdair MacIntyre warns against the propensity among today's citizens to view themselves as merely autonomous moral agents seeking to exert their will upon the world. He argues this outlook trades genuine interdependence for a system where one

37. Augustinus and Dyson, *City of God*, 50.

seeks to manipulate others for their own benefit, while fighting off manipulation by others.[38]

Religious freedom advocacy is sometimes seen by those outside the American evangelical movement as a means of manipulation by the Christian Right to exercise political dominion over other segments of society.[39] Countering this assumption is the argument religious freedom frees religious groups to promote the common good, and do so in accordance with the contemporary norms of human rights. This includes expanding the secular/pluralistic imagination about what is possible when it comes to interactions between otherwise competing groups. Evidence from this study shows that by working across ideological lines, resisting the temptation to restrict the freedoms of outside groups, and solving problems via civil initiatives, religious groups may seize the opportunity to demonstrate an alternative to the cultural warfare that dominates today's political climate.

Niebuhr observed large-group mobilization within the Christian community tends to take the church away from its moral roots and into a power struggle with others. In light of this, he sought a path forward that would "do justice to the moral resources and possibilities in human nature ..." and take account of the limitations of human nature, particularly those which manifest themselves in humanity's collective behavior.[40] In light of this, there are instances observed in this project where Christian leaders have resisted the political temptations Niebuhr warned against in favor of reconciliation and intergroup cooperation.

Niebuhr's prescient skepticism condemned mass political campaigns that promote continual conflict and a will to power against competing groups in a common space. His hypothesis as it relates to seeking the principal justice of religious freedom could be described as follows: Seeking religious freedom for one's religious community without a concern for all members of a pluralistic society defeats the overall project, and ultimately defeats the quest by the group to look after its own religious self-interest. As a result, society is threatened with perennial conflict and a spiral of injustice. Seeking political self-preservation at the expense of others leads to further sectarian differences and even long-term marginalization.

The examples of CEOSS, IGE, and the evangelical effort to craft the 1998 International Religious Freedom Act demonstrate the ability for Christians to work with and seek the common good of all. In each case, those in leadership played a critical role in how the groups defined their

---

38. MacIntyre, *After Virtue*, 68.
39. Castro, "Chairman Martin R. Castro Statement."
40. Niebuhr, *Moral Man and Immoral Society*, xxiv.

approach to a given situation, and outlined a path forward that was both commensurable with the beliefs and understandings of their constituents, and did not seek to trample the rights of others in the pursuit of their own cause. The implication is that a siege mentality among the players in pluralist society leads to harm for all, whereas constructively strengthening the central concepts of universal freedom and dignity can lead to a pluralism that thickens the consensus about what makes society civil.

Christian groups hoping to secure their place in a pluralistic society are in a tough position when it comes to political mobilization. If religious freedom and conscience rights are used as special permission to oppress another group, or merely consist of the state granting special status for religious groups, then the broad assent needed for its long-term survival is endangered. If Christian ideas in the marketplace lose traction through partisanship and political polarization, then what Christians can claim to offer society is dramatically diminished, and religious freedom is imperiled. Yet, if religious groups frame their messages and calls for action according to the principles of Dynamic Engagement drawn from the deep history of religious freedom and conscience rights as well as from current examples, they may help create a larger social framework for constructive engagement in a pluralistic public square.

Bibliography

"20 Years of Vietnam-US Relations: Unforgettable Milestones." 2015. *Vietnam Pictorial*. http://vietnam.vnanet.vn/english/20-years-of-vietnam-us-relations-unforgettable-milestones/192947.html.

Abdel-Tawab, Nahla, and Hegazi Sahar. "Critical Analysis of Interventions against FGC in Egypt." 2000. http://citeseerx.ist.psu.edu/viewdoc/download?doi=10.1.1.175.7826&rep=rep1&type=pdf.

"About IGE." 2017. *Institute For Global Engagement (IGE)*. https://globalengage.org/about.

"ACLJ Films: The Export - Shariah Law Segment." 2011. http://old.aclj.org/Tags/ACLJ?page=30.

Agrama, Hussein Ali. 2012. *Questioning Secularism Islam, Sovereignty, and the Rule of Law in Modern Egypt*. Chicago: University of Chicago Press.

Agreement between the United States of America and the Socialist Republic of Vietnam on Trade Relations. 2000. Washington, DC: Office of the U.S. Trade Representative. https://ustr.gov/sites/default/files/US-VietNam-BilateralTradeAgreement.pdf.

Albanese, Catherine L. 2012. *America, Religions, and Religion*. 5th ed. New York: Wadsworth.

Ali, Yaser. 2012. "Shariah and Citizenship - How Islamophobia is Creating a Second-Class Citizenry in America." *California Law Review* 100 (4): 1027–68. http://scholarship.law.berkeley.edu/californialawreview/vol100/iss4/4.

Alimi, Eitan Y., et al. 2016. *Popular Contention, Regime, and Transition*. New York: Oxford University Press.

Alpert, William T. 2005. *The Vietnamese Economy and its Transformation to an Open Market System*. Armonk, NY: M. E. Sharpe.

al-Salam, Muhammad 'Abd. 2005. "Muslim-Christian Forum in Alexandria: Terrorism Has Nothing to Do with Religions." *Arab West Report*. https://www.arabwestreport.info/en/year-2005/week-40/51-muslim-christian-forum-alexandria-terrorism-has-nothing-do-religions.

Amadeo, Kimberly. 2016. "Three Reasons Why WTO Membership is so Important." *The Balance*. https://www.thebalance.com/wto-membership-benefits-and-importance-3306364.

"American Conservative Union Board Resolution on Frank Gaffney." 2011. *Scribd*. http://www.scribd.com/doc/81353256/American-Conservative-Union-Board-Resolution-On-Frank-Gaffney.

American Public Policy Alliance. 2010. "Representative Civil Legal Cases Involving Shariah Law." http://publicpolicyalliance.org/wp-content/uploads/2010/11/Shariah_Cases_11states_11-08-2010.pdf.

"America's Changing Religious Landscape." 2015. *Pew Research Center*. http://www.pewforum.org/2015/05/12/americas-changing-religious-landscape/.

Anderson, Hannah. 2017. "The Benedict Option Isn't an Evangelical Option." *Christianity Today*. https://www.christianitytoday.com/ct/2017/february-web-only/benedict-option-isnt-evangelical-option.html.

"Annual Report 2013." 2013. CEOSS. https://en.ceoss-eg.org/annual-report-2013/.

Annual Report on International Religious Freedom. 2004. Washington, DC: Department of State. https://www.gpo.gov/fdsys/pkg/CPRT-108JPRT20429/pdf/CPRT-108JPRT20429.pdf.

Anti-Defamation League. 2012. "Anti-Muslim and Anti-Immigrant Speakers to Appear at Religious Right Conference in Dallas." http://blog.adl.org/civil-rights/anti-muslim-and-anti-immigrant-speakers-to-appear-at-religious-right-conference-in-dallas.

"Assemblies of God Receive Permit Covering 40 Provinces." 2009. *Vietnamnews*. http://vietnamnews.vn/society/religion/193105/assemblies-of-god-receive-permit-covering-40-provinces.html.

Assmann, Jan. 2010. *The Price Of Monotheism*. Stanford: Stanford Universtiy Press.

Augustinus, Aurelius, and R. W. Dyson. 2007. *The City of God against the Pagans*. Cambridge: Cambridge University.

"The Avalon Project: The Federalist Papers No. 10." 1787. https://avalon.law.yale.edu/18th_century/fed10.asp.

Awad, Abed. 2012. "The True Story of Sharia in American Courts." *The Nation*. http://www.thenation.com/article/true-story-sharia-american-courts/.

Ayalon, Ami. 2000. "Egypt's Coptic Pandora's Box." In *Minorities and the State in the Arab World*, 53–72. Boulder, CO: Lynne Rienner.

Baehr, Peter. 2001. "The 'Iron Cage' and the 'Shell as Hard as Steel': Parsons, Weber, and the Stahlhartes Gehause Metaphor in the Protestant Ethic and the Spirit of Capitalism." *History and Theory* 40 (2): 153–69.

Barnes, Timothy David. 2011. *Tertullian*. Oxford: Clarendon.

Barth, Karl. 2004. *Community, State, and Church*. Eugene, OR: Wipf and Stock.

———. 1981. *Ethics*. New York: Seabury.

———. 1960. *The Humanity of God*. Louisville: John Knox.

Bartoli, Andrea. 2001. "Forgiveness and Reconciliation in Mozambique." In *Forgiveness and Reconciliation: Religion, Public Policy & Conflict Transformation*, 362–81. Philadelphia: Templeton Foundation.

Bayle, Pierre. 1708. *A Philosophical Commentary on These Words of the Gospel, Luke XIV. 23. Compel Them to Come in, that My House May Be Full. In Four Parts. . . . Translated from the French of Mr. Bayle*. London: J. Darby.

———. 1999. *Bayle: Political Writings*. Cambridge: Cambridge University Press.

Bebbington, David W. 1988. *Evangelicalism in Modern Britain: A History from the 1730s to the 1980s*. New York: Routledge.

Bellah, Robert N. 1988. *Habits of the Heart*. London: Hutchinson.

Benedict XVI. 2010. "44th World Day of Peace 2011, Religious Freedom, the Path to Peace." *Libreria Editrice Vaticana.* http://w2.vatican.va/content/benedict-xvi/en/messages/peace/documents/hf_ben-xvi_mes_20101208_xliv-world-day-peace.html.

Benford, Robert D. 1997. "An Insider's Critique of the Social Movement Framing Perspective." *Sociological Inquiry* 67 (4): 409–30. doi:10.1111/j.1475-682x.1997.tb00445.x.

Benford, Robert D., and David A. Snow. 2000. "Framing Processes and Social Movements: An Overview and Assessment." *Annual Review of Sociology* 26 (1): 611–39. doi:10.1146/annurev.soc.26.1.611.

Berger, Maurits. 2001. "Public Policy and Islamic Law: The Modern Dhimmī in Contemporary Egyptian Family Law." *Islamic Law and Society* 8 (1): 88–136. doi:10.1163/156851901753129683.

Berger, Peter. 2008. "Secularization Falsified." *First Things.* https://www.firstthings.com/article/2008/02/secularization-falsified.

Berlin, Isaiah. 2015. *The Crooked Timber of Humanity*. Princeton: Princeton University Press.

Bernstein, Richard J. 2017. "Nietzsche or Aristotle? Reflections on Alasdair MacIntyre's After Virtue." Soundings: An Interdisciplinary Journal 100 (4): 293–317. doi:10.5325/soundings.100.4.0293.

Bo, Charles Muang. 2015. "Toward a Future of Justice, Peace, and Development in Myanmar: A Christian Perspective." *The Review Of Faith & International Affairs* 13 (4): 91–94. doi:10.1080/15570274.2015.1104956.

Boesenecker, Aaron P., and Leslie Vinjamuri. 2011. "Lost in Translation?: Civil Society, Faith-Based Organizations and the Negotiation of International Norms." *International Journal of Transitional Justice* 5 (3): 345–65. doi:10.1093/ijtj/ijro18.

Bouquet, Mathieu. 2010. "Vietnamese Party-State and Religious Pluralism Since 1986: Building the Fatherland?" *Journal of Social Issues in Southeast Asia* 25 (1): 90–108. doi:10.1355/sj25-1d.

Brown, P. R. L. 1964. "St. Augustine's Attitude to Religious Coercion." *Journal of Roman Studies* 54 (1–2): 107–16. doi:10.2307/298656.

Brown, Peter. 2014. "Costan Lecture 2014 - Peter Brown." https://www.youtube.com/watch?v=6Hu0Ttv7Khc.

———. 2007. *Religion and Society in the Age of St. Augustine*. Eugene, OR: Wipf & Stock.

"Bush, Vietnam President Hold Historic Meeting." 2007. *NPR.* http://www.npr.org/templates/story/story.php?storyId=11278174.

Callahan, Timothy R. 2004. "Vietnam's 'Appalling' Persecution: Activists Want Washington to Confront Communist Leaders for Torturing and Killing Christians." *Christianity Today.* http://www.christianitytoday.com/ct/2004/january/14.30.html.

Carvalho, Nirmala. 2020. "Cardinal Complains of 'Criminal Silence' of Myanmar's Religious Leaders." *Crux.* https://cruxnow.com/church-in-asia/2019/10/cardinal-complains-of-criminal-silence-of-myanmars-religious-leaders/.

Castellio, Sebastian. 1979. *Concerning Heretics*. New York: Octagon.

Castro, Martin R. 2016. "Chairman Martin R. Castro Statement." In *Peaceful Coexistence: Reconciling Nondiscrimination Principles with Civil Liberties*, 29. Washington, DC: U.S. Commission on Civil Rights. http://www.usccr.gov/pubs/Peaceful-Coexistence-09-07-16.PDF.

Center for Development and Population Activities. 1997. "Community Ownership Spurs Girls' Education in Egypt." https://www.ncbi.nlm.nih.gov/pubmed/12320663.

CEOSS Annual Report: 2011. 2011. Cairo: Coptic Evangelical Organization for Social Services. http://en.ceoss-eg.org/annual-report-2011-3/.

Chandler, Russell. 1986. "New World Vision President Named: Robert A. Seiple, 44, Will Replace Ted W. Engstrom, 70." *Los Angeles Times*. http://articles.latimes.com/1986-12-13/local/me-2685_1_new-president.

Chaput, Charles. 2016. "Awakenings: Living as a Believer in the World We Have Now." *First Things*. https://www.firstthings.com/web-exclusives/2016/03/awakenings.

Childs, Brevard S. 2011. *Biblical Theology of the Old and New Testaments*. Minneapolis: Fortress.

"Chris Seiple, President Emeritus." 2018. *Institute for Global Engagement (IGE)*. https://globalengage.org/about/people/dr-chris-seiple1.

"Christian Tract Distribution in Vietnam Brings Arrests." 2003. *Worthy News*. https://www.worthynews.com/379-christian-tract-distribution-in-vietnam-brings-arrests.

Constitution of the Arab Republic of Egypt 2014. 2014. Cairo: Arab Republic of Egypt. http://www.sis.gov.eg/Newvr/Dustor-en001.pdf.

The Constitution of the Arab Republic of Egypt, 1971 (As Amended to 2007). 2007. http://www.constitutionnet.org/sites/default/files/Egypt%20Constitution.pdf.

"The Constitution or Sharia: A Freedom Conference." 2011. https://web.archive.org/web/20150419223444/http://shariafreeusa.com/the-constitution-or-sharia-a-freedom-conference/.

Coxe, A. Cleveland, et al. 1903. *The Ante-Nicene Fathers, Volume III: Latin Christianity: Its Founder, Tertullian*. 10 vols. New York: Scribner's Sons.

Dabla-Norris, Era, et al. 2015. "Causes and Consequences of Income Inequality: A Global Perspective." *IMF Staff Discussion Notes* 15 (13): 3–39. 1. doi:10.5089/9781513555188.006.

Dayton, Donald W., and Robert K. Johnston, eds. 1997. *The Variety of American Evangelicalism*. Eugene, OR: Wipf & Stock.

"Deadly Blast at Egyptian Church." 2010. *BBC News*. http://web.archive.org/web/20110101045135/http://www.bbc.co.uk/news/world-middle-east-12101748.

De Dreu, Carsten K. W., et al. 2011. "Group Creativity and Innovation: A Motivated Information Processing Perspective." *Psychology of Aesthetics, Creativity, and the Arts* 5 (1): 81–89. doi:10.1037/a0017986.

DeGirolami, Marc O. 2017. "Religious Accommodation, Religious Tradition, and Political Polarization." *Lewis & Clark Law Review* 20 (4): 1127–56.

Delhaye, Gregoire. 2012. "Contemporary Muslim-Christian Relations in Egypt: Local Dynamics and Foreign Influences." In *Religious Minorities in the Middle East: Domination, Self-Empowerment, Accommodation*, edited by Anne Sofie Roald and Anh Nga Longva, 71–96. New York: Brill.

de Spinoza, Benedict. 1720. *An Account of the Life and Writings of Spinoza. To Which is Added, an Abstract of His Theological Political Treatise*. London: Boreham.

Diamond, Larry Jay, et al. 2005. *World Religions and Democracy*. Baltimore: The Johns Hopkins University Press.

"Dignitatis Humanae." 2020. *Vatican.Va*. http://www.vatican.va/archive/hist_councils/ii_vatican_council/documents/vat-ii_decl_19651207_dignitatis-humanae_en.html.

Domingo, Eduardo. 2009. "Intertextuality and the Sociology of Religion: Amazing Sociological Contexts as Text." *Philippine Sociological Review* 57: 79–103. http://www.jstor.org/stable/23898345.

Donaldson, James, and Alexander Roberts. 1872. *Ante-Nicene Christian Library: Translation of the Writings of the Fathers Down to A.D. 325*. 25 vols. Edinburgh: T. & T. Clark.

Dreher, Rod. 2017. *The Benedict Option*. New York: Sentinel.

Dreisbach, Daniel L. 2003. *Thomas Jefferson and the Wall of Separation between Church and State*. New York: New York University Press.

Dutton, George Edson. 2006. *Tây Son Uprising: Society and Rebellion in Eighteenth-Century Vietnam*. Honolulu: University Press of Hawaii.

Edwards, Bob, and David Snow. 2007. "Resources and Social Movement Organization." In *The Blackwell Companion to Social Movements*, edited by David Snow et al., 116–52. Kindle. Malden, MA: Blackwell.

"Egypt Eases Restrictions on Repairing Churches: Mubarak Reforms 19th-Century Law." 2006. *The Christian Century*. https://www.christiancentury.org/article/2006-01/egypt-eases-restrictions-repairing-churches.

El-Fekki, Amira. 2015. "3 Copts Face Charges for Giving Muslims Dates to Break Fast - Daily News Egypt." *Daily News Egypt*. http://www.dailynewsegypt.com/2015/07/14/3-copts-face-charges-for-giving-muslims-dates-to-break-fast/.

"The End of White Christian America." 2017. *Public Religion Research Institute*. https://www.prri.org/end-white-christian-america.

Esposito, John. 2012. "'Bachmann Affair' on Clinton Aide Abedin is a Wake-Up Call." *Onfaith*. https://web.archive.org/web/20180504064754/https://www.onfaith.co/onfaith/2012/07/26/bachmann-affair-against-clinton-aide-huma-abedin-is-a-wake-up-call/10649.

"Evangelicals & Catholics Together: The Christian Mission in the Third Millennium." 1994. *First Things*. https://www.firstthings.com/article/1994/05/evangelicals-catholics-together-the-christian-mission-in-the-third-millennium.

Farr, Thomas F. 2001. "Designation of Countries of Particular Concern Under the International Religious Freedom Act." *Federal Register*. https://www.federalregister.gov/documents/2001/05/01/01-10833/designation-of-countries-of-particular-concern-under-the-international-religious-freedom-act.

———. 2009. *World of Faith and Freedom: Why International Religious Liberty is Vital to American National Security*. New York: Oxford University Press.

Federico, Christopher M., et al. 2012. "Ideological Asymmetry in the Relationship Between Epistemic Motivation and Political Attitudes." *Journal of Personality and Social Psychology* 103 (3): 381–98. doi:10.1037/a0029063.

Fioina, Morris P. 2016. *The Temptation to Overreach*. Stanford, CA: Hoover Institution. https://www.hoover.org/sites/default/files/research/docs/fiorina_temptationtooverreach.pdf.

Form 990: Institute for Global Engagement. 2003. Arlington, VA: Internal Revenue Service. https://projects.propublica.org/nonprofits/display_990/233042456/2015_10_EO%2F23-3042456_990_201412.

Form 990: Institute for Global Engagement, Internal Revenue Service (2014). 2014. Arlington, VA: Internal Revenue Service. http://990s.foundationcenter.org/990_pdf_archive/233/233042456/233042456_201412_990.pdf.

"Form 990: Samaritan's Purse." 2018. https://projects.propublica.org/nonprofits/display_990/581437002/09_2019_prefixes_54-59%2F581437002_201812_990_2019092716698487.

Forster, Greg. 2011. *John Locke's Politics of Moral Consensus*. Cambridge: Cambridge University Press.

Fox, Richard Wightman. 1996. *Reinhold Niebuhr: A Biography*. Ithaca, NY: Cornell University Press.

"From the President: Strategy, Evangelism, and Freedom." 2005. *Institute for Global Engagement (IGE)*. https://globalengage.org/news-media/from-the-president/from-the-president-strategy-evangelism-and-freedom.

Gaffney, Frank. 2018. "Frank Gaffney in the Washington Times: American Mosques, Jihad's Incubators." *Mappingsharia.Com*. http://mappingsharia.com/?p=412.

Galli, Mark. 2007. "Chris Seiple on Relational Diplomacy." *Christianity Today*. http://www.christianitytoday.com/ct/2007/may/25.30.html.

———. "A New Day In Vietnam." 2007. *Christianity Today*. https://www.christianitytoday.com/ct/2007/may/24.26.html.

Gamson, William A. 1990. *The Strategy of Social Protest*. Belmont, CA: Wadsworth.

Garrity v. New Jersey, 385 U.S. 493 (1967).

Gaubatz, David P., and Paul Sperry. 2009. *Muslim Mafia: Inside the Secret Underworld that's Conspiring to Islamize America*. Los Angeles: WND.

George, Robert. 2014. "Muslims, Our Natural Allies." *First Thoughts (blog)*. http://www.firstthings.com/blogs/firstthoughts/2014/02/muslims-our-natural-allies.

Gershoni, Israel, and James P. Jankowski. 2011. *Egypt, Islam, and the Arabs*. New York: Oxford University Press.

Gilman, Sarah E. 2004. "Peddling the Promise Along the Nile: The Ambivalent Mission of American Evangelicals in Egypt, 1854–1954." Presentation, American Sociological Association Annual Meeting, San Francisco, August 16, 2004.

Glendon, Mary Ann. 2002. *A World Made New*. New York: Random House.

Goertzen, Peggy. 2014. "Inola Mennonite Brethren Church." *Global Anabaptist Mennonite Encyclopedia Online*. https://gameo.org/index.php?title=Inola_Mennonite_Brethren_Church_(Inola,_Oklahoma,_USA).

Gracey, Celeste, and Jeremy Weber. 2014. "World Vision: Why We're Hiring Gay Christians in Same-Sex Marriages." *Christianity Today*. http://www.christianitytoday.com/ct/2014/march-web-only/world-vision-why-hiring-gay-christians-same-sex-marriage.html.

———. 2014. "World Vision Reverses Decision to Hire Christians in Same-Sex Marriages." *Christianity Today*. http://www.christianitytoday.com/ct/2014/march-web-only/world-vision-reverses-decision-gay-same-sex-marriage.html.

Graham, Franklin. 2015. "Four Innocent Marines." *Facebook*. https://www.facebook.com/FranklinGraham/posts/967305353325646.

Greenslade, S. L., ed. 1956. *Early Latin Theology: Selections From Tertullian, Cyprian, Ambrose and Jerome*. Philadelphia: Library of Christian Classics.

Grim, Brian J., and Roger Finke. 2011. *The Price of Freedom Denied*. New York: Cambridge University Press.

Hadi, Amal Abdel. 2006. "A Community of Women Empowered: The Story of Deir El Basha." In *Female Circumcision: Multicultural Perspectives*, edited by Rogaia Mustafa Abusharaf, 104–24. Philadelphia: University Press of Pennsylvania.

Hanford, John. 2018. "Has IRFA Succeeded? Lessons from the First 20 Years." Speech given at the Religious Freedom Institute, Washington, DC, November 9, 2018.

Hannigan, John A. 1991. "Social Movement Theory and the Sociology of Religion: Toward a New Synthesis." *Sociological Analysis* 52 (4): 311–31. doi:10.2307/3710849.

"Hanoi Officially Recognises Baptists and Mennonites." 2007. *Asianews*. http://www.asianews.it/index.php?l=en&art=10466.

Harnack, Carl Gustav Adolf von, and Thomas Bailey Saunders. 1901. *What is Christianity? Sixteen Lectures . . . Translated Into English By T. B. Saunders.* New York: Putnam & Sons.

Harries, Richard, and Stephen Platten. 2010. *Reinhold Niebuhr and Contemporary Politics*. Oxford: Oxford University Press.

Hatina, Meir. 2006. "In Search of Authenticity: A Coptic Perception." *Middle Eastern Studies* 42 (1): 49–65. doi:10.1080/00263200500399553.

Hauerwas, Stanley. 2014. *Approaching the End: Eschatological Reflection on Church, Politics and Life*. Grand Rapids: Eerdmans.

———. 2010. *A Community of Character*. Notre Dame: University of Notre Dame Press.

———. 2002. "September 11, 2001: A Pacifist Response." *South Atlantic Quarterly* 101 (2): 425–33.

———. 2001. *With the Grain of the Universe: The Church's Witness and Natural Theology: Being the Gifford Lecture*. Grand Rapids: Brazos.

"HB 2582: An Act Amending Title 12, Chapter 1, Arizona Revised Statutes, By Adding Article 5; Relating to Judicial Determinations." 2011. *Arizona State Legislature*. http://www.azleg.gov//FormatDocument.asp?inDoc=/legtext/50leg/1r/bills/hb2582p.htm&Session_ID=102.

Hertzke, Allen D. 2006. *Freeing God's Children: The Unlikely Alliance for Global Human Rights*. Lanham, MD: Rowman & Littlefield.

———. 2013. *The Future of Religious Freedom: Global Challenges*. Oxford: Oxford University Press.

"HFH Egypt Celebrates Completion of 6,000 Houses." 2005. *Habitat for Humanity - Egypt*. http://habitategypt.org/stories/egypt_6000_houses.aspx.

Hieatt, Kathy. 2018. "Bills to Ban Use of Foreign Laws Rile Groups." *Virginian-Pilot*. https://www.pilotonline.com/government/virginia/article_a9a77f3f-14cf-59d2-8576-4a486fa803d8.html.

Hobbes, Thomas. 1969. *Behemoth*. New York: Franklin.

———. 1651. *Leviathan*. [London]: Andrew Crooke at the Green Dragon in St. Pauls Church-yard.

Hooker, Richard. 1907. *Of the Laws of Ecclesiastical Polity*. London: Dent.

Horowitz, Michael. 1995. "New Intolerance between Crescent and Cross." *Wall Street Journal*, July 5, 1995, A8.

"Horus Hospital مستشفى روح." https://www.youtube.com/watch?v=1jkC6td1ryE.

"H.R.1587 - 108th Congress (2003–2004): Vietnam Human Rights Act of 2004." 2004. *Library of Congress*. https://www.congress.gov/bill/108th-congress/house-bill/1587.

"H.R.5602 - 114th Congress (2015–2016): To Amend Title 31, United States Code, to Authorize the Secretary of the Treasury to Include All Funds When Issuing Certain Geographic Targeting Orders, and for Other Purposes." 2018. *Library of Congress*. https://www.congress.gov/bill/114th-congress/house-bill/5602.

Human Rights Watch. 2002. "Nigeria: First Execution Under Sharia Condemned." http://www.hrw.org/news/2002/01/08/nigeria-first-execution-under-Sharia-condemned.

Hung, Do Quang. "The Importance of Partnership (Part 1)." 2016. https://www.youtube.com/watch?v=3YO5lJa-FTg.

Hussein, Aziza. 2018. "NGOs and Development Challenges of the 21st Century." In *Egypt in the Twenty First Century: Challenges for Development*, edited by M. Riad El-Ghonemy, 199–217. New York: Routledge.

Ibrahim, Raymond. 2015. "'Incensed' Muslims Surround Christian Home Accused of Being Turned into Church." *Coptic Solidarity*. https://www.copticsolidarity.org/2015/07/02/incensed-muslims-surround-christian-home-accused-of-being-turned-into-church/.

"IGE Co-Convenes 'Peace, Security & Co-Existence' Conference in Myanmar." 2013. *Institute for Global Engagement (IGE)*. https://globalengage.org/news-media/press-release/ige-co-convenes-peace-security-co-existence-conference-in-myanmar.

"IGE Extends Partnership on Religious Freedom Projects in Vietnam." 2006. *Institute for Global Engagement (IGE)*. https://globalengage.org/news-media/press-release/vietnamese-delegation-visits-u.s.-to-build-friendships-engage-religious-fre.

"IGE's Work: Highlights." 2013. *Institute for Global Engagement (IGE)*. https://globalengage.org/news-media/video/iges-work-highlights.

'Ila, Abu 'Ila Madi Abu, et al. 1996. "We are a Civil Party with an Islamic Identity: An Interview with Abu 'Ila Madi Abu 'Ila and Rafiq Habib." *Middle East Report* 199: 30. doi:10.2307/3012891.

Imai, Lynn, and Michele J. Gelfand. 2010. "The Culturally Intelligent Negotiator: The Impact of Cultural Intelligence (CQ) on Negotiation Sequences and Outcomes." *Organizational Behavior and Human Decision Processes* 112 (2): 83–98. doi:10.1016/j.obhdp.2010.02.001.

"Institute for Global Engagement: Brandywine Forum." *Spirit: The Eastern University Magazine* (Fall 2003) 13.

International Religious Freedom Act. 1998. Vol. 112. Washington, DC: U.S. Statutes at Large 112: 2787.

"International Religious Freedom Report 2002: Vietnam." 2002. *U.S. Department of State*. https://www.state.gov/j/drl/rls/irf/2002/13916.htm.

Jeavons, Thomas H. 1994. "Stewardship Revisited: Secular and Sacred Views of Governance and Management." *Nonprofit and Voluntary Sector Quarterly* 23 (2): 107–22. doi:10.1177/089976409402300203.

Jefferson, Thomas. 1785. "Act for Establishing Religious Freedom." https://founders.archives.gov/documents/Madison/01-08-02-0206.

———. 1776. "Declaration of Independence: A Transcription." ://www.archives.gov/founding-docs/declaration-transcript.

———. 1802. "Jefferson's Letter to the Danbury Baptists." Library Of Congress. https://www.loc.gov/loc/lcib/9806/danpre.html.

———. 1781. "Notes on the State of Virginia." https://docsouth.unc.edu/southlit/jefferson/jefferson.html.

Jefferson, Thomas, and Henry A. Washington. 1853. *The Writings of Thomas Jefferson*. Washington DC: Taylor & Maury.

Jenkins, Brian. 2017. *The Origins of America's Jihadists*. Santa Monica, CA: RAND.

Jenkins, Philip. 2011. *The Next Christendom: The Coming of Global Christianity.* 3rd ed. New York: Oxford University Press.
Jenson, Robert. 2018. "Hauerwas Examined." *First Things.* https://www.firstthings.com/article/1992/08/004-hauerwas-examined.
"Jerry Boykin: Islam Deserves No First Amendment Protections." 2010. https://youtu.be/qaNjU9TmQ_A.
Johnson, Todd M., and Cindy M. Wu. 2015. *Our Global Families.* Grand Rapids: Baker Academic.
Johnson, Toni, and Mohammed Aly Sergie. 2014. "Islam: Governing under Sharia." *Council on Foreign Relations.* http://www.cfr.org/religion/islam-governing-under-Sharia/p8034.
Jones, Robert P. 2017. *The End of White Christian America.* New York: Simon & Schuster.
Jones, Robert P., and Daniel Cox. 2017. *America's Changing Religious Identity.* Washington, DC: Public Religion Research Institute.
Jones, Sidney, et al. 2018. *Repression of Montagnards: Conflicts over Land and Religion in Vietnam's Central Highlands.* Reprint, 2002. New York: Human Rights Watch.
Juhnke, James. 1977. "Mob Violence and Kansas Mennonites in 1918." *Kansas History* 43 (3): 344–50. https://www.kshs.org/p/mob-violence-and-kansas-mennonites-in-1918/13278.
Juzwik, Mary M. 2014. "American Evangelical Biblicism as Literate Practice: A Critical Review." *Reading Research Quarterly* 49 (3): 335–49. doi:10.1002/rrq.72.
Kang, Dake. 2020. "Leaked Data Shows China's Uighurs Detained Due to Religion." *Associated Press News.* https://apnews.com/890b79866c9eb1451ddf67b121272ee2.
Kant, Immanuel. 1917. *Idee Zu Einer Allgemeinen Geschichte In Weltbürgerlicher Absicht.* Leipzig: Meiner.
Kant, Immanuel, and Theodore M Greene. 2011. *Religion within the Limits of Reason Alone.* Stilwell, KS: Neeland Media LLC.
Katkin, Wendy F., et al. 1998. *Beyond Pluralism.* Urbana: University of Illinois Press.
Keith, Charles Patrick. 2008. *Catholic Vietnam: A Church from Empire to Nation.* Berkeley: University of California Press.
Kennedy, Bud. 2011. "There's No Room for Hate at Christian-Muslim Get-Together." *Fort Worth Star-Telegram.* http://www.star-telegram.com/living/family/moms/article3828982.html.
Kessler, Sanford. 2002. "Religious Freedom in Thomas More's Utopia." *The Review of Politics* 64 (2): 207–30. doi:10.1017/s0034670500038079.
Khalifa, Sherif. 2015. *Egypt's Lost Spring: Causes and Consequences.* New York: Praeger.
Khalīl, Emād. 2011. "Pope Shenouda Leaves Hospital After Medical Checkups." *Arab West Report.* https://www.arabwestreport.info/en/year-2011/week-15/2-pope-shenouda-leaves-hospital-after-medical-checkups.
Khan, Ali. 2003. "The Reopening of the Islamic Code: The Second Era of Ijtihad." *University of St. Thomas Law Journal* 1 (2003) 341–85.
Kierkegaard, Søren, and David F. Swenson. 2007. *Philosophical Fragments, Or, a Fragment of Philosophy.* Vancouver: Emerald Knight.
Kierkegaard, Søren, and Robert W. Bretall. 1946. *A Kierkegaard Anthology.* New York: Modern Library.
Kingsley, Patrick. 2018. "Egyptian Activists Hope for 'Second Revolution' a Year After Morsi's Election." *The Guardian.* http://www.theguardian.com/world/2013/jun/27/egyptian-activists-hope-revolution-morsi.

Kirchgaessner, Stephanie. 2018. "Vatican: Pope's Only 'Audience' Was with Gay Former Student – Not Kim Davis." *The Guardian*. http://www.theguardian.com/world/2015/oct/02/pope-francis-kim-davis-audience-gay-student.
Kirkpatrick, David. 2012. "Coptic Church Chooses Pope Who Rejects Politics." *New York Times*. http://www.nytimes.com/2012/11/05/world/middleeast/coptic-church-chooses-pope-who-rejects-politics.html.
Kirkpatrick, David D., and Heba Afify. 2011. "A Top Egyptian Minister Quits in Protest over Killings." *New York Times*. http://www.nytimes.com/2011/10/12/world/middleeast/egypts-finance-minister-resigns.html.
Kniss, Fred, and David Todd Campbell. 1997. "The Effect of Religious Orientation on International Relief and Development Organizations." *Journal for the Scientific Study of Religion* 36 (1): 100–1. doi:10.2307/1387885.
Kuruvilla, Shyama, et al. 2012. "The Millennium Development Goals and Human Rights: Realizing Shared Commitments." *Human Rights Quarterly* 34 (1): 141–77. doi:10.1353/hrq.2012.0010.
Lahusen, Christian. 1996. *The Rhetoric of Moral Protest: Public Campaigns, Celebrity Endorsement, and Political Mobilization*. Berlin: de Gruyter.
Land, Richard. 2018. "A Mosque Near Ground Zero is Unacceptable." *On Faith*. http://www.faithstreet.com/onfaith/2010/07/22/a-mosque-at-ground-zero-is-inappropriate-and-counterproductive/7432.
Larimer, Sarah. 2015. "Pope Francis: Government Workers Have 'Human Right' to Deny Gay Marriage Licenses." *Washington Post*. https://www.washingtonpost.com/news/acts-of-faith/wp/2015/09/28/pope-francis-conscientious-objection-is-a-human-right-even-for-government-workers/.
"The Lausanne Covenant." 1974. *Lausanne Movement*. https://www.lausanne.org/content/covenant/lausanne-covenant.
Leirvik, Oddbjørn. 2010. *Human Conscience and Muslim-Christian Relations: Modern Egyptian Thinkers on Al-Damir*. New York: Routledge.
Lenski, Gerhard. 1977. *The Religious Factor: A Sociological Study of Religion's Impact on Politics, Economics and Family Life*. Westport, CT: Greenwood.
LEO XIII. 1891. "Rerum Novarum." *Vatican.Va*. http://www.vatican.va/content/leo-xiii/en/encyclicals/documents/hf_l-xiii_enc_15051891_rerum-novarum.html.
Liên, Trần Thi. 2005. "The Catholic Question in North Vietnam: from Polish Sources, 1954–56." *Cold War History* 5 (4): 427–49. doi:10.1080/14682740500284747.
Lightfoot, Joseph Barber. 1889. *The Apostolic Fathers*. London: Macmillan.
Lilla, Mark. 2008. *The Stillborn God*. New York: Knopf.
Lindbeck, George A. 2009. *The Nature of Doctrine: Religion and Theology in a Postliberal Age*. Louisville: Westminster John Knox.
Lindsay, D. Michael. 2009. *Faith in the Halls of Power*. New York: Oxford University.
"Little Sisters of the Poor v. Azar." 2018. *Becket Fund for Religious Liberty*. http://www.becketfund.org/littlesisters/.
Livingston, James C. 2006. *Modern Christian Thought*. Minneapolis: Fortress.
"Local Development." 2013. CEOSS. https://en.ceoss-eg.org/local-development/.
Locke, John, and William Popple. 2018. *Two Treatises of Government & a Letter Concerning Toleration*. Warsaw: Adansonia.
Lombardi, Federico. 2015. "A Statement Regarding a Meeting of Pope Francis and Mrs. Kim Davis at the Nunciature in Washington, DC." *Vatican.va*. http://press.vatican.va/content/salastampa/en/bollettino/pubblico/2015/10/02/0749/01616.html.

Lovin, Robin W. 2011. *An Introduction to Christian Ethics*. Nashville: Abingdon.
Luther, Martin. 2020. "Disputation against Scholastic Theology." http://courses.washington.edu/hsteu402/Luther%20against%20scholastic%20philosophy.pdf.
Luther, Martin. "Martin Luther: 'On War against The Turk' on Fighting Unbelief Rather Than the Turk." https://berkleycenter.georgetown.edu/quotes/martin-luther-on-war-against-the-turk-on-fighting-unbelief-rather-than-the-turk.
———. 2013. *On Secular Authority*. Waltham, MA: Fig.
———. 2020. "On Secular Authority: How Far Does the Obedience Owed to it Extend?" on Use of Force to Prevent Heresy." https://berkleycenter.georgetown.edu/quotes/martin-luther-on-secular-authority-how-far-does-the-obedience-owed-to-it-extend-on-use-of-force-to-prevent-heresy.
Luther, Martin, et al. 1982. *Works of Martin Luther*. Grand Rapids: Baker.
Lyotard, Jean-Francois. 1997. *The Postmodern Condition*. Minneapolis: University of Minnesota Press.
MacArthur, John. 1995. "Evangelicals and Catholics Together." *Master's Seminary Journal* 6: 7–37.
MacIntyre, Alasdair C. 1981. *After Virtue*. London: Bloomsbury.
Madison, James. 1787. "The Federalist Papers No. 10." *The Avalon Project*. https://avalon.law.yale.edu/18th_century/fed10.asp.
———. "Memorial and Remonstrance against Religious Assessments." https://founders.archives.gov/documents/Madison/01-08-02-0163.
Mahmood, Saba, and Peter G. Danchin. 2014. "Politics of Religious Freedom: Contested Genealogies." *South Atlantic Quarterly* 113 (1): 1–8. doi:10.1215/00382876-2390401.
Manini, Mark. 2010. *U.S.-Vietnam Relations in 2010: Current Issues and Implications for U.S. Policy*. Washington, DC: Congresssional Research Service. http://www.usvtc.org/info/wb/CRS%20US-Vietnam%20relations%202010-8%20R40208.pdf.
Manyin, Mark E. 2010. *U.S.-Vietnam Relations in 2010: Current Issues and Implications for U.S. Policy*. Washington, DC: Congresssional Research Service. http://www.usvtc.org/info/wb/CRS%20US-Vietnam%20relations%202010-8%20R40208.pdf.
———. 2005. *The Vietnam-U.S. Normalization Process*. Washington, DC: Congressional Research Service. https://fas.org/sgp/crs/row/IB98033.pdf.
Marty, Martin E. 1981. *The Public Church*. New York: Crossroad.
"Masked Men Fire at the Evangelical Church in Fayoum (مسلحون يطلقون النيران على الكنيسة الإنجيلية بالفيوم)." 2015. *Calam1.Org*. http://bit.ly/1MInRhB.
Mathewes, Charles T. 2012. "Interview with Peter Berger." *The Hedgehog Review*. https://hedgehogreview.com/issues/after-secularization-special-double-issue/articles/interview-with-peter-berger.
McAdam, Doug, et al. 2008. *Dynamics of Contention*. Cambridge: Cambridge University Press.
McConnell, Michael W. 1990. "The Origins and Historical Understanding of Free Exercise of Religion." *Harvard Law Review* 103 (7): 1409–1517. doi:10.2307/1341281.
McLoughlin, William G., Jr. 1959. *Modern Revivalism: Charles Grandison Finney to Billy Graham*. Reprint, 2004. Eugene, OR: Wipf & Stock.
Meecham, Henry George. 1949. *The Epistle to Diognetus*. Manchester: Manchester University Press.
Michalson, G. E., Jr. 1979. "Lessing, Kierkegaard, and the 'Ugly Ditch': A Reexamination." *The Journal of Religion* 59 (3): 324–34. doi:10.1086/486707.

Michaud, Jean. 2000. "The Montagnards and the State in Northern Vietnam from 1802 to 1975: A Historical Overview." *Ethnohistory* 47 (2): 333–68. doi:10.1215/00141801-47-2-333.

Milbank, Dana. 2012. "Religious Right Has Lost its Political Influence." *Washington Post*. https://www.washingtonpost.com/opinions/religious-right-has-lost-its-political-influence/2012/01/20/gIQAsnMrDQ_story.html?utm_term=.4854283fb4a1.

Miller, Kevin D. 1998. "De-Seiple-Ing World Vision." *Christianity Today*. http://www.christianitytoday.com/ct/1998/june15/8t7049.html.

Minh, Gia. 2013. "Thêm Một Người Chết Tại Đồn Công an Tỉnh Dak Nông (One More Person Died at Dak Nong Police Station)." *Radio Free Asia*. https://www.rfa.org/vietnamese/in_depth/a-new-case-of-death-at-the-police-station-03232013143358.html.

Mitchell, Curtis. 1957. *God in the Garden: The Story of the Billy Graham New York Crusade*. New York: Doubleday.

"Montagnard Christians in Vietnam: A Case Study in Religious Repression." 2011. *Human Rights Watch*. https://www.hrw.org/report/2011/03/30/montagnard-christians-vietnam/case-study-religious-repression.

Montange, Renee. 2015. "Pope's Meeting with Kim Davis Disappoints LGBT Catholics." *NPR.Org*. http://www.npr.org/2015/10/01/444912558/popes-meeting-with-kim-davis-disappoints-lgbt-catholic.

Moynihan, Robert. 2018. "Letter #38, 2015: Kim and Francis - Inside the Vatican." *Inside the Vatican*. https://insidethevatican.com/news/letter-38-2015-kim-and-francis/.

Mufford, Tina. 2017. *Religious Freedom in Vietnam: Assessing the Country of Particular Concern Designation 10 Years After its Removal*. Washington, DC: U.S. Commission on International Religious Freedom.

Munson, Ziad. 2001. "Islamic Mobilization: Social Movement Theory and the Egyptian Muslim Brotherhood." *The Sociological Quarterly* 42 (4): 487–510. doi:10.1525/tsq.2001.42.4.487.

Munson, Ziad W. 2009. *The Making of Pro-Life Activists*. Chicago: University of Chicago Press.

Murch, James DeForest. 1956. *Cooperation without Compromise*. Grand Rapids: Eerdmans.

Murphy, Sophia. 2012. *Changing Perspectives: Small-Scale Farmers, Markets and Globalization*. London: International Institute for Environment and Development.

Murphy, Tim. 2011. "Meet the White Supremacist Leading the GOP's Anti-Shariah Crusade." *Mother Jones*. http://www.motherjones.com/politics/2011/02/david-yerushalmi-sharia-ban-tennessee.

Musaji, Sheila. 2012. "Islamic Sharia and Jewish Halakha Arbitration Courts." *The American Muslim*. http://theamericanmuslim.org/tam.php/features/articles/islamic_Sharia_and_jewish_halakha_arbitration_courts.

"Muslims in the American Public Square: Shifting Political Winds & Fallout from 9/11, Afghanistan, and Iraq." 2004. Washington, DC: Project MAPS. https://web.archive.org/web/20050118031542/http://www.projectmaps.com/AMP2004report.pdf.

Musselman, John. 2011. "American Muslims: A (New) Islamic Discourse on Religious Freedom." *The Review of Faith & International Affairs* 9 (2): 17–24. doi:10.1080/15570274.2011.571420.

Neroulias, Nicole. 2010. "Quietly, Another Mosque Operates in the Shadow of Ground Zero." *Houston Chronicle*. http://www.chron.com/life/houston-belief/article/Quietly-another-mosque-operates-in-the-shadow-of-1714428.php.
"New Crackdown on Montagnards in Vietnam." 2002. *Human Rights Watch*. https://www.hrw.org/news/2002/09/20/new-crackdown-montagnards-vietnam.
Newbigin, Lesslie. 2014. *The Gospel in a Pluralist Society*. New York: SPCK Classics.
Ng, T. T. 2018. *The New Way: Protestantism and the Hmong in Vietnam*. Seattle: University of Washington Press.
Ngo, Tam T. T. 2015. "Protestant Conversion and Social Conflict: The Case of the Hmong in Contemporary Vietnam." *Journal of Southeast Asian Studies* 46 (2): 274–92. doi:10.1017/s0022463415000089.
Niebuhr, Reinhold. 2013. *Faith and History: A Comparison of Christian and Modern Views of History*. New York: Read.
———. 2015. *Major Works on Religion and Politics*. New York: Literary Classics of America.
———. 2013. *Moral Man and Immoral Society*. New York: Westminster John Knox.
Niebuhr, Reinhold, and D. B. Robertson. 1967. *Essays in Applied Christianity*. New York: Meridian.
Nietzsche, Friedrich. 2014. *Beyond Good and Evil*. New York: HarperTorch.
"Northwood Church Hosts Vietnam Delegation." 2007. *Institute for Global Engagement (IGE)*. https://globalengage.org/news-media/press-release/northwood-church-hosts-vietnam-delegation.
Oaks, Dallin H. 2015. "Elder Oaks Transcript at Sacramento Court and Clergy Conference #Fairness4all." http://www.mormonnewsroom.org/article/transcript-elder-oaks-court-clergy-conference.
"Operation Christmas Child 2019 Special Report." 2020. https://www.samaritanspurse.org/operation-christmas-child/occ-2019-special-report/.
"Outcome of 'The Constitution or Sharia: Preserving Freedom' Conference, Nashville, November 11." 2011. https://www.usjf.net/outcome-of-%E2%80%9Cthe-constitution-or-sharia-preserving-freedom-conference%E2%80%9D-nashville-november-11.
"The Partisan Divide on Political Values Grows Even Wider." 2018. *Pew Research Center*. http://www.people-press.org/2017/10/05/the-partisan-divide-on-political-values-grows-even-wider/.
"PC(USA) Mission History in Egypt." 2014. *Presbyterian Mission Agency*. http://www.presbyterianmission.org/ministries/global/egypt-history/.
Penn, William, and Andrew R. Murphy. 2002. *The Political Writings of William Penn*. Indianapolis: Liberty Fund.
Perkins, Tony. 2014. "David Limbaugh, Michele Bachmann, Todd Starnes." *FRC*. http://www.frc.org/wwlivewithtonyperkins/david-limbaugh-michele-bachmann.
Pew Forum on Religion and Public Life. 2018. "Lobbying for the Faithful: Religious Advocacy Groups in Washington, D.C." Washington, DC: Pew Forum on Religion and Public Life. http://www.pewforum.org/2011/11/21/lobbying-for-the-faithful-exec/.
Pew Research Center. 2015. "America's Changing Religious Landscape." http://www.pewforum.org/2015/05/12/americas-changing-religious-landscape/.
———. 2012. "Controversies over Mosques and Islamic Centers Across the U.S." http://www.pewforum.org/2012/09/27/controversies-over-mosques-and-islamic-centers-across-the-u-s-2/.

———. 2011. "How Many Christians are There in Egypt?" http://www.pewresearch.org/2011/02/16/how-many-christians-are-there-in-egypt/.

———. 2015. "Latest Trends in Religious Restrictions and Hostilities." http://www.pewforum.org/2015/02/26/religious-hostilities/.

———. 2018. "Muslim Americans: Middle Class and Mostly Mainstream." http://www.pewresearch.org/2007/05/22/muslim-americans-middle-class-and-mostly-mainstream/.

———. 2014. "Political Polarization in the American Public." http://assets.pewresearch.org/wp-content/uploads/sites/5/2014/06/6-12-2014-Political-Polarization-Release.pdf.

———. 2017. "Political Polarization, 1994–2017." http://www.people-press.org/interactives/political-polarization-1994-2017.

———. 2014. "Religious Hostilities Reach Six-Year High." http://www.pewforum.org/2014/01/14/religious-hostilities-reach-six-year-high/.

———. 2017. "Religious Landscape Study." http://www.pewforum.org/religious-landscape-study/religious-tradition/evangelical-protestant.

———. 2012. "Rising Tide of Restrictions on Religion." http://www.pewforum.org/2012/09/20/rising-tide-of-restrictions-on-religion-findings/#america.

Philpott, Daniel. 2009. "When Faith Meets History: The Influence of Religion on Transitional Justice." In *the Religious in Response to Mass Atrocity: Interdisciplinary Perspectives*, edited by Thomas Brudholm and Thomas Cushman, 174–212. New York: Cambridge University Press.

"Political Polarization in the American Public." 2014. *Pew Research Center*. http://www.people-press.org/2014/06/12/political-polarization-in-the-american-public/.

"Political Polarization, 1994–2017." 2017. *Pew Research Center*. http://www.people-press.org/interactives/political-polarization-1994–2017.

Presbyterian Church in America. 1996. "Statement of Conscience of the National Association of Evangelicals Concerning Worldwide Religious Persecution." http://www.pcahistory.org/pca/3-476.pdf.

"Presidential Vote By Religious Affiliation and Race." 2018. *Pew Research Center*. http://www.pewresearch.org/fact-tank/2016/11/09/how-the-faithful-voted-a-preliminary-2016-analysis/ft_16-11-09_relig_exitpoll_religrace/.

"President Morsi Visits CEOSS Pavilion in the First Ngos Forum." 2013. *CEOSS*. http://en.ceoss-eg.org/president-morsi-visits-ceoss-pavilion-in-the-first-ngos-forum/.

"Pro-Democracy Activists to Be Charged with Terrorism in Vietnam." 2008. *Human Rights House*. http://humanrightshouse.org/Articles/8653.html.

Putnam, Robert D. 2000. *Bowling Alone: The Collapse and Revival of American Community*. New York: Simon & Schuster.

Raftery, Bill. 2012. "Bans on Court Use of Sharia/International Law: Signed Into Law in Kansas, Sent to Study Committee in New Hampshire, Still Technically Alive in MI, NC, PA." *Gavel to Gavel*. http://gaveltogavel.us/2012/05/29/bans-on-court-use-of-shariainternational-law-signed-into-law-in-kansas-sent-to-study-committee-in-new-hampshire-still-technically-alive-in-mi-nc-pa-sc/.

Ramsey, Jacob. 2004. "Extortion and Exploitation in the Nguyễn Campaign against Catholicism in 1830s-1840s Vietnam." *Journal of Southeast Asian Studies* 35 (2): 311–28.

"Rating for World Vision." 2018. *Charity Navigator*. https://www.charitynavigator.org/index.cfm?bay=search.summary&orgid=4768.

Ratliff, Martha. 2004. "Vocabulary of Environment and Subsistence in the Hmong-Mien Proto-Language." In *Hmong-Miao In Asia*, edited by Nicholas Tapp et al., 147–65. Ann Arbor: University of Michigan Press.
Ratliff, Walter. 1998. "Congress May Merge Efforts." *Christianity Today*. http://www.christianitytoday.com/ct/1998/september7/8ta27a.html.
———. 2007. "Crisis In Kaduna." Video. https://www.youtube.com/watch?v=EIBt1X-yU5g.
———. 1998. "New Religious Liberty Bill Unveiled." *Christianity Today*. https://www.christianitytoday.com/ct/1998/august10/8t915a.html.
Rauschenbusch, Walter. 1913. *Christianizing the Social Order*. New York: MacMillan.
Rawls, John. 2005. *Political Liberalism*. New York: Columbia University Press.
———. 2004. *A Theory of Justice*. New York: Oxford.
Rawlyk, George A. 1994. *Amazing Grace: Evangelicalism in Australia, Britain, Canada, and the United States*. Montreal: McGill-Queen's University Press.
"Refused War Service, Get Long Prison Terms." 1918. *New York Times*. https://timesmachine.nytimes.com/timesmachine/1918/06/11/102708489.html?pageNumber=9.
Renard, John. 2011. *Islam and Christianity: Theological Themes in Comparative Perspective*. Berkeley: University Press of California.
Reynhout, Kenneth A. 2015. *Interdisciplinary Interpretation*. Lanham, MD: Lexington.
Ricoeur, Paul. 1992. *The Symbolism of Evil*. Boston: Beacon.
Rivers, Tess. 2009. "Baptists Celebrate 50 Years in Vietnam with Hugs, Tears." *Baptist Press*. http://www.bpnews.net/31767/baptists-celebrate-50-years-in-vietnam-with-hugs-tears.
Roberts, Bob. 2019. "The Wycliffe School for Global Engagement." https://www.youtube.com/watch?v=h2_i8V5pAjE.
Rowe, Paul. 2009. "Building Coptic Civil Society: Christian Groups and the State in Mubarak's Egypt." *Middle Eastern Studies* 45 (1): 111–26. doi:10.1080/00263200802548147.
Rupp, Kelsey. 2015. "Influential Christian Scholar Explains Exactly Why Kim Davis Actions Weren't Civil Disobedience." *IJR - Independent Journal Review*. http://www.ijreview.com/2015/10/451379-dignity-dissension-robert-george-christians-respond-gay-marriage-court-ruling.
Samile, Zakia. 2011. *Between Feminism and Islam: Human Rights and Sharia Law in Morocco*. Minneapolis: University of Minnesota Press.
Schmidt, Melvin. 1969. "Tax Refusal as Conscientious Objection to War." *Mennonite Quarterly Review* 43 (3): 234–46.
Schneider, Jo Anne. 2012. "Comparing Stewardship across Faith-Based Organizations." *Nonprofit and Voluntary Sector Quarterly* 42 (3): 517–39. doi:10.1177/0899764012461399.
Scott, James. 2010. *The Art of Not Being Governed: An Anarchist History of Upland Southeast Asia*. New Haven, CT: Yale University Press.
Scott, Rachel M. 2010. *The Challenge of Political Islam: Non-Muslims and the Egyptian State*. Stanford, CA: Stanford University Press.
Sedra, Paul. 1999. "Class Cleavages and Ethnic Conflict: Coptic Christian Communities in Modern Egyptian Politics." *Islam and Christian–Muslim Relations* 10 (2): 219–35. doi:10.1080/09596419908721181.

Seiple, Chris. 2012. "Building Religious Freedom: A Theory of Change." *The Review of Faith & International Affairs* 10 (3): 97–102. doi:10.1080/15570274.2012.706437.

———. 2009. "IGE: Your Global Neighborhood Weather Station." *Institute for Global Engagement.* https://globalengage.org/news-media/from-the-president/ige-your-global-neighborhood-weather-station.

———. 2006. "IGE in Vietnam: 2001–2006: Relational Diplomacy at Work." *Bethel University.* https://web.archive.org/web/20140217173226/https://cas.bethel.edu/dept/religious-studies/chrisseiple.

———. 2013. "International Good Faith: An Introduction to the 10th Anniversary Issue." *The Review of Faith & International Affairs* 11 (1): 1–8. doi:10.1080/15570274.2012.760981.

———. 2012. "Theology, Strategy & Engagement: Some Interim Reflections." In *Sorrow and Blood: Christian Mission in Contexts of Suffering, Persecution, and Martyrdom*, edited by William Taylor et al., 902–17. Pasadena, CA: William Carey Library.

Seiple, Robert A. 2004. *Ambassadors of Hope: How Christians Can Respond to the World's Toughest Problems.* Downers Grove, IL: InterVarsity.

"Seven Ways Religious Freedom Contributes to Sustainable Development." 2015. *Religious Freedom and Business Foundation.* http://religiousfreedomandbusiness.org/2/post/2015/08/seven-ways-religious-freedom-contributes-to-sustainable-development.html.

Shah, Timothy Samuel. 2003. "Evangelical Politics in the Third World: What's Next for the 'Next Christendom?'" *The Brandywine Review of Faith & International Affairs* 1 (2): 21–30. doi:10.1080/15435725.2003.9523160.

Shah, Timothy S. 2009. "For the Sake of Conscience: Some Evangelical Views of the Church." In *Church, State, and Citizen: Christian Approaches to Political Engagement*, edited by Sandra F. Joireman, 136–37. Oxford: Oxford University Press.

Sharkey, Heather J. 2008. *American Evangelicals in Egypt: Missionary Encounters in an Age of Empire.* Princeton: Princeton University Press.

Shellnutt, Kate. 2017. "Most White Evangelicals Don't Believe Muslims Belong in America." *Christianity Today.* http://www.christianitytoday.com/news/2017/july/pew-how-white-evangelicals-view-us-muslims-islam.html.

Shimron, Yonat. 2020. "Franklin Graham on His Central Park Field Hospital: 'We Don't Discriminate. Period.'" *Religion News Service.* https://religionnews.com/2020/04/01/franklin-graham-on-his-central-park-field-hospital-we-dont-discriminate-period/.

———. "Samaritan's Purse Sets Up Emergency Field Hospital in New York's Central Park." 2020. *Religion News Service.* https://religionnews.com/2020/03/30/samaritans-purse-sets-up-second-emergency-field-hospital-in-new-yorks-central-park/.

Shin, Chan Woong. 2014. "America's New Internationalists?: Evangelical Transnational Activism and U.S. Foreign Policy." PhD diss., Syracuse University Press.

Shortland, John H. 1875. *The Persecutions of Annam.* London: Burns and Oates.

Sider, Ronald J., and Diane Knippers. 2005. *Toward an Evangelical Public Policy: Political Strategies for the Health of the Nation.* Grand Rapids: Baker.

Silk, Mark. 2012. "Islamo-Fearmongering 2012." *Religion News Service.* https://religionnews.com/2012/07/20/islamo-fearmongering-2012/.

Smith, C. Henry. 1920. *The Mennonites.* Berne, IN: Mennonite Book Concern.

Smith, Steven D. 2018. *Pagans and Christians in the City: Culture Wars From the Tiber to the Potomac*. Grand Rapids: Eerdmans.

———. 2014. *The Rise and Decline of American Religious Freedom*. Cambridge, MA: Harvard University Press.

Snow, David. 2013. "Identity Dilemmas, Discursive Fields, Identity Work, and Mobilization: Clarifying the Identity-Movement Nexus." In *the Future of Social Movement Research: Dynamics, Mechanisms, and Processes*, edited by Jacquelien van Stekelenburg et al., 263–80. Minneapolis: University of Minnesota Press.

Snow, David A., et al. 1986. "Frame Alignment Processes, Micromobilization, and Movement Participation." *American Sociological Review* 51 (4): 464–81. doi:10.2307/2095581.

Sommer, Elisabeth. 2018. "Review: European Mennonites and the Challenge of Modernity over Five Centuries." *Sixteenth Century Journal* 49 (1): 147–49.

Spector, Ronald H. 2013. "Phat Diem: Nationalism, Religion, and Identity in the Franco-Viet Minh War." *Journal of Cold War Studies* 15 (3): 34–46.

Sperry, Paul E. 2008. *Infiltration: How Muslim Spies and Subversives Have Penetrated Washington*. Nashville: Thomas Nelson.

Spinoza, Baruch. 2013. *Theological-Political Treatise*. Cambridge: Cambridge University Press.

Springborg, Robert. 1989. *Mubarak's Egypt*. Boulder, CO: Westview.

"S. Rept. 109-321 - A Bill to Authorize the Extension of Nondiscriminatory Treatment (Normal Trade Relations Treatment) to the Products of Vietnam." 2006. *Library of Congress*. https://www.congress.gov/congressional-report/109th-congress/senate-report/321/1.

Stakelbeck, Eric. 2018. "The Watchman: 'ISIS in Your Backyard.'" *Christian Broadcasting Network*. http://www.cbn.com/tv/4457412543001.

State Information Service, Arab Republic of Egypt. 2015. "Sisi Probes Civil Society's Role in Achieving Development." http://www.sis.gov.eg/Story/91928?lang=en-us.

Stearns, Richard. 2014. *The Hole in Our Gospel, Special Edition: The Answer That Changed My Life and Might Just Change the World*. Nashville: Thomas Nelson.

Stepan, Alfred. 2018. *Arguing Comparative Politics*. New York: Oxford University Press.

Stephanous, Andrea Zaki. 2014. "A Middle-Eastern Evangelical Perspective on the Cape Town Congress: from Minority Mentality to Active Participation." In *the Lausanne Movement: A Range of Perspectives*, edited by Lars Dahle et al., 331–37. Oxford: Regnum.

———. 2012. *Political Islam, Citizenship, and Minorities*. Lanham, MD: University Press of America.

Stetzer, Ed. 2010. "Monday is for Missiology: Evangelism and Social Justice." *The Exchange (blog)*. http://www.christianitytoday.com/edstetzer/2010/march/monday-is-for-missiology-evangelism-and-social-justice.html.

———. 2012. "Rick Warren Interview on Muslims, Evangelism & Missions (Responding to Recent News Reports)." *The Exchange (blog)*. http://www.christianitytoday.com/edstetzer/2012/march/rick-warren-interview-on-muslims-evangelism-missions.html.

Stoltzfus, Duane C. S. 2014. *Pacifists in Chains*. Baltimore: Johns Hopkins University Press.

Su, Anna. 2014. *Exporting Freedom: Religious Liberty and American Power*. Cambridge, MA: Harvard University Press.

Sullivan, Winnifred. 2014. "The Impossibility of Religious Freedom." *SSRC the Immanent Frame*. http://tif.ssrc.org/2014/07/08/impossibility-of-religious-freedom/.

Summers, Juana. 2011. "GOP Litmus Test: Sharia Opposition." *Politico*. http://www.politico.com/story/2011/05/gop-litmus-test-sharia-opposition-054605.

Tadros, Samuel. 2013. *Motherland Lost*. Stanford, CA: Hoover Institution.

Tang, Didi. 2015. "Severe Crackdown in China on Church Crosses Draws Backlash." *The Journal*. https://the-journal.com/articles/26725.

Tarek, Sherif. 2012. "Pope Shenouda III: Four Decades of Coptic History." *Al Ahram*. http://english.ahram.org.eg/WriterArticles/NewsContentP/1/125438/Egypt/Pope-Shenouda-III-Four-decades-of-Coptic-history.aspx.

Tarrow, Sidney G. 2012. *Power in Movement*. Cambridge: Cambridge University Press.

Taylor, Charles. 2007. *A Secular Age*. Cambridge, MA: Harvard University Press.

Tilly, Charles. 2008. *Contentious Performances*. New York: Cambridge University Press.

"Timeline." 2018. *Embassy of the Socialist Republic of Vietnam in the United States*. http://vietnamembassy-usa.org/vietnam-us-relations/timeline.

"Timeline: US-Vietnam Relations." 2010. *Contemporary Southeast Asia* 32 (3): 350–53.

Tocqueville, Alexis de. 1998. *Democracy in America*. Charlottesville: University of Virginia Press.

Trigg, Roger. 2020. "Threats to Religious Freedom in Europe." *Public Discourse*. http://www.thepublicdiscourse.com/2013/06/10439/.

Tripp, Linda. 1999. "Gender and Development from a Christian Perspective: Experience from World Vision." *Gender & Development* 7 (1): 62–68. doi:10.1080/741922931.

Troeltsch, Ernst. 1991. *Religion in History*. Minneapolis: Fortress.

Turner, Bryan S. 1996. *The Blackwell Companion to Social Theory*. Oxford: Blackwell.

Turton, Shaun, and Phak Seangly. 2017. "Montagnards Flee to Thailand, Fearing Return to Persecution in Vietnam." *Phnom Penh Post*. http://www.phnompenhpost.com/national/montagnards-flee-thailand-fearing-return-persecution-vietnam.

Tutu, Desmond. 2010. "The First Word: To Be Human is to Be Free." In *Christianity and Human Rights*, edited by John Witte Jr. and Frank S. Alexander, 1–7. New York: Cambridge University Press.

United States Conference of Catholic Bishops. "Discrimination against Catholic Adoption Services." 2017. http://www.usccb.org/issues-and-action/religious-liberty/discrimination-against-catholic-adoption-services.cfm.

United States Department of Labor. 2015. "Child Labor and Forced Labor Reports: Egypt." https://www.dol.gov/agencies/ilab/resources/reports/child-labor/egypt.

"Universal Declaration of Human Rights." 2018. *United Nations*. http://www.un.org/en/universal-declaration-human-rights/index.html.

van der Schalk, Job, et al. 2010. "The More (Complex), the Better? The Influence of Epistemic Motivation on Integrative Bargaining in Complex Negotiation." *European Journal of Social Psychology* 40 (7): 1110–19. doi:10.1002/ejsp.633.

Vandrunen, David. 2004. "The Context of Natural Law: John Calvin's Doctrine of the Two Kingdoms." *Journal of Church and State* 46 (3): 503–25. doi:10.1093/jcs/46.3.503.

"Vietnam." 2016. *Institute for Global Engagement (IGE)*. https://globalengage.org/relational-diplomacy/countries/vietnam.

"Vietnam: Religious Freedom Denied." 2008. *Human Rights Watch*. https://www.hrw.org/news/2008/05/08/vietnam-religious-freedom-denied.

"Vietnam: USCIRF Testifies on Capitol Hill." 2003. *United States Commission on International Religious Freedom.* http://www.uscirf.gov/news-room/press-releases/vietnam-uscirf-testifies-capitol-hill-0.

"Vietnamese Delegation Visits U.S. To Build Friendships, Engage Religious Freedom Issues." 2006. *Institute for Global Engagement (IGE).* https://globalengage.org/news-media/press-release/vietnamese-delegation-visits-u.s.-to-build-friendships-engage-religious-fre.

"Vietnam Sentences Four Hmong Christians to Prison After Praying in Worship Service." 2004. *Hudson Institute, Center for Religious Freedom.* https://www.hudson.org/research/4776-vietnam-sentences-four-hmong-christians-to-prison-after-praying-in-worship-service.

Violations of Religious Freedom in Vietnam. 2013. Göttingen, : Gesellschaft für bedrohte Völker. https://www.gfbv.de/fileadmin/redaktion/UN-statements/2013/Vietnam_Verletzung_der_Religionsfreiheit_in_Vietnam_Violations_of_religious_freedom_in_Vietnam.pdf.

Virtue, David W. 2011. *A Vision of Hope: The Story of Samuel Habib.* Eugene, OR: Wipf & Stock.

"VN-US Economic & Trade Relations: Milestones in Vietnam-U.S. Economic and Trade Relations." 2015. *Vietnam Trade Office in the USA.* http://www.vietnam-ustrade.org/index.php?f=news&do=detail&id=87&lang=english.

Voss, Kim. 1996. "The Collapse of a Social Movement: The Interplay of Mobilizing Structures, Framing, and Political Opportunities in the Knights of Labor." *Comparative Perspectives on Social Movements,* edited by Doug McAdam et al., 227–58. doi:10.1017/cbo9780511803987.012.

Vu, Hien. 2012. "The Institute in Vietnam." *Institute for Global Engagement (IGE).* https://globalengage.org/attachments/005_Vietnam%201%20Pager_05_2012.pdf.

Vu, Michelle. "Rick Warren to Muslims: Talk is Cheap, Let's Work Together." 2009. https://www.christianpost.com/news/rick-warren-to-muslims-talk-is-cheap-lets-work-together.html.

Wagner, William. 2016. "Islam, Shariah Law, and the American Constitution." *Intermountain Christian News.* http://www.imcnews.org/downloads/issues/vol14n1.pdf.

Wald, Kenneth D., et al. 2005. "Making Sense of Religion in Political Life." *Annual Review of Political Science* 8 (1): 121–43. doi:10.1146/annurev.polisci.8.083104.163853.

Wegemer, Gerard B., and Stephen W. Smith. 2012. *A Thomas More Source Book.* Washington, DC: Catholic University of America Press.

Weil, Simone. 1951. *Waiting for God.* London: Routledge & Paul.

Weil, Simone, and Siân Miles. 1986. *Simone Weil: An Anthology.* New York: Weidenfeld & Nicolson.

Westbrook, Robert. 2013. "Pragmatists and Politics: The Richards Bernstein and Rorty." *Raritan* 32 (4): 104–22.

Westmoreland-White, Michael. 2018. "Is 'Evangelical' Still a Useful Term?" *Pilgrim Pathways.* https://pilgrimpathways.wordpress.com/2012/07/15/is-evangelical-still-a-useful-term.

White, Hayden. 1997. *The Content of the Form.* Baltimore: The Johns Hopkins University Press.

Williams, Roger. 1846. *Bloudy Tenant of Persecution for Cause of Conscience*. London: Haddon.
Williams, Elisha, and Thomas Cushing. 1744. *The Essential Rights and Liberties of Protestants*. Boston: Printed and sold by S. Kneeland and T. Green in Queenstreet.
Witte, John. 2012. "Shari'ah's Uphill Climb." *Christianity Today*. http://www.christianitytoday.com/ct/2012/november/shariahs-uphill-climb.html.
Wolterstorff, Nicholas. 2012. *The Mighty and the Almighty*. Cambridge: Cambridge University Press.
Wood, Michael. 1998. "The Use of the Pharaonic Past in Modern Egyptian Nationalism." *Journal of the American Research Center in Egypt* 35 (1998) 179–96. doi:10.2307/40000469.
Yerushalemi, David. 2006. "On Race: A Tentative Discussion." *The Mcadam Report* 585 (2006): 7. http://archive.is/y4KX5.
Yerushalemi, David, and Mordechai Kedar. 2011. "Sharia Adherence Mosque Survey: Correlations between Sharia Adherence and Violent Dogma in U.S. Mosques." *Perspectives on Terrorism* 5 (6): 81–138. http://www.terrorismanalysts.com/pt/index.php/pot/article/view/sharia-adherence-mosque-survey/340.
Yoder, John Howard. 1994. *The Politics of Jesus*. Grand Rapids: Eerdmans.
Younan, Patrick Alexander. 2014. "The Coptic Christians of Egypt: Dhimmitude and Discrimination." http://scholarship.shu.edu/cgi/viewcontent.cgi?article=1608&context=student_scholarship.
Young, Michael K. 2002. "Testimony: Communist Entrenchment and Religious Persecution in China and Vietnam." *United States Commission on International Religious Freedom*. http://www.uscirf.gov/advising-government/congressional-testimony/communist-entrenchment-and-religious-persecution-in.
Yount, Kathryn M. 2004. "Symbolic Gender Politics, Religious Group Identity, and the Decline in Female Genital Cutting in Minya, Egypt." *Social Forces* 82 (3): 1063–90. doi:10.1353/sof.2004.0062.
Zald, Mayer N. 2000. "Ideologically Structured Action: An Enlarged Agenda for Social Movement Research." *Mobilization: An International Quarterly* 5 (1): 1–16.
Zald, Mayer N., and John McCarthy. 1987. "Religious Groups as Crucibles of Social Movements." In *Social Movements in an Organizational Society*, edited by Mayer Zald, John McCarthy, 67–96. New Brunswick, NJ: Transaction.
"التنمية المحلية." 2018. *CEOSS*. http://ceoss-eg.org/local-development/.

Index

Abou El Fadl, Khaled, 96
Abuja. *See* Nigeria
American Center for Law and Justice (ACLJ), 100
Anabaptist, 3
Aquinas, Thomas, 20
Augustine, 19, 31, 75, 185
Aurelius, Marcus, 17

Bachmann, Michele, 101
Barth, Karl, 39
Bayle, Pierre, 27
Bebbington, David, 91
Becket Fund for Religious Liberty, 102
beit din, 95
Benford, Robert, 61
Berger, Peter, 81, 174
Bernstein, Richard, 49
Beyond Good and Evil, 46
Bill of Rights, 23
Bo, Charles, 5
Boykin, Jerry, 89, 102
Brown, Peter, 70

Calvin, John, 22
Carnell, E. J., 71
Castellio, Sebastian, 23
Canon Law, 95
Centesimus Annus, 39
Civil Rights Era, 79
Clement of Alexandria, 18
Colson, Chuck, 90, 110

Coptic Evangelical Organization for Social Services (CEOSS), 4, 60, 66, 113
Coptic Orthodox, 115, 121

Declaration of Independence, 30
Descartes, Rene, 23
Dignitatis Humanae, 38
Dobson, James, 92
Dreher, Rod, 74

Establishment Clause, 33
Evangelicals and Catholics Together, 180

Falwell, Jerry Jr, 179
Family Research Council, 98
Far East Broadcasting Company, 150
First Amendment, 98
First Indochina War, 149
Freeing God's Children, 92

Gaffney, Frank, 97
Gana, Jerry, 2
George, Robert, 106, 110
Graham, Billy, 44, 71, 102, 109, 180
Graham, Franklin, 87
Grim, Brian, 93, 168
Grotius, Hugo, 24

Habib, Rafiq, 130, 137, 175
Habib, Samuel, 116, 122, 130, 131, 178
Hanford, John, 90, 93

Harnack, Adolf von, 44
Hauerwas, Stanley, 52, 72, 82, 173
Hertzke, Allen, 92
Hmong Christians, 150
Hobbes, Thomas, 25
Hooker, Richard, 29
Horowitz, Michael, 90
human dignity, 2

Institute for Global Engagement (IGE), 60, 66, 101, 140
International Religious Freedom Act (IRFA), 3, 6, 60, 65, 85, 89, 92, 107, 111, 171, 177, 186
intertextuality, 13, 14, 71
Isaiah, 76

Jackson-Vanik Amendment, 153
Jefferson, Thomas, 29, 35
Jeffress, Robert, 179
Jenkins, Philip, 113, 175
Jesus, 16, 77
Job, 14

Kaduna. See Nigeria
Kant, Immanuel, 31
Kennedy, D. James, 92
Kierkegaard, Søren, 42

Land, Richard, 102, 110
Leviathan, 24, 25, 37, 53, 82
Lilla, Mark, 37
Lindsay, D. Michael, 106
Locke, John, 29, 30
Lovin, Robin, 69
Luther, Martin, 21, 76, 83
Lyotard, Jean-François, 47

MacIntyre, Alasdair, 185
Madison, James, 29, 35
Magna Carta, 34
McCarthy, John, 61
Mennonite Central Committee, 181
Mennonites, 3
Montagnard, 150
Moral Man and Immoral Society, 68, 72, 79, 174
More, Thomas, 22

Munson, Ziad, 63
Murch, James, 109, 141, 179
Muslim Brotherhood, 63, 101, 131, 133, 135

National Association of Evangelicals, 92, 109
Neuhaus, Richard John, 110
Newbigin, Lesslie, 114
Niebuhr, Reinhold, 53, 68, 71, 79, 173
Nietzsche, Friedrich, 46
Nigeria, 1

Pan-Arabism, 134
Paul the Apostle, 16, 24, 73, 142
Peace of Westphalia, 23
Penn, William, 34
Perkins, Tony, 86
Philosophical Fragments, 43
Philpott, Dan, 181
Political Liberalism, 40
Pope Benedict XVI, 108
Pope John Paul II, 39
Pope Leo XIII, 38
Pope Shenouda III, 117, 118
Pope Tawadros II, 119
Putnam, Robert, 91

Rawls, John, 40, 53
Religion Through the Limits of Reason Alone, 52
Rerum Novarum, 38
Ricoeur, Paul, 50
Roberts, Bob Jr., 109, 157, 179
Rohingya, 4, 5
Romans, 17, 40

Samaritan's Purse, 87
Saperstein, David, 92
Scillitan Martyrs, 17
Second Great Awakening, 55
Second Vatican Council, 38
Secularization Thesis, 81
Seiple, Chris, 142, 152, 154, 168, 183
Seiple, Robert, 145, 152, 153
Sermon on the Mount, 16, 46, 178
Shah, Timothy, 70
Sharia, 94, 117

Shea, Nina, 90
Snow, David, 61
Spinoza, Benedict de, 26
Stakelbeck, Erik, 87
Stepan, Alfred, 93
Stephanous, Andrea Zaki, 115, 132, 175
Sullivan, Winifred, 93

Tarrow, Sidney, 61
Tây Sơn Rebellion, 147
Taylor, Charles, 85
Tertullian, 18, 178
The Bloody Tenant, 29
Tilly, Charles, 64
Treaty of Saigon, 148

Universal Declaration of Human Rights, 11, 129

Wagner, William, 98
Warren, Rick, 86, 105, 109, 179
Weil, Simone, 51
Williams, Elisha, 34
Williams, Roger, 23, 28
Wolterstorff, Nicholas, 53
World Trade Organization (WTO), 158
World Vision, 142, 145, 180

Xinjiang, 169

Yerushalemi, David, 96
Yoder, John Howard, 77, 173

Zald, Mayer, 61

www.ingramcontent.com/pod-product-compliance
Lightning Source LLC
Chambersburg PA
CBHW062027220426
43662CB00010B/1500